PARENTS NOT GUILTY!

OF THEIR CHILDREN'S NEUROSES

Books by DR. EDMUND BERGLER

CURABLE AND INCURABLE NEUROTICS

TENSIONS CAN BE REDUCED TO NUISANCES

PRINCIPLES OF SELF-DAMAGE

THE PSYCHOLOGY OF GAMBLING

HOMOSEXUALITY: DISEASE OR WAY OF LIFE?

LAUGHTER AND THE SENSE OF HUMOR

THE REVOLT OF THE MIDDLE-AGED MAN

KINSEY'S MYTH OF FEMALE SEXUALITY
(in collaboration with W. Kroger)

FASHION AND THE UNCONSCIOUS

THE SUPEREGO

MONEY AND EMOTIONAL CONFLICTS

COUNTERFEIT-SEX

THE WRITER AND PSYCHOANALYSIS

THE BASIC NEUROSIS

CONFLICT IN MARRIAGE

DIVORCE WON'T HELP NEUROTICS

THE BATTLE OF THE CONSCIENCE

UNHAPPY MARRIAGE AND DIVORCE

PSYCHIC IMPOTENCE IN MEN

TALLEYRAND-NAPOLEON-STENDHAL-GRABBE

FRIGIDITY IN WOMEN
(in collaboration with E. Hitschman)

JUSTICE AND INJUSTICE
(in collaboration with Joost A. M. Meerloo, M.D.)

PARENTS

NOT GUILTY!

OF THEIR
CHILDREN'S NEUROSES

by

EDMUND BERGLER, M.D.

LIVERIGHT PUBLISHING CORPORATION

NEW YORK

Library of Congress Catalog Card Number: 64-23333

PRINTED IN THE UNITED STATES OF AMERICA

CONTENTS

PREFACE

PARENTS are afraid of their children. Fear completes the furnishings of every modern nursery. Unfortunately it is a sophisticated fear and more difficult to contend with than the simple apprehensions of our grandparents. They were chiefly worried about the child's physical condition.

Today the psychic apparatus of the child is regarded with great anxiety. One "mistake" by father and mother might cause irreparable damage. One suppression of the child's effort to "express himself" could be catastrophic. Parents approach their child training duties with dread and panic.

The incorrect assumption is that there is a direct connection between acts, words, attitudes of parents toward the child's behavior and later development. This is not the case. If children actually reflected the benevolence or the cruelty of parental conduct, the end product of the educational process could be foreseen easily. Kind, loving, understanding parents would always produce normal, well-balanced children. Harsh, unkind, unloving parents would consequently produce neurotic children who grow into neurotic adults.

Such a belief is not supported by clinical evidence, although the popular fallacy is widespread. Neurotic children frequently do emerge from comparatively normal environments and mentally healthy children often emerge from neurotic families.

It is a cookbook recipe logic that supposes the use of correct ingredients must produce a successful result. In human behavior, however, the one ingredient that cannot be measured is the particular and unique personality of each individual. We begin there with an imponderable and unknown quantity.

The troubled parents ask, "Does not childhood experience have decisive results that remain influential from youth to adulthood?" Yes, the experience does leave its mark upon the psyche of the child. But it is experience *as the child sees it,* and what he perceives and retains is not necessarily the facts of reality. What often is remembered is not a true photographic copy of the events and the environment.

Modern psychiatry, basing its conclusions on Freud's fundamental research, holds that it is the child's *inner elaborations* of his experiences, the fantasies that he chooses to create of the world around him, that have such tenacious effect.

This explains why the results of external influence are limited, even contradictory, and why *parents and educators have less control over the child's future than is generally assumed.*

Parental influence is only one of a trio of forces that combine to shape the child's fate. Parents represent *environment;* they have no voluntary part in the child's *biological endowment,* which determines the rate and direction of his development. Neither do they play any part in his unconscious elaboration of these influences. Parents are truly helpless against the decisive force: the child's *unconscious elaboration* of his fantasies.

Since, of these three, only environment can be externally manipulated, people who want progress have energetically called for such changes. In their frantic campaign to change parents' attitudes they have ignored the fact that only one influence affecting the child was being encountered. To improve the environment was not enough.

The modern theory of pedagogy—active demands by parents and teachers and passive leniency on the part of the child—has been of some superficial advantage to the child. The brutal, one-sided punitive technique of child rearing is gone, although the child is paying heavily for this improvement by being subjected to several less fortunate changes.

In exchange for an official slogan of hopefulness, parents have had to acquire angelic, superhuman patience and have had to accept fear as the companion to each educational effort, as they weigh the amount of "error" that may have crept into each "possibly atavistic" attitude. This constant apprehension is entirely out of proportion to any damage the parents' "errors" may inflict upon the child.

However painful the real facts may be to the defenders of contemporary theory, the truth is that the reality presented to the child is merely raw material. *What the child does with this raw material depends entirely upon his own unconscious decisions.*

Given an unfavorable home situation, one child might grow into adulthood correcting the frustrating influences. Another, starting with an ideal home situation, could magnify small incidents into "injustices" and later, as a neurotic adult, continue to feel that he has been wronged.

Two brothers, brought up together by a disagreeable, domineering mother, handled the same problem differently. One boy *corrected* his childhood experience by marrying a kind, loving girl. The other brother *perpetuated* his infantile disappointment by marrying a cold, unpleasant woman who made his life miserable.

A commercial artist, age twenty-eight, consulted me. In great excitement he tried to explain why he was a homosexual. He proceeded to diagnose his own case. His mother had been responsible for his distaste for women. According to him, she was a cruel person who "reduced poor father to a pulp." He described her attitude toward his father as that of a cat playing with a mouse before eating it. The atmosphere of the household had been one of unrelieved coldness, equally painful to both the patient and to his twin brother.

At the age of eleven both boys began homosexual practices. They continued until they were about eighteen when they separated to go to different colleges. From that time on little communication passed between the brothers. A short time before seeing me, however, the patient had taken a long trip back to his home town to attend his brother's wedding.

"So your brother isn't a homosexual?" I asked.

"No, he married a rather nice girl."

"Where does this leave your theory that your mother is responsible for your homosexuality? Wasn't your twin brother under the identical influence, and for the same period of time?"

The young man looked startled. Rather reluctantly he admitted that he had attended his brother's wedding to check up and determine whether the girl was "really nice." An extensive "search" failed to reveal any "incriminating material." All this evidence against his theory did not prevent him from going on, immediately afterward, with his indictment of his "cruel" mother.

It is logical to ask: "Why wait for the child to correct unfavorable influences? Why not prevent the need from arising by making certain parental influence is favorable? Two obstacles arise: first, the *personalities of the parents,* and second, the *child's inability to see reality as it exists.* To elaborate:

Parents are average people, and like everybody else they have their own marked neurotic tendencies to contend with. No amount of indoctrination with the principles of modern pedagogy can teach them more than lip-service understanding; nor can one analyze all parents. The child is much less affected by permissive words than by an intuitive impression of his own. A gesture, an inflection, a look that flows from exasperation into anger—all these are taken very seriously by him, nullifying the assurance of any friendly words that may accompany such nonverbal communication.

Even when parental neuroticism does not interfere, permissive education puts such intolerable burdens on naturally kind parents that outbursts of impatience and anger are unavoidable. This excessive strain became so obvious that the original doctrine of permissiveness was modified. The latest pedagogic rule seems to be: "Don't suppress your disapproval of the child's 'impossible' actions. Make it clear that you love him *in general,* though you strongly object to his unacceptable deed." Not even the devisors of this precept can satisfactorily explain how the child can be kept from overlooking the underlying love and selectively concentrating on the disapproval.

The ingenious idea from which permissive education grows is based on *adult* concepts of reciprocity: be nice to me and I'll be nice to you. Very reasonable, but entirely inapplicable to children. The assumption is that children are capable of seeing reality. This is simply not so. All children imbue their personal lives with fantasies, misconceptions, and misinterpretations, shifting these to the world around them whether favorable or unfavorable. The child sees all reality through the spectacles of his own inner conflicts. *His* reality, his standards, are not the adult's, just as his conflicts are not the adult's.

The growing child must cope with a multiplicity of inner problems of which two are unreachable by parental influence. These are *psychic masochism* and *projection*. These terms will be discussed in detail in the body of this book, but here is a brief outline of their practical application.

Every child begins by living on the basis of "infantile megalomania," the illusion that he controls his universe. Infuriated by the need to submit to "foolish" adults, unable to express his anger externally because of the inadequacy of his body and the personalities of the "people with haloes" (parents and educators) who surround him, he becomes the target of his own rebounding fury—a phenomenon made inevitable by the fact that anger, once aroused, must find an object. (A drive, as Freud stated, is more "interested" in being discharged than in the object against which it is directed.) Victim of his own fury (aggression) and at the same time a seeker of pleasure, the child must find a way out of his uncomfortable situation. He does so by sugar-coating his self-aggression with a patina of pleasure. In this way, unconsciously, he fits himself into a pattern of "pleasure in displeasure," a pattern scientifically known as *psychic masochism*. As a result he develops an inner tendency that is not acceptable to his unconscious conscience (superego). When the pattern is firmly set, the child cannot give it up, and he therefore creates an ingenious fiction to make it acceptable; he maintains, unconsciously, that he is not a lover of displeasure but an innocent victim of outside malice. This accounts for the fantastic provocations of some children, provocations not deterred by parental punishment.

I once asked an adherent of the no-deterrence theory: what

would you do if your three-year old established this routine: favorite sleeping hours, eight A.M. to six P.M.; favorite eating habit, dissecting raw meat with his fingers; favorite sport, setting the house on fire with matches, exclusively provided by his mother; favorite approach to his baby brother, poking a fork into its eyes? Don't you agree that after the arsenal of kindness, understanding, and persuasion had proved ineffective, and after you had assured the child that you love him even though you disapprove of a particular action, even *you* would have to proceed to some kind of punishment? And what on earth can prevent the child from misconstruing your behavior as a terrible injustice? And what on earth can prevent him from remaining unimpressed by punishment and repeating the same routine, provocatively?

In other words, the child's conduct represents the results of his own solution to his inner conflicts and not the results of his parents' attitudes. If a child is devoted to considerable quantities of psychic masochism, he will extract punishment from the most benevolent upbringers.

On the other hand, as has already been mentioned, parents without realizing it often provide what is conceived as punishment in the facial expressions, tones of voice, and exasperated glances that are evoked by protracted "naughtiness." The child reckons with covert as well as overt manifestations of the parents' attitude. Hence many parents who "never punish" a child are nevertheless meting out what the child construes as punishment.

The punitive educational methods of the past made it easy for the child to "be punished." Today the child bent on extracting unconscious pleasure from conscious displeasure has difficulties. In spite of recurring nostalgic letters to editors, the difference does not justify or recommend the old system. It is, however, a difference with a wry implication.

The unconscious maneuvers involved in the masochistic "solution" are closely connected with the phenomenon of *projection*. This is a process in which one attributes one's own unacceptable feelings to another person. As the English school of analysis has shown, the child uses projection extensively in order to dispose of some of his own aggression. If, for inner reasons, he does this by attributing his own aggressive tendencies to his parents, he will perceive his mother and father as mean, malicious, and cruel even though they may be objectively kind, devoted, and forgiving. Because he builds up parts of his inner conscience by identifying with his parents *as he perceives them,* projection causes him an added difficulty in its distortion of realistic facts.

Recently I witnessed the spectacle of a woman who gave up her profession in order to devote herself entirely to her little boy. She insisted on administering all his feedings herself. She thought this would "avoid frustration." After a few weeks of this regime of constant vigilance, she found herself with a child who cried inconsolably when she left him for a minute. The poor woman had been trapped by her failure to understand the real meaning of "frustration"; she did not realize that too much indulgence can disappoint the child as painfully as too little. Too much indulgence leaves the child insatiable; when the best is not good enough there is no way out for either child or parent. Unhappily, the child cannot be spared all disappointment. *Some frustrations are inherent in his adjustment to reality—especially the unavoidable offenses to his fantasy of megalomania.*

How he accepts these inevitable frustrations seems to be decisive. Given a child who perceives a few minutes of waiting for his milk as a major affront (as he will if he starts life with a substantial endowment of megalomania), and you have an individual upon whom any deprivation may have marked effects.

Curiously enough, one of the complications arising from the recent principles of child rearing has been the too literal acceptance by parents. Scientific findings are not, after all, formulas with success guaranteed. But for two or three decades they have been so considered. These have been decades of discovering that the formulas, no matter how faithfully followed, still result in the usual quota of neurotic children. That this discovery should be followed by over-violent reaction is not surprising. And it is more likely now that the general attitude will be one of condemning the principles rather than readjusting their application.

It is undue optimism, shared by both parents and educators, that is the real snare, since it ensures disappointment. There are many ways of making one's life miserable but none more reliable than neurotic expectation. Some of this unwarranted hopefulness can be eliminated by accepting the fact that the parents have only a relative part in the psychic development of the child. *Children may be sources of joy to their parents; only too often they are manufacturers of unhappiness.* There are biological reasons for the wish to have children, but parenthood has a complicated unconscious structure of which parents are unaware. They see their children as investments in gratitude, when they should consider them only as investments in possible identification. Unless their expectations remain modest and limited, parents may eventually discover that raising a family has been an investment in injustice collecting.

The controversy over the dominant or limited influence of parents is not new in psychoanalysis. From the scientific point of view the core of the problem has been the question of how accurately or how distortedly the parental influence is stored in the child's unconscious conscience (superego). Freud had this to say on the subject in 1932:

> The superego seems to have made a one-sided selection, to have chosen only the harshness and severity of the parents, their preventive and punitive function, while their loving care is not taken up and continued by it. When the parents actually were stern taskmasters, we believe it easily understandable that a severe superego should develop in the child. Experience shows, however, against our expectations, that the superego can acquire the identical character of merciless hardness even when education was mild and kind and threats and punishments were as far as possible avoided. (*Gesammelte Schriften* XII, p. 216.)

The English school of psychoanalysis has constantly pointed out the projective character of the child's "observations." Freud partly accepted this thesis. In *Civilization and Its Discontents* he wrote:

> Experience proves that the severity of the superego developed by the child by no means mirrors the severity of the treatment he actually experienced, as correctly stated by Melanie Klein

and other English writers (the last part of this sentence is a foot-note). This severity of conscience seems independent of it; even when the education was a mild one, a child can develop a very severe conscience.

What is missing in these discussions is the paramount role played by the psychic-masochistic solution, in which the uncon-scious ego accepts the torture meted out by the superego and short-changes it into "masochistic pleasure." This process I have emphasized in earlier publications. It is independent of all educa-tional media.

To come back to the basic question, whether parents are responsible for their children's neuroses—my unequivocal opin-ion is that they are *not. The worst that even neurotic parents can do is to force the child to create specific, temporary uncon-scious defenses, while at best even normal parents cannot prevent specific infantile misconceptions.* Whether the child perpetuates the misconceptions or the spur-of-the-moment defenses or relin-quishes them depends upon *his own unconscious elaboration.* Indeed, this is the crucial question, the unconscious tendency which, more than any other, differentiates the not-too-neurotic from the neurotic child. A neurotic defense, devised to meet a specific situation, may be discarded when the situation changes, or it may be retained as a permanent part of the psychic structure even after the situation that prompted it has become part of the past. The masochistic solution is used in both cases—but in differing degrees. And it is only in the second case that the child is so deeply committed to the masochistic pattern that all his ac-tions are colored by it.

During more than thirty years of psychoanalytic practice on two continents, I have witnessed the transition from the punitive to the lenient form of education and have seen the products of both systems on the analytic couch. The results, as far as the basic scourge of psychic masochism is concerned, have been identical.

This book is devoted to re-evaluating the problems of parents and clearing away the misconceptions that burden them today with unjustified and damaging feelings of guilt. All that can be reasonably asked of parents is that they do their best for their children. The rest is out of their hands.

EDMUND BERGLER, M.D.

New York City
January, 1962

PARENTS NOT GUILTY!

OF THEIR CHILDREN'S NEUROSES

CHAPTER 1

THE INFANT'S MULTIPLE INNER TROUBLEMAKERS AND THE LONELY TROUBLE-SHOOTER

"TOO LITTLE and too late," the prevailing complaint, ranks as a minor tragedy when compared with its opposite, the "too much, too soon" that characterizes almost every aspect of the world inhabited by the infant, baby and small child. The child comes into the world endowed with powerful drives that clamor for expression, but with a physical apparatus incapable until much later in life, of carrying out the demands of these drives. If the result were merely a stalemate, it would be bad enough. But the infant's drives insist upon some outlet, some target. Since they cannot be expressed outwardly, they turn inward, against the child himself.

This is the succession, inexorable as the tide, that controls every new chapter in the unfolding history of the child. Adults take for granted, as of course they should, the biological facts of growth, the prolonged maturation time of the human being, and the protracted dependence of the child. The extreme helplessness of the infant only adds to his appeal, and to the pride and pleasure of parenthood. But the fact that the human infant, unique among mammals, must inhabit an artificial womb for almost a year after he has emerged from his real one, is the greatest of his psychological troublemakers.

This does not mean that if the young child, like the young foal, could rise unsteadily to his feet a short while after birth and give vent to his bewilderment and fear by butting his head angrily against his mother's belly, the course of his psychological development would be automatically and entirely smoothed. Psychologically speaking, the child is born with—or very soon acquires—other difficulties. But the essential contradiction between his powerful endowment of drives and his negligible endowment of physical control colors and directs his entire approach to the new world in which he finds himself.

That new world, in itself, is a problem which the newborn child must solve. In a very real sense, the human being begins to fend for himself the instant he is born. Although his physical apparatus is ready for life, he is not psychologically prepared for even the simplest necessities of existence—the burden of breathing, eating and adjusting. We know that within the womb all wants are automatically satisfied; oxygen and nourishment are directly channeled into the unborn infant's blood vessels, and he is nurtured and protected to the utmost extent. It would be merely romantic to speculate on his possible mental activity, but it can be deduced from the actions after birth that he recognizes —quite bitterly—a "before" and "after" and retains an insistent reminiscence of the Eden from which he has been expelled.

What the infant wants, and what he gets—to the extent the parents can make it possible—is a repetition of the prenatal situation. Some miracles are gone for good; the child must breathe for himself, suck at breast or bottle and eliminate for himself. But warmth, darkness and quiet are all preserved for him by his parents, and other needs are cared for as promptly as possible. The child's rudimentary thinking processes classify all these phenomena, and it is a measure of human intelligence that he is able to construct a fable in which all the mysterious events of his new life submit to a comprehensive, if fantastic, explanation.

As the newborn child sees his new reality, it is a world peopled at first by himself alone; he sees himself as an omnipotent sorcerer. A little later comes the first compromise—the precursor of many others. He half acknowledges the outer world. Now he discerns two forces; himself and the Other, which is not an individual but the environment as a whole. The Other is at times his servant, at times his wicked antagonist. The Other serves him, the child believes, because of his magical powers. From the infant's early viewpoint, therefore, food, warmth and comfort are all self-given, and he himself rules an unknown but controllable world. This *illusion of omnipotence*—the human being's first exercise in illogic—dominates the initial stage of the child's growth and persists, in more or less rudimentary form, throughout life, even after repeated amendments have been made necessary by the realities of existence.

The first of these amendments is dictated by the infant's recognition that the magic does not always work. Sometimes his wishes are "refused"; he makes his will known and nothing, or the wrong thing happens. This is a double crisis, since his wish remains unsatisfied and a new problem arises—what has happened to his omnipotence? Since the newborn child is also equipped with a store of inborn aggression, the result is fury.

This factor, again, represents a biological "mistake." The intensity of the eight-pound child's aggression is the potential measure of the aggression he will possess as a full-sized adult. To put it another way: If Samson had been a mild and philosophical baby, he could not have grown up to command the fury that made him capable of killing a thousand Philistines with the jawbone of an ass. The tragedy is that Samson and all lesser Samsons, as babies, must bottle up their fury because they are not able to expend it on the outside world. The baby can scream, he can vomit, he can make ineffectual movements with his arms and legs, and when his spasm of temper is over, he is still left with a substantial deposit of his original fury. Part of this unexpended aggression accumulates within his unconscious. Eventually it is used, but the external path has been temporarily blocked so that it can only be used against the child himself.

The young child's anger arises from a standard sequence of events. He wants something; the wish is not fulfilled *instantly*. He feels deprived—where is his milk?—and he feels humiliated—has he lost his magical powers? He has suffered a defeat on every possible front, and his only recourse is fury.

The pitiful part of this entire sequence is the fact that the "frustration" the baby has suffered is a frustration only from the point of view of his own limited wisdom and understanding. The baby has no sense of time and no information about the routine manipulations required before his wishes can be satisfied. An instant of time to the adult may be an eternity to the child. And if, after two or three minutes of furious crying, his bottle finally does appear before him, the humiliation of subjectively perceived failure is not wiped out by eventual success. The desired object now is in his possession, yes; but he cannot forget that as a sorcerer he has lost the game.

Here is the first of the situations in which the parent, whether he wishes to or not, must fail the child "for his own good." The fact that the fantasy of omnipotence is the young child's dearest possession does not help. Reality, personified by the parents or upbringers, must whittle away at this illusion, substituting its own truths and forcing the child to acknowledge them. No system of education can condone for long a child's refusal to recognize his dependence on the outside world and to submit to restrictions made necessary by objective facts.

This is, of course, what eventually happens. The child's theory of autarchy or omnipotence—his cherished illusion that he is self-sufficient and independent of outside help—gives way, bit by bit, under the onslaughts of experience. A certain amount of natural erosion, one could say, helps the process along as the child grows older and wiser and of his own accord makes a few careful amendments to his original theory. The most important of these divides outside phenomena into "good" and "bad." The "good" he still claims as his own, but the "bad" situations, he acknowledges, are not of his doing. This must mean that a rival magician exists in his universe. Gradually he finds a name for the supposed rival magician; gradually he admits that his rival can mete out some good in addition to the bad. Eventually he settles into the standard nursery compromise between life as he would like it to be and as it insists on being: he makes the absolutely necessary concessions to the giants of the nursery, the mother or nurses who have repeatedly proved that they have the power to give or deny, punish or reward, admire or reject. He knows, by now, that his alleged magic will bring him neither peace nor rewards. To stay on the good side of the giants he must accept the fact of his dependence and abide by their rules of conduct. He must inhibit his aggression, which means giving up "naughtiness" and stubbornness, and become "a good boy." And, since he is the weaker, he gives in.

What happens to the illusion of omnipotence? It retreats from the center of the stage but by no means disappears from the scene. To a greater or lesser extent, later on it colors even the adult's unconscious attitudes. And throughout childhood it tends to reappear suddenly and spontaneously, though never in the forefront of events.

A lesser troublemaker than inborn aggression or inborn infantile megalomania is one popularly assumed to cause more difficulty than either. I am referring to the much misunderstood *libido*.

The term *libido* denotes sexual energy in its widest meaning. The typical misunderstanding of it ignores all but its narrowest sense, assuming that it applies only to the final culmination in adults, genital union in intercourse. Libido, however, includes all the *precursors* of sex. The word was originally used to mean "pleasurable excitation of the mucous membranes," in the usual succession of the mouth zone, the urethral and anal region, and the sexual organs. Parallel excitations are transmitted by eye, ear, skin, muscles, etc.

The child discovers these sources of pleasure in the sequence in which he learns to use his various organs. For a time, all his pleasure energy is concentrated on one, newly discovered source; the focus then shifts, leaving a small deposit of libido behind. Normally, the concentration on each phase is transitory; when a shift fails to take place on schedule or the sequence of excitation secondarily reverses itself, returning to positions previously given up, the result is neurotic regression. The real catch here is that even the small deposit of libido thus reinforced is outlawed as "infantile" and repressed. Some pleasure persists, but it is now unconscious and guilty pleasure.

The fourth of the child's troublemakers is a fully unconscious mechanism which has decisive consequences: the "unconscious

repetition compulsion." A better term is *"repetition in reverse."*
Curiously enough, this mechanism is largely unknown or has
been neglected, even in psychologically oriented circles. Repetition in reverse is the tendency to repeat *actively* what one has
had to experience passively. The reversal is accomplished in response to an unconscious impulse; it is a purely automatic counteraction to a humiliating experience.

The purpose of the procedure is to heal the wound that has
been dealt to one's self-esteem (meaning one's infantile illusion
of omnipotence) by the painful experience. The important element here is the enforced passivity; no ruler of a universe can
accept the role of slave or puppet with equanimity. If the experience is physically unpleasant as well as humiliating, anger
and resentment are of course heightened, but this consideration
takes second place to the all-important matter of authority over
one's environment and one's own self. According to the standards
of the unconscious, only one means of restitution is possible. The
situation must be repeated in reverse, with the formerly passive
victim playing the active role. Curiously enough, the other person involved in the original experience need not be the victim
in the repetition; this role can be filled by anyone.

Even when the passive situation is not objectively disagreeable, there is an imperative need to restore self-esteem. Pleasure
is not the aim, nor is it accepted as a sop. Nothing can make
up for a blow to omnipotence except proof that the blow has
been eradicated—and a specific proof exactly tailored to fit the
situation.

Freud was the first to describe the unconscious repetition compulsion, although it was a mechanism he never used clinically in
his later researches. His original observation referred to a little
girl who was taken to the dentist's office, where she was forced
against her will to open her mouth for his ministrations. Upon
returning home she played dentist with a younger child. This
time she was the dentist; the other child was the patient, forced
to open her mouth unwillingly. Freud saw the twist in this apparently simple game: the little girl wiped out her own passivity by

actively forcing the younger child to submit passively to a re-enactment of the dentist's "torture."

Historically speaking, these four troublemakers are almost as old as the child himself. They appear regardless of the method of upbringing. The endowments of megalomania, aggression, libido, and the tendency to enact repetitions in reverse seem to be biologically determined. The quantities too are biologically set. All four are domiciled in the part of the unconscious known as the "id," the department of repressed wishes.

The fifth troublemaker in the child's world belongs to a different category. Although it is an inevitable arrival, it is a late-comer and is, in a sense, artificially acquired. It is a structure manufactured unconsciously by the child himself in an effort to resolve his problems—a creation that in the end dominates its creator. This self-constructed inner mechanism is the *unconscious conscience*, in scientific terms the "superego." To understand its function and its prominence within the unconscious mind one must first trace the path of the young child's psychological development.

From the magical simplicity of his earliest conception of his environment the child advances bit by bit towards the real outer world. At first he denies that an outer world exists. Then he reluctantly begins to concede that he is not alone in his universe. This admission represents a compromise in which everything "good" comes from himself and everything "bad"—that is, every refusal—from that mysterious other power, the giantess of the nursery. The division of good from bad is intensified by his always insistent need to dispose of his great stock of inexpressible aggression. One of the ways in which he can do this is through the process of *projection*. He shifts great parts of his own aggression and fury to the figure of the giantess, thus making her the embodiment of cruelty. None of his alleged wrongs is perceived by him as merely casual. As he sees it, the unknown enemy is always malicious and out for blood.

This state of affairs prevails in what is called in analytical terminology the *pre*-Oedipal stage in the growth of the child. In these first two years his idea of his mother is entirely controlled by the peculiar misconceptions described above. The mother's actual role impresses itself very slowly on the child's mind, so slowly, indeed, that in the many months before it is fully acknowledged he builds up fantasies, a "septet of baby fears," in which the mother is a cruel and vengeful witch and the baby her helpless victim. In a succession of inner dramas, changing and undergoing some revision as he grows older and learns to come to terms with a few inescapable facts, the child sees himself as the innocent victim of an ogress who is capable of first starving, then devouring, poisoning, choking him, chopping him to pieces, draining and finally castrating him.

Clinical proofs fully verify this statement. Other proofs, of a different kind, are found in folklore. The world mirrored in the immature mind of the young child is closer to the world of Alice in Wonderland or Grimm's fairy tales than to the adult's knowledge of things as they really are. Allowing for distortions and embellishments, a good many myths and fairy tales are presentations of repressed infantile fantasies. It is this that makes them timeless. The perennial appeal of "Hansel and Gretel," for instance, is that it expresses fantastic baby fears that are universal in the unconscious. A stepmother convinces her reluctant, poverty-stricken husband that the way out of this dilemma is to abandon his two hungry children in the trackless forest to die of starvation or be eaten by wild animals; a witch lures the starving children to her house made of tempting food, and there feeds them generously so that they will become plump enough to provide her with a delicious cannibalistic meal.

These infantile fears have little or no connection with reality factors, the actions or attitudes of the mother. The starting point for all such painful fantasies is in the infant's desperate struggle to maintain his picture of himself as an autarchic sorcerer, in the face of the realities that constantly reveal it as false. For example, the basic necessity of feeding the child is a source of conflict. A creature who has known only the absolutely effortless comfort of the womb and whose limited perception includes no recognition of a world outside himself must find even the offer of breast or bottle a bewildering and threatening intrusion. Luck-

ily for human beings, the pleasures of sucking and feeding—
"oral libidinous pleasure"—reconcile the baby to at least some
aspects of the new order.

The earliest of the baby fears is the *fear of starvation.* Without the complication of the child's fantasy of omnipotence, of
course, there would be no basis for this fear: mothers do not let
their children starve. For the child, however, making him wait
even a few seconds underlines his dependence and reduces his
alleged magic to absurdity. It is therefore taken as an act of extreme malice: in other words, "starvation."

This infantile fury against the mother tends to reappear in a
modified form in later life. It is then disguised as an accusation
that the child (or the neurotic adult) has been refused love, kindness, gifts or attention. In some neurotics, the game of claiming
refusal becomes a major unconscious theme.

Next to the fear of starvation comes the *fear of being devoured,* which may actually represent a shift of the child's own
aggressive designs on the breast or bottle (as emphasized by the
English school of analysis, but without considering the psychic-
masochistic elaboration). The formula reads: "I don't want to
bite; Mother wants to devour me." Fairy tales and dreams, unconscious fantasies, and animal phobias are built upon this particular infantile misconception.

Sooner or later, when the child is forced by reality to acknowledge that he is being fed and not starved, he modifies his fear of
starvation to fit his new understanding. Now he accuses his
mother of *poisoning* him: "Yes, mother feeds me, but the food
is harmful." Remnants of the *fear of poisoning* reappear in adult
life in neurotic intestinal disturbances, hypochondriacal complaints centering around food, and other similar difficulties.

The fear of being choked also persists in hidden form in later
life. Neurotics afraid of confined places, whether they suffer
from genuine claustrophobia or merely have a neurotic fear of
elevators, subways and trains, are unconsciously still dominated
by the infantile fantasy of being *choked* or smothered by the
mother's breast or body. Again, this does not begin as a reality
fear; the problem does not arise because the mother's body seems

enormous to the child or because mother or nurse have been clumsy or over-forceful in feeding him.

This phobia can take strange forms. One of my patients, after seeing an old horror movie, had developed a fear of being choked in his sleep. In the movie a man went to sleep in a flour mill. During the night the valves that kept the flour piled up were opened and it slid down over him and smothered him. The patient, fearing that particles of plaster from his bedroom wall might choke him while he slept, protected himself against this possibility by wearing a gas mask to bed. It was this "foolishness" that finally convinced him that analysis was indicated.

The baby's *fear of being chopped to pieces* grows out of the washing and cleaning procedures to which his mother subjects him. These seem to him dangerous, and therefore malicious. Once again, his misapprehension is not caused by his mother's clumsiness. The evil design is projected by the child.

The *fear of being drained* is perhaps, to an adult, the most surprising of these fears. It arises because of the baby's "helplessness" when he feels the need to eliminate urine and feces. There are "propelling forces," as he sees it, that "drain" him against his will. He combats his fear in slightly later childhood by adopting both proprietary and aggressive attitudes towards the products of elimination. In neurotic adults this fear, now repressed and quite unconscious, reaches the surface as miserliness in money, sex, and even words.

The *fear of castration*, the last of the seven, is the culmination of the baby fears. It appears during the "Oedipal phase," when the child reaches the age of three or four and readjusts his conception of the world to admit the importance of other inhabitants besides himself and his mother. Here again it is clear that his frightening fantasy does not depend on an actual threat or warning. Analytical literature today is in agreement that this universal fear of castration is connected with a a series of precursors. The sheltered Eden of prenatal existence disappears; the breast or bottle is withdrawn, stool is "drained," milk teeth eventually fall out. Putting the evidence together as well as he can, the child bitterly concludes that "pleasure leads to the loss of the pleasure-giving organ" (F. Alexander). Moreover, the child's fear and suspicion of his mother, revised from time to time and made into new accusations as he himself learns to see the flaws in his earlier fantasies, remains very much alive in spite of his repeated concessions. Much of what is termed castration fear actually consists at bottom of undigested terror identical with the terror that gave rise to the other items in the septet of baby fears.

The period of the baby fears (*pre*-Oedipal) is also that in which the child learns to extract pleasure from displeasure and fear (see Preface). Thus the kernel of psychic masochism is in existence at an amazingly early age.

It is a measure of the richness and complexity of the human mind that these very real fears do not prevent the child from learning that his mother does regard him with loving kindness. Though her role of necessity remains primarily that of the great refuser, the child's welfare requiring that she forbid and control at least as often as she is generous and permissive, the child can somehow bring himself to admit that his mother "also gives." But, curiously enough, this recognition increases his conflict instead of lessening it. From straightforward enmity and distrust, his attitude changes to one of ambivalence. At the same time that he fears and resents her, he loves and appreciates her. The meeting of these two extremes cannot help bringing an inner disturbance. Despite the child's growing friendliness, affection, and trust, he cannot fully discard his old fantasies.

This contradictory double portrait of the mother as "good" and "bad" can still be perceived in the attitudes of many neurotic adults. It played the major part in a curious minor drama enacted by one of my patients some years ago.

This man had gone with a friend to see a movie depicting a crisis in the lives of a "nice" woman and her child. The woman was being blackmailed; if she failed to pay up, the child would be kidnapped. After a good deal of painful suspense the blackmailer was caught and the crisis ended happily. During the performance the patient's friend remarked that he had seen another movie starring the same actress, in which she had been an aggressive, alluring siren. The patient insisted that his friend was wrong and the siren could not have been played by this actress, refusing to admit that a talented woman could play two widely different roles with equal effect. His refusal was not only vehement but emotional, and his friend tactfully changed the subject.

This did not end the incident for the patient. The next day, still indignant over his friend's "obvious mistake," he went to a good deal of trouble to discover where the other picture was playing. Tracking it down to an obscure theater in Brooklyn, he got into his car for the tedious, hour-long trip, unable to explain to himself why he was wasting so much time in order to see a boring movie for the second time. After watching a few scenes he left. Of course his friend was right. It was the same actress.

At this point he realized that his actions had been too odd to pass over. At his next analytic appointment he asked for an explanation.

He was married to a kind, loving, and devoted wife. Their conflicts were never anything but minor and had nothing to do with his need for analysis. He had come into treatment because of recurring depressions, set off by commonplace, small-scale disappointments. Unconsciously he misused these disappointments masochistically, deriving unconscious pleasure from his conscious unhappiness and, to increase his masochistic profit, making minor reverses into decisive defeats. His infantile history, partly remembered and partly reconstructed in analysis, pointed to an unsolved conflict with his domineering mother dating back to earliest childhood.

When the patient asked me why he had been so insistent that the same actress could not have been "nice" in one movie and "cruel" in another, I answered him by referring to his infantile past:

"You let yourself become masochistically attached to the image of the 'cruel' woman and tried to escape this danger by creating the fantasy of the 'nice' woman. You married a nice woman—as a defense. Your friend presented the actress to you as a single figure who combined the 'cruel' image and the 'nice' image. To protect your defense you refused to believe that the two could be one."

"I cannot accept that. My wife and my mother are completely dissimilar."

"Granted. But you escaped the danger on only one front. In every situation except your marriage you are still a prey to the fantasy of malice, and it operates against you in perpetual motion. Haven't we discussed, again and again, your way of misusing harmless incidents, making them into 'terrible injustices,' which you then exploit masochistically?"

"That's what you claim."

"That's what the record shows. Let's recapitulate. I told you that adult psychic masochists follow a certain unvarying pattern. The pattern consists of three parts. First, through their behavior, or the misuse of an external situation, they unconsciously provoke disappointment and refusal, identifying the outer world with the allegedly refusing mother of earliest infancy. Next, not realizing that they themselves have brought about their disappointment, they put up a show of activity and aggression, apparently full of righteous indignation and self-defense. Finally, they consciously indulge in self-pity, while unconsciously enjoying psychic masochism. The theme in this last scene is 'This can happen only to poor little me.'"

The patient interrupted impatiently. "Yes, I know the story. What has it got to do with my not recognizing that the same actress played those two parts?"

"Impatience does not solve problems. The connection—what you think of as the 'missing' connection—consists in the fact that putting the two parts of the picture together, combining the kind mother image with the cruel one, undoes a job that you have unconsciously done. Unconsciously you have taken your ambivalent attitude towards your mother and divided it into two apparently unconnected attitudes. And this split is the basis of your 'outlook on life'—the masochistic technique you are defending so desperately. By the way, I don't believe that you never, 'but never,' feel ambivalence towards your admittedly loving wife."

He became gloomy. After a pause he told me of a "peculiar misuse of words" that had suddenly come into his mind. Some years earlier he had been involved in a trivial conflict in his office, the result of one of the innumerable chips on his shoulder. He came home and recited the story to his wife. Even in this account his exaggeration had been so patent that his invariably benevolent wife interposed a mild objection. Infuriated, he shouted, "Don't act the part of your mean mother with me!" This in turn infuriated his wife; her mother had died in giving her birth, and the tragic event had left a scar of guilt. "You must be losing your mind!" she retorted. Now you are confusing your mother with mine!" The patient had to apologize profusely. The incident, long forgotten, now came to the fore again.

The patient then asked, "What's so tragic about ambivalence?"

I explained: "These contradictory feelings are tragic for the child and highly disagreeable to the adult. Freud has dealt with this problem; in his opinion, seeing in the single person of the mother a giving *and* refusing, a loving *and* hating, a loved *and* hated being leads to an unbearable situation. If the child is a boy, he finds a way out by concentrating his hatred on his father; this shift separates the contradictory feelings originally aroused by his mother. If the child is a girl, the same splitting procedure takes place, except that the mother gets the hatred and the father the love. Now in the earliest stages the only significant relationship for the child is the duality of himself and his mother. After the splitting process this duality becomes a triangle: mother, father and child. As you know, this triangular relationship marks the Oedipal phase."

"Do you mean to say that the movie actress in two editions, the cruel and the nice, reminded me of this early conflict?"

"Precisely."

If we were to look for the common denominator of all the child's varied conflicts and experiences in the first two years of life, we would find it in the word "passivity." The young child is entirely dependent on his mother. As already pointed out, he feels that he is being passively victimized even by the process of feeding, a burden which he was spared in the womb (this is typically counteracted by the newly discovered libidinous pleasure of sucking). Moreover, he is passively dependent on someone else for his milk; he may be subjected to a time schedule for his feedings; eventually he is compelled to undergo the tragedy of weaning. The list of enforced outrages does not end with nutritional wrongs. Functions which to the adult seem both natural and inevitable—urination, defecation, and even sleep—appear quite differently to the immature child. Some unknown power remorselessly "drains" parts of his body from him from time to time (libido again provides a counteraction; in time he discovers the libidinous pleasure of elimination). At other intervals some other inexorable power "forces" him to sleep. The young child has a meager frame of reference in which to place these experiences. He can merely relate them to his only reality: his illusion of omnipotence. With this as his sole criterion, it is not remarkable that he should regard even the commonplace events of his life with suspicion and distrust. The result can be seen in the septet of baby fears.

By the time the child has reached the approximate age of two, his fear and his ambivalence combine to make his entire attitude towards life untenable. This time he makes a radical amendment in his point of view, learning to see himself as part of the Oedipal triangle instead of the mother-child duality.

The child is now aware of his father and realizes that in this new figure he confronts a powerful competitor for the prize of his mother's love. As a competitor he is a formidable and intimidating enemy, but the very fact of his strength now enables the boy to perform an extraordinary tour de force. Remembering that he has repeatedly been the "victim" of that threatening and fear-inspiring "witch," his mother, the boy borrows strength from his father, pulls his mother down from her position of power, and turns her into a caricature and image of his own frightened, defenseless self. This demotion is an interesting variation on the unconscious "repetition in reverse"; the boy achieves a reversal of roles by identifying with the father who, he believes, cruelly conquers his supposedly passive victim, the mother, in the sexual act.

In its popular interpretation the Oedipal stage is widely believed to be a period in which the boy desires his mother sexually. This limited view unduly simplifies a complex process. The real key to the boy's identification with his father's alleged sexual cruelty is his need to reverse the roles which have so far been played by his mother and himself, and to wipe out his history of passivity by turning her into the "victim."

Thus the importance of the Oedipal period is that it represents a rescue station from earlier perils; its purpose is to save the child from the unbearable baby fears connected with the giantess.

At about this time the boy discovers another reality factor which he can turn into proof of his mother's weakness. He now learns that the female does not have sex organs like his own. This knowledge underlines his new picture of his mother as helpless and passive. Now he possesses the "magic" organ, and she does not.

The child's comforting illusion that poetic justice has been achieved and his passivity banished lasts for only a few years. By the time he is five he has realized that eliminating one fear-inspiring authority has only opened the door to another. Now his father is the power he must contend with. And the father is not only fear-inspiring but punishment-threatening. After the principle of "an eye for an eye, a tooth for a tooth," the boy fears that the father's retaliation will be aimed at the "criminal organ," his sex organ. The child must now decide which is more important to him, the security of his organ or his Oedipal wishes towards his mother. The choice is made easy for him; he abandons his wishes, which in any case have not been taken seriously by his mother and have at worst been received with irritation and anger. But the end result is a return of passivity. Normally the intense rivalry of the Oedipal period disappears and the emotional situation is adjusted to a calmer level. The child's hatred for his father (the so-called rival of the Oedipal stage inherits a good deal of the anger piled up during the *pre*-Oedipal period) is supplanted by friendliness; his intense feeling for his mother becomes nonsexual and merely affectionate.

At this point the child has run through the last of his expedients; he has no new way to rescue himself from his baby fears. Now the whole problem goes into storage for the next few years. During the latency period, from the age of about five until the onset of puberty, the problem makes only shadowy and temporary reappearances. With puberty, however, the old conflicts unconsciously revive. Again the child fights to resolve the problems first encountered in early infancy, and this time the final results are recorded in indelible ink. Whether or not these early conflicts can be successfully minimized and triumphantly absorbed will determine the adult's neurotic index: too neurotic, which will make for infinite trouble, or not-too-neurotic, in which case he will somewhat charitably be classified as emotionally "normal." Not that the individual's destiny is "decided" in the course of this revival of his early conflicts. The direction of his course was foreshadowed in early childhood; adolescence generally does no more than confirm or amend the previous determination. The inner tribunal that judges his case in the first place carries a good deal of weight, and, as in real life, few of its decisions are upset by a superior court.

Long before the time comes for this final decision, however, the fifth great inner troublemaker has entered the child's life. This troublemaker consists of the series of demands presented by the *unconscious conscience.*

The *unconscious* conscience is not to be confused with ordinary conscience, meaning the set of conventional, fully conscious precepts of right and wrong that the child learns from his parents and his environment. It is instead an inner tyrant constructed by the child himself in the mistaken hope that it will be an ally.

The development of the unconscious conscience (or superego, a more precise term) is a highly controversial subject. Originally Freud connected it with the benevolent institution which insisted only on the renunciation of Oedipal wishes. Freud's opinions changed later on, as can be seen from the quotations in the Preface. The development of the child's psychic life, and especially the account of the superego's development as presented in these preceding pages, corresponds to my personal opinions, which have been elaborated in my previous books.

Even the abridged outline of early development given here makes it clear that the child's inner life proceeds from expedient to expedient, each step necessitated either by an unchangeable biological factor or by the steps that have preceded it. This is true, also, of the construction of the inner conscience. The propelling reason here is the child's original endowment of aggression. As already mentioned, the newborn child possesses a store of aggression that he cannot use because of his physical helplessness. Unexpended aggression accumulates within his unconscious, clamoring to be used. It is a portion of this unexpended and malicious energy that empowers the unconscious conscience (a smaller part is projected; the third, and smallest, part is retained by the ego). Since its fuel is malice, its function must of necessity be that of cruelty.

This is not an easy conclusion to accept; one can admit without argument that the whole process is fantastic. But years of observation have convinced me that "man's inhumanity to man" is equaled only by man's inhumanity to himself, and man's inhumanity to himself is engineered and initiated by his inner conscience.

We have seen how the realities of life whittle away at the infant's cherished illusion of omnipotence and magic power. No matter where he turns, he constantly finds himself in conflict with an environment stronger than he is, and in consequence his life becomes an endless succession of humiliating defeats. The unknown political master mind who pronounced the rule, "If you can't lick 'em, join 'em," must unconsciously have been remembering what he did when he was a two-year-old child. For at about two, every child figures out this simple way to save face and preserve the remnants of his illusion of autarchy from new defeats. He unconsciously identifies with the precepts laid down by his adult governors—precepts which till now have appeared to him as autocratic commands, even when in the form of coaxing, "reasoning," or simple information. In this way he substitutes an inner warning voice for the external voice of authority.

What he hears is the identical "don't!" of the past; what he excludes is the element of surrender. He has rearranged the trappings of obedience so that he himself allegedly orders his actions, saves face and avoids punishment. Having triumphantly restored a little corner of his ruined autarchic castle, the child is happy; having apparently scored a major educational coup, the parents and upbringers are happy; life in the nursery becomes tranquil and contented—for a time.

The creation of this inner *department of don'ts* is the first stage in the growth of the inner conscience. The next stage, which arises naturally from it—and, indeed, with it—is marked by the development of an inner agency with access to the deposit of cruelty and aggression that has been accumulating within the child since birth. This second agency, the *department of torture,* makes its first appearance long before the child adopts his own inner precepts. Perhaps a pre-stage is under way when children turn their damned-up aggression against themselves by hitting themselves in frustration, as they are often observed to do. Even very young children do this; many infants, for example, are habitual head-bangers.

The "torturer" soon finds a target both vulnerable and tempting. The "department of don'ts," since it was installed to preserve self-esteem, necessarily incorporates the child's portrait of himself, which he has built up to suit the enormous vista of his illusion of absolute power and absolute perfection. Part of this conception of himself includes the future, embodying his grandiose and confident ambitions and expectations, expressed in superlatives. The child will not become a mere seaman but the captain of the largest ocean liner afloat; he does not see himself as a mere jet pilot but as the first man to reach Mars. Because of this, it would be more precise to call this inner sector the *department of don'ts and great expectations* (it corresponds to Freud's "ego ideal"). This sector and the department of torture constitute the superego.

It is the combination of a self-imposed inner code of conduct and a self-constructed (and impossible!) standard of achievement that invites the department of torture to attack. Repeatedly, thereafter, the inner torturer asks: "Have you achieved all your great expectations? Have you lived up to the code of don'ts you set up for yourself?" The child has rescued himself from one dilemma and walked directly into another—from which he will never, even as an adult, emerge. Any time the inner torturer can prove a discrepancy between the rules and promises enumerated in the department of don'ts and great expectations and the individual's external actions or accomplishments it can impose punishment. This punishment takes the conscious form of dissatisfaction, guilt, and depression.

What makes this an inescapable trap is the fact that neither the self-imposed code nor the naive promises made to himself can be changed by the individual in later life. The adult is helplessly bound to the promissory note he signed when he was an ignorant child, helplessly bound because the entire structure is fully unconscious. He cannot amend his early standard because he does not know what it contains.

To add to the irony of the situation, the inner definition of success has nothing whatever to do with success as it is recognized in the external world. If the department of great expectations contains a pledge to become President, it is not an acceptable inner excuse to be able to explain, "But I am Chief Justice!" Anything short of literal fulfillment ranks as a discrepancy, and is punished as such by the malicious inner torturer.

The department of torture, therefore, is a powerful fifth column within the personality, meting out punishment whenever an excuse can be provided. In consequence, guilt—the manifestation of the power of the inner torturer—becomes the child's companion, following him into maturity like a shadow. Unconsciously every individual makes desperate attempts to solve his specific problem of inner guilt. There are literally hundreds of techniques and countermeasures ("defense mechanisms") which he can and does use. *The most important of these is psychic masochism.*

Psychic masochism consists of an unconsciously acquired taste for rejection, refusal, humiliation and defeat. It is a technique for nullifying the inner tyrant's torture by deriving pleasure from it. The purpose of the torture is to impose pain and prevent repetition of an offense; but to a glutton for punishment, severe suffering is actually alluring. This ingenious technique is highly successful, highly dangerous and infinitely self-damaging.

The confirmed psychic masochist (a decidedly too-neurotic individual) devotes his life to provoking "injustices." These "injustices" give him *conscious pain and unconscious pleasure.* All of them are ascribed to figures which he unconsciously identifies with the infantile image of the allegedly cruel mother.

He must, of course, pay for his peculiar pleasures. The inner tyrant, which is made up exclusively of cruelty, declares masochistic enjoyment to be taboo and the worst of all possible crimes. It then prepares to impose a penalty. The psychic masochist, attempting to avoid the additional penalty, defends himself by constructing an alibi. This consists of a pattern of conduct; it is visible in every act of "injustice collecting" and never changes.

This is the secondary internal drama enacted by the psychic masochist:

Act I: Through his behavior, or the misuse of an external situation, he unconsciously provokes disappointment and refusal, identifying the outer world with the allegedly refusing mother image of earliest infancy.

Act II: Unaware that he himself has brought about his disappointment, he becomes aggressive, putting up a convincing show of righteous indignation and appearing to act in self-defense. (This anger is false aggression, or pseudo-aggression.)

Act III: After defeat, which is inevitable because he always stacks the cards against himself, he indulges in conscious and ignorant self-pity while unconsciously enjoying his humiliation. "This can happen," he reflects, "only to poor little me."

One of the most amazing of the characteristics of unconscious adherence to the pattern of deriving unconscious pleasure from conscious unhappiness is the need to drive on to defeat once a possible opening has been glimpsed and anticipation aroused. It seems that the individual *must* spend whatever psychic masochistic energy has been mobilized by a specific circumstance, such as the expectation of danger. Sometimes the unused masochism shows up in consciousness as a "senseless" feeling of depression, sometimes as a pseudo-moronic action in people who are far from morons. It may also explain why some people "cannot take success," reacting to it with depression instead of exhilaration.

Two other situations illustrate this tendency. One is the commonplace reaction of "tears of happiness"; the other, predictable depressions of psychic masochists who have expected but then escaped an unpleasant crisis.

Everybody accepts the fact that people can and do cry when they are unhappy. Paradoxically, everybody accepts without astonishment the opposite explanation: "I'm crying because I am happy."

As far as tears of happiness are concerned, they do not appear unless the specific happy event has been *preceded* by long periods of worry, uncertainty, despair, failure, or lack of success. Unless the stage has been set in this way, the reaction to the fortunate event is complacency and not happiness.

Worry, despair, lack of success unconsciously mobilize a good deal of psychic masochism within the affected person. Once the pleasure-in-displeasure pattern has been activated, it cannot be immobilized until the store of energy accumulated has been discharged. If the individual's dreary expectations are climaxed by failure, the masochistic discharge is absorbed by the subsequent depression. But what happens if his expectations perversely result in success? He then looks for a new point of deposition for his masochism. He invariably finds it, discounts the happy event, and behaves externally in a way suited to the misery which preceded his success.

In inner reality, therefore, tears of happiness represent three unconscious ingredients:

a. Unconscious discharge of psychic masochism, prepared in expectation of a negative outcome;

b. Unconscious pleasure derived from masochistically tinged self-pity, repeating in inner review the suffering preceding the favorable outcome;

c. Conscious rationalization of the paradox: since the individual is not conscious of mechanisms (a) and (b), he must construct an explanation which satisfies logical thinking. The fact that the logic too is faulty is gratuitously disregarded.

Why should the dreary prelude to tears of happiness serve to mobilize a substantial show of psychic masochism? The imminent prospect of failure signals a warning to the unconscious: "Here we go again! Again the inner tyrant is going to prove a discrepancy between your achievement and the promises you made when you were a child!" In a preventive move, the inevitable punishment is transformed into pleasure-in-displeasure; once this has been done, the masochistic energy thus produced must find an external point of deposit. It cannot be dismissed like a servant who is not needed at the moment. When the psychic masochist greets his "happiness" with tears, he is completing the unconscious transaction prepared when he expected disaster.

Here is an example of a more complicated phenomenon—depression as an aftereffect of missed masochistic opportunities.

A woman of thirty-five had entered psychoanalysis because of "dissatisfaction with everything and inability to make decisions" (her own diagnosis). Constantly she would brood on the supposed injustices done her by her mother, who had been her main educator. Her father had died when she was still very young. She described her mother as a "self-centered, always demanding, always indignant" woman. This description was confirmed by her husband; the patient did not falsify facts but merely misused them to further her own ends.

Every day the patient would have a long telephone conversation with her mother. This was inflexible routine, and it survived the fact that neither woman ever had anything to say. The tone of voice used by the older woman in these talks, the inflection she lent to a word, what she said or left unsaid would provide the daughter with her "masochistic dish" for the day. So assiduous was she in collecting injustices of this type that she put her twins under the care of an energetic nurse who intimidated her to such a degree that she did not dare to "interfere" in nursery affairs.

The daily telephone calls to her mother, she reasoned, represented "reassurance." All her life she had feared that "something might happen to mother," a fear implanted in her in childhood by her mother's attitude. Punishment had been threatened whenever her actions seemed likely to "excite" the older woman. Since anything she did might achieve this dire result, she was blamed for her mother's suffering when it was no more than a cold or slight headache. She could not explain why, after twenty-five or thirty years, she should still cling to infantile don'ts or so tenaciously hold on to her guilty feelings about her mother, which seemingly arose from aggressive thoughts.

As was to be expected, this layer of false aggression against the older woman covered a more deeply repressed, truly fantastic masochistic attachment.

The patient's "indecision" turned out to be an inner sarcasm directed at her mother. As a child and young girl, having been forced to submit to her mother's wishes in every way, even about the choice of clothing, she reduced herself to a masochistic nonentity in later life. She was unable to choose her clothes, she could not furnish the luxurious country house her husband had built for her; she could not enjoy his love.

After a few months of analysis, when some of the "injustices" she complained of had been analytically explained and worked out and her infantile past (including Oedipal fantasies) linked with its repetitions in her present life, the patient showed some improvement. She bought clothes and some furniture—a great advance.

Her resistance in treatment was very pronounced, although it followed the standard pattern. As is usual in cases like hers, she accepted the interpretation of her repressed aggression against her mother but failed to "understand" its substratum, her masochistic attachment to that same provider of injustices. She found it difficult to grasp the fact that her enormous burden of guilt pertained to this masochistic, unconsciously chosen perpetuation and was only secondarily shifted to the crime of pseudo-aggression: a crime less heinous than psychic masochism according to the inner lawbook, and therefore invariably used as an unconscious alibi by psychic masochists under attack by the inner torturer.

The whole idea that she could be a devotee of pleasurably perceived self-torture was abhorrent to the patient. It was rather pathetic to observe how anxiously this incarnation of psychic masochism longed to be considered an "aggressive" person. It took a long time before she appeared to understand what analysis was driving at in her case.

Then came a rather long interruption in treatment, made necessary by my summer vacation. In the middle of August I heard her voice on the telephone. She had been getting along "fine," she reported, until two weeks earlier, "when a change came over me—mind you, without any external reason." My response was a question: "What's going on with your mother?"

That question was prompted by my knowledge that the mother habitually spent the summer months with another daughter, one who was "cold and indifferent to mother's peculiarities," but that this year the program had had to be changed. The husband of the "cold and indifferent" sister was less tolerant than his wife and had issued an ultimatum with regard to his mother-in-law's visit: she had to be out of their summer home by the time his vacation began in August. "Either she goes or I do" was his threat. Under this pressure, the sister gave in and began to bombard my patient with warnings that their mother would be *her* responsibility during August. My patient was frantic. She consulted her husband, and they agreed that the older woman was under no condition to stay at their house. Instead, they would suggest that she allow them to take a room for her at a nearby resort; the patient's husband was to accept the blame for the absence of any invitation to their home. (The mother was financially independent, by the way.) This had been the situation —unresolved but covered by plans—before my summer vacation began.

The patient answered my question ("What's going on with

your mother?") with a surprised, "Why do you ask? Mother is in a resort near my sister's."

"And are you in no way connected with this decision?"

"Well, just to keep up appearances, I invited her. She refused."

"Does the beginning of your depression—two weeks ago—coincide with the day your mother moved out of your sister's house?"

"Yes, but . . ."

"There is your answer. You were prepared for a great masochistic fiesta—your mother's visit. It did not materialize. Now you are mourning over a lost opportunity."

Masochistic anticlimaxes such as this are invariably predictable. In people as severely neurotic as this patient, it is not enough to prevent masochistic acts; they must also be made familiar with depressions that will arise after they have avoided these very actions.

The mocking writer Saki said of a character who showed all the scars of the psychic masochist: "He simply has the instinct for being unhappy highly developed." Saki was of course inaccurate; what he could not have known was that psychic masochism is not an "instinct" but a complex inner defense against the punitive campaigns of the inner department of torture. The price of this unconscious defense is conscious unhappiness, and even when the defense appears to have been rendered superfluous by a favorable event, payment in kind (a consolation prize!) is exacted for the preparatory period.

The psychic masochist's inner life is directed by a number of curious bargains and equally curious, or illogical, conventions. His unconscious can be described as the scene of an unending battle between two unmatched protagonists. The more powerful by far is his inner torturer, the malevolent force within his unconscious conscience. *This antagonist's weapons consist of unending malice, absolute absence of scruples, and the power to inflict punishment.* All of these weapons are enormously effective; they rank as the intercontinental ballistic missiles of the psychic conflict. Against them the individual can muster a small range of countermissiles, mostly defensive rather than offensive in character, and generally of only temporary effectiveness. The most tragic aspect of this psychic warfare lies in the fact that the aggressor—the department of torture—can be temporarily halted but never damaged or disarmed, while the defender must pay heavily for every losing engagement.

The individual does learn, however, how to keep up some semblance of "business as usual" under a perpetual state of siege. He discovers, for example, which actions make him vulnerable to attack and which leave him more or less undisturbed. The inner tyrant will not be aroused by actions which give him a modicum of unconscious pleasure; only a substantial amount of inner pleasure arouses the inner tyrant to an all-out attack.

A good deal of parleying takes place in the course of this warfare within the individual between his department of inner wishes and that of inner torture. The intermediary is the *unconscious ego,* which plays the role of inner lawyer. These three departments constitute the "unconscious" in the clinical meaning of the term.

This is what happens when the inner tyrant accuses the individual of having committed a "crime," and in this way signals that it is about to impose punishment: The inner lawyer intervenes with a defense. Knowing that a mere accusation is tantamount to conviction, it makes no attempt to clear its "client" of all guilt. The defense, using the legal technique known as "copping a plea," concedes that a crime has been committed, but presents an alibi to prove that guilt arises from a crime quite different from that mentioned in the indictment. The crime admitted to is, of course, less serious than the offense alleged. (The standards here are internal, not external; psychic masochism, which does not appear as a crime in any external code, is the crime of crimes in the unconscious law book, simply because it neutralizes the torturer's torture.) The inner lawyer's aim—and the best it can do for its client—is to make the punishment fit the crime chosen by the defense, instead of fitting the crime detected by the inner torturer. In the language of external courts, he has his client plead guilty to a misdemeanor, so that he will escape possible conviction for a felony.

There is a certain formalism about the substitute crime chosen to serve as a defensive alibi. The alibi is invariably the exact opposite of the accusation. This formalism can be seen at work in the unconscious schedule of the psychic masochist. After having committed the major crime of provoking conscious defeat in order to reap unconscious masochistic profit, the individual loses no time in putting up a show of aggression—the exact opposite of passive pleasure-in-displeasure—by demonstrating his external anger and indignation. This anger is no more than skin deep; its real aim is internal advantage—an alibi.

This explanation should not be taken to mean that the inner tyrant's list of crimes comprises only forbidden external actions. A crime may also consist of a forbidden intention. Here, too, the standard rejoinder calls for providing proof that the department of wishes harbors the opposite intention. This technique accounts for the immense difficulty that accompanies any attempt to evaluate human actions and reactions. Unconscious wishes never enter the arena of action directly; they appear in consciousness thoroughly masked by double defenses. To take an unconscious defense for its exact opposite, an unconscious wish, spells utter confusion.

A young man in a state of depression and despondency consulted a physician after he suddenly found himself impotent with his wife. This had all come about, he explained, as a result of seeing a movie based on Emile Zola's novel *The Human Beast*. In this movie the main character shrinks from having intercourse with a girl because he is afraid that he may strangle her in his sexual frenzy. (Zola erroneously attributed this attitude to "hereditary alcoholism.") The patient could not get this part of the movie out of his mind. He applied the situation to himself. The physician he consulted was interested in analysis and sent the young man to me. In a telephone conversation, he explained the case as he saw it: "This man identifies himself with the murderer; his guilt makes him impotent." I questioned that assumption immediately. If this had been the patient's real conflict, he never would have become aware of it. I suspected that deep masochistic passivity was hidden behind the facade of extreme aggression, and the patient's analysis confirmed this suspicion. His impotence disappeared after a period of treatment, conducted in accordance with my interpretation of his deep inner passivity. It was obvious that there would never have been any change in him if his false aggression had been taken at face value. Such a course of treatment would have strengthened his neurotic defense and not have destroyed it.

(This example shows, how wide the discrepancy between inner and outer codes may be. Here the wish to murder was successfully passed off as a lesser *inner* crime than passivity.)

The inner lawyer's list of available defenses includes a few that succeed in eliminating any punishment, at least for a time. "That's no crime; everybody does it" provides complete exoneration, but only for a breathing space; very rarely indeed can the inner tyrant find no flaw in this defense, no deviation from correct pattern. To a limited extent, however, social approval does confer immunity. But there is one defense that can leave the individual entirely free of guilt and punishment for an appreciable length of time. This is the defense of *tender and romantic love*. The key to this success lies in the fact that tender love hits at one of the inner tyrant's most reliable accusations: the charge that the individual has failed to live up to the achievements promised when he set up his department of don'ts and great expectations. The discrepancy between expectation and accomplishment —between the confident belief that one would be the first Earthman on Mars and the drab reality of one's job as pilot for an airline that ferries passengers from Buffalo to Poughkeepsie— has always been the basis and justification for imposing punishment and has always been self-evident. But when tender love appears on the scene it becomes possible for the first time to argue that there is no discrepancy, and the basis for punishment vanishes.

The argument which demolishes the so-evident discrepancy is provided by the other member of the romantic duo. The young girl in love sees in her lover the incarnation of all possible virtues. In her eyes his promise has become his achievement. The illusion of achievement works after the principle: "He'll do it—in the future." The girl's confidence in him, her eagerness to grant him success on his promissory note, can thus be used as an inner witness for the defense. "There is no failure," this inner witness declares. And as long as love lasts, the inner tyrant cannot use the department of great expectations as an excuse for imposing punishment. Unfortunately for them, neurotics are incapable of using normal love as an antidote. Their emotional life exhausts itself in repetition of infantile conflicts, projected on innocent bystanders.

If one looks through this account of the workings of the inner mind for a hint of purpose or logic on the part of the department of torture, it will not be found. There is an undeviating aim, of course—the aim of "as little pleasure as possible" for the individual—but this aim is not part of a larger structure which, taken as a unit, can be seen as furthering the growth or development of the human being. The remorselessness of the inner tyrant appears to be *cruelty for the sake of cruelty*. It can display the extreme of useless, gratuitous malice. And this makes the irony complete: if the inner tyrant cannot prevent the victim's success, it devaluates it with a contemptuous "so what?"

It accepts no excuse and even blames the victim for situations beyond his control. Here is an example:

A French patient in his mid-forties, in analysis because of masochistic personality conflicts, had to be operated on to remove a dangerous tumor. The tumor involved the facial nerve, and this nerve had to be removed. Half his face was partially paralyzed. This was a severe shock to him, especially since he had not known of this possible result when he underwent the operation. While still in the hospital he had the following dream:

> I am in a tough neighborhood. I enter a bar; an intellectual is talking to a gangster, and there is some kind of disagreement. The gangster threatens the other man with a knife and starts cutting up the intellectual's thigh. The intellectual is incredulous; he goads the gangster on by saying ironically, "So what? You

cut my trousers." The gangster answers, "You want more?" and drives the knife so deeply into the intellectual's thigh that it reaches the genital region. I was horrified and woke up in intense fear.

When the patient was out of the hospital, he resumed his analysis. His depression was so deep that he was unable to see his operation as a whole and recognize that some good had come out of it: a dangerous tumor had been removed. He could think of nothing but the disastrous effect on his appearance. As he put it, he had entered the hospital a whole person—and "look what they did to me."

His dream was still vivid to him and he recited it in detail. His associations to it pointed directly to an identification of the gangster with his surgeon. In the patient's opinion all surgeons were butchers. The intellectual in the dream was the patient himself, thinly disguised; he prided himself on his culture and intellect and actually possessed a large stock of rather confused knowledge.

The salient point in the dream was the phrase, "tough neighborhood." His inner tyrant, evidently, reproached him for having entered this doubtful and dangerous area: if only he had avoided any contact with "gangsters" everything would have been fine. The identical reproach comes through in the encounter with the gangster, for it is the intellectual who starts the discussion. The final clause in the inner tyrant's accusation presents the same reproach, rephrased still more tellingly: "Because of your masochism, you asked for your wound; you even dared the gangster to do his worst."

This dream is sheer cruelty, except for one small sector in which the inner lawyer can be perceived at work presenting a pitifully ineffectual alibi. The scene of the dream is set in a bar, indicating that the man cannot be all psychic masochist since he wants to get, not to be refused.

Can anything be more cruel than a dream in which the victim of a dangerous disease is accused of having senselessly provoked his own mutilation? In this example the inner torturer entirely disregards reality and pronounces the victim the maker of his own tragedy.

The inner structures of the personality, to be sure, are not entirely independent of reality, since they are largely constructed under the pressure of what the child perceives as reality situations. But the parent's participation here is necessarily incidental. The reality situation, to begin with, is distorted by the child's ignorance and fear. His picture of his environment is a projection from scraps of evidence, like an early map of the American continents. What is even more important, the scraps of evidence that first impress themselves on the child do not represent parental actions but unchangeable factors which are at the same time broad and general. Examples are the whole implacable routine of feeling that frightened need, hunger, of satisfying it in a new, fumbling way, of experiencing its mysterious aftermath, elimination. These problems, with which the child must come to terms in the first months of life, are followed by others which the parents are equally unable to manipulate.

There is no way of avoiding this conclusion: the majority of the child's inner troublemakers are beyond the reach of external influence, either for good or for evil. (And external influence is his sixth troublemaker.) The parents can do their best to minimize the child's problems, but they cannot eliminate all the factors that push him into constructing his dangerous inner "solutions." And once these have been set in motion, the emergence of the inner tyrant becomes the major factor in his unconscious life. He must then rely on his inner defender, his unconscious lawyer (the unconscious ego), to handle his continuing battle with his entrenched torturer and his department of wishes. The "lawyer" does so, preparing endless inner compromises, inner defenses and counterdefenses. These influence and often dominate the child's external actions.

The greatest danger, in the perilous internal journey which the child embarks on as soon as he is born, is that his unconscious solutions will climax with the construction of an inner tyrant so powerful that inner defenses and alibis can never be more than delaying actions. When this occurs, it means that the child's appetite for pleasure-in-displeasure—his psychic-masochistic in-dex—is so insatiable that he has provided the tyrant with an unbeatable weapon. In my opinion, such an overdose of psychic masochism develops when the child cannot take the constant offenses to megalomania which make up such a large proportion of the educational process. Clinical reality proves that these offenses cannot be eliminated, and it is no help to sugar-coat them (as parents always hopefully do) with tender explanations. Persuasion can never be so friendly that a specific child will be unable to turn it into an offensive or unfriendly decision, imposed on him against his will.

One of the most banal situations in childhood is the child's request for a treat—candy, ice-cream, cake—which must be denied to him for the sake of his physical well-being—when, for example, he has an upset stomach. There are times when the parents, performing their function as custodians of the child's bodily health, must sacrifice his wishes—and perhaps their own —to that end. Few children will accept this refusal—and how can one expect them to?—on the adult level of understanding which permits one calmly to renounce an immediate pleasure in order to safeguard future comfort. The child operates within his own framework of understanding, and according to his own pri-vate system of priorities. And his illusion of omnipotence (which in practical application expresses itself in terms of his whims as well as his needs) determines whether the masochistic route is *also* taken (which means relative normality) or becomes the *leading* pattern (which means neurosis).

CHAPTER 2

INNER SOLUTIONS
VERSUS EDUCATIONAL MEASURES

MUCH of the educational process consists of an attempt to mold the child into conformity with the cultural dicta accepted in his parents' specific stratum of society. In favorable circumstances this process takes place by means of the child's identification with parental models. This is by no means a recent scientific observation; as far back as 1842 Joseph Joubert noted in his *Pensées:* "Children need models more than critics."

These models are incorporated in the child's department of don'ts and great expectations. But this department of don'ts is not a teletype, faithfully reproducing every item fed into it at the other end. A highly individual element of selectivity operates here, making meaningless the indignant question so often posed to a delinquent child. "Didn't your parents teach you the difference between right and wrong?" The factual answer to this question must be "yes." The real question—the pertinent one—should have to do with a more complicated process than the enunciation of rules of conduct. That process consists of the internal acceptance of parental precepts, and the parents, whether they are rock-bound, old-style New England disciplinarians or new-style and highly permissive, have no material influence over it.

If, for example, a specific child solved his infantile conflict with an overdose of psychic masochism, he will be driven to transgression against parental precepts in order to get his daily requirement of injustice collecting. There would be no provocation of the punishment he needs if he were obedient to nursery rules. Can the parents be responsible for the inner elaboration which rules the child's attitudes?

Very often, in such children, the inner plot to provoke punishment is subtly disguised. The French writer, Stendhal, tells of such an elaboration in *La Vie de Henri Brulard,* his autobiography.

Stendhal grew up in the small town of Grenoble during the French Revolution; he was seven when his father, whose sympathies were with the aristocrats, was put on the local list of suspects. This meant that he was a candidate for the guillotine. When this became known, Stendhal wrote, the family expressed its horror. All but the child:

> "But what do you want?" I said to my father. "Amar has put you on the list as notoriously suspect of not loving the Republic; it seems to me that it is certain that you do not love it." At this remark the whole family turned red with anger. They were on the point of banishing me to confinement in my room; and during supper, which was soon announced, nobody spoke a word to me. I pondered deeply. Nothing can be truer than what I said; my father glories in execrating the "new order of things" (a term then fashionable among aristocrats); what right did they have to get angry?

There can be no possible doubt that Stendhal's parents had "taught" the child to mourn Louis XVI and to sympathize with the aristocrats. Nevertheless, because of inner conflicts, the boy became an enemy of the old regime.

The child does not identify with a whole but with an aspect of the whole, and therefore any single identification may be balanced by a counteridentification. The Republican or Democratic Party does not automatically gain a new member when one becomes a father.

Who or what does make the decision? The answer is always the same: the specific means which the specific child unconsciously uses to solve his inner conflict. In other words, the dictator is the unconscious.

So far, people have entirely overlooked the highly important matter of *sequence:* the fact that solutions to inner conflicts have an absolute priority over educational measures. One can only reach a dead end if one explains a person exclusively in terms of parental and educational influences, for in doing so one ignores a formidable fact: the punitive power of the inner conscience.

The chief inner enemy within the human psyche is a specific reproach of the inner conscience. To ward off this reproach, and to formulate the indispensable (but ever changing) inner alibi, the child both uses and misuses educational dicta. This may be dismaying to educators, but it is a clinical fact.

It is easy to see how the inner priority prevails over the external precept if one is familiar with a mechanism called "the pseudo-moral connotation in neurotic symptoms."

Here is the "connotation" at work in what may seem to be merely an amusing anecdote; in actuality it is a very revealing and rather tragic clinical fact.

In analysis a young woman recalled a crisis dating from her childhood, when she had lived in the country with her parents. Her father, a rigid educator, had declared his apple orchard out of bounds for the children. This particular year, the trees had borne well and promised a bountiful harvest. When the time came to gather the crop, the father discovered that, although the apples still remained on the trees, his daughter had been climbing up and nibbling the fruit as it hung from the stem. When accused, she readily admitted what she had done but offered an unanswerable excuse: "You didn't say anything about eating. All you said was—'Don't pick'!"

The marked disparity between intention and interpretation here by no means represents an innocent error. When an adult cries out a warning "Hold it!" (intending the phrase to mean "Stop!") and the listening child responds by clutching at the nearest object, we are witnessing an innocent and straightforward error. But it takes subtlety—the kind that involves unconscious intention—to misinterpret a precept so that it sanctions the exact opposite of a specific command.

The unconscious intention involved in this tendency has to do with creating acceptable alibis to offer to the punitive inner tyrant. It will be remembered that the department of punishment makes use of the individual's own moral code (his sub-department of don'ts) and his own idealized self-portrait (his sub-department of great expectations) as torture material, reproaching him for all failures to live up to these promises and imposing penance for all lapses. Whenever possible, the inner lawyer attempts to deny the lapse; when this first line of defense fails, an attempt is made to justify the alleged wrong. Often such a secondary defense is built around a very real educational precept; depending on the specific situation, it is either accurately reproduced or deliberately and ironically distorted. The highly effective slogan here reads: "My parents told me to!" This useful technique constitutes a combined defense and attack. It is a defense against the accusation of the inner tyrant; it is a mocking attack against the educators who prescribed and to an extent enforced the binding precepts in the first place. It reduces both educators and inner tyrant to absurdity by literally reproducing moral precepts at the wrong time, in the wrong place, and by quoting them out of context.

The child's internalized moral code plus his naive certainty of his own value to the world provide his inner tyrant with abundant material for torture, since even under the best of circumstances lapses and discrepancies cannot be avoided. But these detailed promissory notes also set limits for the invisible enemy. It has already been pointed out that the punishable discrepancy between promise and accomplishment vanishes, temporarily, in the haven of romantic love, when a witness appears who takes the word for the deed. In the same way, an apparent lapse from the code of conduct is transformed into acceptable conduct when some educational precept can be twisted so that it flashes a go-ahead signal.

An amusing, though unrecognized, analogous literary example appears in a story by Alexander Woollcott. At the casino in Monte Carlo he noticed an elderly English gentleman actively engaged at the roulette table. He was wearing gloves. Discreet inquiries uncovered his reason. He had promised his dying mother "never again to touch a roulette chip." He remained an inveterate gambler, but he fulfilled his promise and at the same time reduced it to absurdity by doing all his gambling with gloved hands.

These unconscious ironic manipulations can eventually be used to justify an enormous variety of neurotic attitudes.

The psychic masochist, for example, self-righteously justifies the show of false aggression which he uses to ensure a retaliatory injury or humiliation by quoting his parents: "Didn't they teach me to fight back when attacked?"

The cynic maintains that his parents pointed the way for him: "Everybody secretly agrees with my forbidden views; besides, wasn't I told always to look for truth, and always to see the humorous side of things?"

The hypocrite has a trump card: "Didn't they teach me not to offend people?"

The neurotic optimist, using his invariably rosy expectations as a down payment on certain disappointment, declares: "Didn't my parents always tell me that people are nice and kind?"

The neurotic reconteur, who infuriates his environment by seizing the center of the stage and holding it until his audience melts away, cites his parents in his unconscious defense: "Didn't they always say, 'Don't just sit around; look alive, get into things'?"

The neurotic gambler unconsciously points out: "Wasn't I told time and again to take chances, to be ambitious?"

In the analysis of a good-looking girl, pathologically overweight, a good many discussions had to do with her inability to reduce. Her voracity ("I want to get") was her standard alibi against the charge of psychic masochism ("I want to be refused."). This was pointed out to her, but she would not admit that she ate excessively. A friend's evidence was resorted to here. When the two girls had lunch together, they ordered the same meal, but the friend, a slim woman, ate only part of each dish while my patient ate every crumb. The friend pointed this out to her, and in recounting it she explained: "But I had to eat everything. My mother told me it was bad manners to leave anything on my plate." This rule, it turned out, had been laid down when, at the age of eight, she needed to be "fattened up," and she was applying it years later when she obviously needed to reduce. In the next three months of analysis she lost thirty-five pounds.

A woman analyst who specialized in children's problems asked my opinion of a child who stubbornly persisted in not chewing his food properly. The patient was a boy of four. The analyst had very intelligently uncovered a number of determining factors, but the symptom remained unchanged. She then placed special emphasis on the interpretation of guilt connected with biting people (the child habitually bit his younger brother and often bit others). The symptom still persisted. I suggested that the boy was making use of an underlying irony. He was taking the familiar injunction "don't bite" and applying it to a situation it was not meant to fit: to eating, where of course his mother wanted him to "bite" his food.

Clearly the child—and the adult, later on—accepts the parents' values for what they are worth to him, as props, defenses, pretexts, and even sanctions for their exact opposite. Just as clearly the parents can do no more than present these precepts and values to the child; both whether and how the child accepts them must remain a question. Straightforward acceptance, or mocking literal acceptance, emerges in accordance with the child's inner necessities.

This does not complete the list of inner mechanisms which tend to undermine the parents' influence. Another significant mechanism is one I have described as *the theory of details*. It arises from the fact that, emotionally, only small, detailed experiences have any real, decisive impact on the unconscious personality.

To find the reasons for this, it is necessary to go back to the nursery again.

To the very young child, nothing ranks as an experience unless it enters directly into his extremely limited frame of reference. His world is built up of small perceptions, of sharp flashes of recognition. These perceptions and recognitions are of necessity simple and direct; he is not yet capable of gradations or subdivisions or of acknowledging that an infinite number of stages intervene between full pleasure, which is one extreme, and outright rejection, which is the other. His emotional vocabulary includes no "yes, buts" or "if, therefores."

To take a banal nursery event as an example: A child asks for candy at a time when it is necessary that the mother refuse him. No matter how carefully the mother explains that the refusal is "for his own good," no matter how philosophically the child appears to accept the refusal, the incident to him is climaxed with her "no." His reaction is based entirely on the fact of rejection; the aftermath registers externally but not on his inner record. Unconsciously he has replied to the refusal with hatred, hatred which does not pertain to the mother's action in this single instance but to the mother herself, regardless of her actions in the past and regardless of the "reasons" (really excuses in the child's opinion) she offers for her present conduct. It would be logical to expect that as the child's horizon widens, the tendency of the detail to dominate the whole will diminish. It is true that in time the child becomes capable of a purely intellectual—not emotional—distinction between a general attitude and an individual situation. He does learn to say and even to believe that his anger in a specific instance does not outweigh and cancel out his over-all affection for the person who has aroused his anger. Under the surface, however, he still reacts to the detail with his total personality.

The main reason for this emotional standstill is to be found in the child's inner feeling of guilt. The original anger was inevitable; it arose when the mother offended his illusion of omnipotence by refusing him. But hatred of the mother is forbidden; when this hatred appeared it was therefore accompanied by guilt. To get rid of the guilt the child had to justify it by *magnifying the importance of his disappointment*. When the inner torturer charged, "You hate your parents, who are so good to you," the child was then able to retort: "That may be so, but see what they have just done to me! This was terrible, this was unforgettable. How can they be loving if they are capable of such cruelty?"

To give basis to his inner alibi, the child must enlarge the importance of the trifle that has aroused his hatred of his parent or parents. It is this defense that is reflected in his external conduct. It becomes his emotional pattern—a pattern that remains unchanged throughout life, unless the individual is analyzed.

This magnification of details to provide an inner alibi explains why objectively trifling irritations should tend to arouse so much resentment, and why objectively unimportant detail-observations should so frequently make profound impressions on people. The detail fits the inner emotional pattern; the overcrowded vista does not. External logic does not change this state of affairs; even while saying to ourselves, "Why should this small crumb of irritation affect me so?" we go on being deeply affected.

The young child, of course, has no common-sense qualms about the importance he is assigning to a trifling detail. He inflates a routine and unavoidable denial until it grows into an injustice severe enough to balance his inner feeling of guilt. In so doing he cannot help distorting the adult's intention, whatever it was—and the adult's intention, in the fullest sense, was educational. Again, the parent can do no more than present the lesson; what the child makes of it depends on his own inner needs.

To demonstrate the naïveté of some pedagogic enthusiasts, here are descriptions of four typical neurotic or half-neurotic personality traits—exaggeration, snobbishness, blushing, and shyness—and the unconscious attitudes underlying them. In each it will be seen how strongly these unconscious imperatives outweigh educational influences.

1. EXAGGERATION

Exaggeration as a characterological trait is tacitly tolerated as one of the less deadly social sins; as such, it is understandable that few attempts have been made to uncover its psychological reasons. In analysis, however, one does encounter patients given to rather ridiculous exaggeration, and in treating a series of such patients I have come to the conclusion that they are unconsciously using the pseudo-moral connotation technique: they are mocking the educational authorities who once stated the law to them in no uncertain terms. This overemphasis was seen by these children as exaggeration; as adults they ironically dramatize the alleged exaggeration of their educators. Another unconscious mechanism is also reflected in their conduct: their exaggeration demonstrates to the educators how they did *not* want to be treated when they were children. (This is known as a "negative magic gesture.")

Both the unconscious irony and the dramatic demonstration, however, are defensive aspects of this personality trait. They are aggressive alibis and as such are only superficially repressed, although they are still unconscious. Still more deeply repressed is the trait's real starting point: masochistic elaboration of the infantile conflict. When the department of torture threatens to exact punishment for the crime of psychic masochism, the standard machinery of defense is put in operation, and the inner lawyer attempts to show that its client is not passive-masochistic, but aggressive—he *hates* his upbringers. To make sure that punishment is imposed for this lesser crime of aggression (in reality, false aggression) instead of the greater crime of masochism, the dramatized caricature of parental overemphasis makes its appearance.

The environment, of course, imposes penalties for constant exaggeration: it reacts with reserve, irony or disbelief. Apparently these penalties are accepted as proper retaliation for the show of false aggression. The real inner conflict remains hidden and unpunished—and the exaggerator goes on exaggerating.

A forty-year-old editor, in analysis because of personality conflicts, complained one day that he "had not slept a wink" the preceding night.

"I assume that your sleep was interrupted," I said.

"Why do you assume that I'm exaggerating?"

"Because that's your style. Remember you dreamed, a few nights ago, that you were holding forth at a party and someone said, 'There are people so addicted to exaggeration that they can't tell the truth without lying.' You woke up in a sweat, allegedly because you could not remember who quoted whom—

the other fellow Josh Billings' witticisr , or you the other fellow.

"Why do you catch me on a dream?"

"That's a slight mistake. Your conscience was catching you in a dream."

"According to your book, 'The Superego,' the inner conscience is a cruel torture machine. Why couldn't the accusation be sheer malice?"

"Because the inner torturer, though bent on torture, is bound by some restrictions. Before the tyrant can punish you for a crime, a rather formal proof that you have really committed the crime must be provided. Let's check: how many hours did you actually sleep last night?"

"Very few. That's a fact."

"Quite possible. But sleeping very little and 'not sleeping a wink' are not identical. Why do you exaggerate?"

"It makes a better case."

"That's a secondary rationalization. Can you give some other reason?"

"Don't be such a stickler for precision!"

"Your tone of voice is so indignant that the suspicion of repetition of some infantile scene is in order. Who was such a stickler for facts and precision at home?"

"Nobody."

"Nobody reproached you for exaggeration and half-lies?"

"Never."

Another tack was taken at this point, but the question of exaggeration came up again a few days later. Rather ironically, but still with signs of righteous indignation, the patient was describing how educational precepts had been drilled into him during childhood. His mother especially had used "ridiculous overemphasis," he said. "Today, having children of my own, I know what I didn't know as a boy—educating children is a thankless task. Whatever you do may turn against you. As a boy I couldn't help feeling that my mother constantly made mountains out of molehills. What used to get me was not what she said but how she said it. Once when I was an adolescent, I got a great deal of pleasure out of showing her two quotes from Mark

Twain. One was: 'There are 869 different forms of lying, but only one of them has been squarely forbidden: Thou shalt not bear false witness against thy neighbor . . .' The second quote was even better: 'Carlyle said a lie cannot live; it shows he did not know how to tell them.'"

"How does this tally with your statement that nobody reproached you in your childhood for exaggerations and half-lies? If the quotes from Mark Twain, dealing with lies, were an argument against your mother, she must have done so often."

"Believe it or not, the problem of lies wasn't an important issue. Mother's overemphasis was."

"O.K. Would you accept the suspicion that in your exaggerations you are caricaturing—unconsciously, to be sure—what you call 'Mother's overemphasis'?"

A long silence followed. When the appointment was over, the patient bowed himself out with a smile and a compliment: "Today you earned your fee."

At his next appointment he was still enthusiastic about this newly observed facet in his personality. He became much less enthusiastic when its masochistic basis was called to his attention.

"Oh for God's sake! Don't start that again! I'll have to take back the compliment I paid you!"

"Not even this threat can change clinical facts. If aggression—and guilt because of aggression—really were the basis of your conflicts, how could we explain your constant masochistically provoked difficulties? Your whole 'leading-with-the-chin' technique, which has brought you into innumerable conflicts, including lost jobs, unhappy marriage, etc., etc.?"

"The only thing I can say is: Aggression is acceptable, masochism isn't."

"Quite true—consciously. The pseudo-aggressive defense supports your conscious picture of yourself as a he-man; the masochistic basis invalidates the picture—which, by the way, is a self-delusion."

A woman who said she was in her "late thirties," an assistant editor of a nationally read publication, came into analysis. Her story was a sad succession of marital fiascos. All her husbands had disappointed her, but none so successfully as the current one. He was cold, reticent, refusing both sex and money. This report was freely punctuated with tears; in the subsequent discussion each new detail was the signal for nearly uncontrollable weeping.

"All this is very tragic," I said. "You left out only one point—why did *you* choose all these impossible men?"

"Are you blaming me? I have been the victim!"

"Nobody is 'blaming' you. The purpose of the question is to find out how much you cooperated in your disappointments."

"I like that! If a brick falls on a pedestrian's head, you blame the head and not the brick!"

"Your example is poor. Anybody can find himself involved in an unhappy accident through no fault of his own. But when a person is involved in repeated marital failures, the extent of his or her cooperation cannot be excluded. You knew your future husbands before you married them. If you want to fit your situation into the example of the brick, you will have to add that you saw a sign reading, 'Danger, Keep out,' but stood on the pavement waiting for the brick to fall on your head."

"None of these men had warning signs hanging around their necks. They were all charming—on the surface. How was I to know that they would prove to be stinkers—if you'll excuse the word; it's vulgar but accurate."

"I disagree. Inwardly everyone has some kind of automatic warning apparatus, telling him or her to keep out of the way of 'impossible' people."

"If this automatic warning apparatus really exists, it was not installed in my case."

"Again, I cannot agree. Isn't it strange that you have always—without a single exception—chosen men who have disappointed you? At best you can say that you have an excellent signal system—for finding disappointing men. And the only conclusion possible is that disappointment is what you are unconsciously looking for."

"That's not fair!"

By this time the patient had used up all three of her handkerchiefs (she had prudently come with some equipment). To keep the "discussion" going, I provided her with a small pile of tissues. She was half through the pile before she stopped sobbing, got her second wind, and asked:

"Can you tell me how I 'cooperated' in the scene we had last night? My husband came home very preoccupied; he is all tied up in a silly business venture which can only end in his losing money. I have warned him about this repeatedly. To cheer him up, I planned a bed party. Nothing doing. My darling husband got into bed and started reading some idiotic financial report without paying any attention to me. I started to cry, which made him furious. He accused me of hysteria and what not."

"You simply chose an inopportune moment for your advances. A man preoccupied with business worries is not the ideal lover. If you hadn't been bent on disappointment, you would have left him in peace."

"He is an albatross hanging around my neck!"

"You chose him, remember?"

"I also remember that marriage is supposed to mean companionship. What kind of companionship can I expect from a perpetual reader of financial reports in amorous situations?"

"Why do you pick the wrong time for your amorous efforts?"

"Efforts, that's the right word. I just wanted to console him."

"Does he usually react positively to such consolations when he is worried?"

"Sometimes."

"What's the approximate percentage of his positive and negative reactions—external circumstances and worry being identical?"

"I don't keep book."

"That's an evasion. May I assume that your 'sometimes' refers to an approximate ratio of one 'yes' to ten 'no's'?"

There was no answer.

"May I therefore also assume that you had exactly a one-in-ten chance of getting what you wanted? And still, you reacted as though the ratio were reversed, and a terrible injustice had been done you."

"Just pile it on me! I'm guilty!"

"If this goes on, you will prove, first, that all men are fellow conspirators; second, that I'm a brute because I'm not impressed by your tears; third, that I don't understand the fine texture of your feelings."

"You guessed right. And that's no joke, either." After a second's pause: "Please give me some more tissues."

It was just as well that there was an ample supply of these; otherwise the list of the analyst's crimes would certainly have included "malicious refusal of help in a situation where I needed it badly."

This appointment might have been an abridged history of the lady's emotional life—not so abridged, however, that it overlooked some highly revealing details. Clearly, she was an injustice collector, bent on disappointment and assiduous in finding the paths that led to it. Clearly, too, she was not one to soft-pedal the third act of the unconscious masochistic drama, since she took such pains, with her copious tears, to show that she was a helpless victim, unable to dodge the vicious blows of fate. What was unusually interesting about her tear technique was this: it was part of a more general pattern of exaggeration. This tendency was a byword in her social and business circles. A story she told me illustrates this. A colleague had asked her, absent-mindedly, "Is today Monday or Tuesday?" She replied, "Monday," and he commented ironically, "That must be an exaggeration of yours."

Her crying spells constituted exaggerations because she led up to them by magnifying self-constructed nuisances until they loomed as tragedies. Just as in the first case cited, the neurotic elaboration of the infantile situation was decisive here. The patient's mother was an "intense" person in general; she had been "impossibly intense" about drilling cultural precepts into her daughter. This trait subsequently became the target of the patient's unconscious irony, and in her mocking reproduction, intensity became exaggeration.

There is another interesting detail connected with the patient's weeping. Her abundance of tears was a means of reducing her mother to absurdity, for in the course of intensely putting forward her educational aims the mother had often "had tears in her eyes." The patient later expanded these few drops to repeated floods.

Strangely enough, these and similar cases show that the offending element was not the content of the educational command but the manner in which it was communicated. It is the manner that the exaggerator subsequently misuses. The identical parental attitude can be, and often is, disregarded. The decisive point seems to be whether or not the child needed an inner argument against the educator.

The objection, "But Mother actually acted that way," misses the point. If the child had no inner need for masochistic elaboration, nor for a pseudo-aggressive defense against that elaboration, he would calmly have discounted his mother's overemphatic attitude. In listening to her statements, he would automatically have followed the recommendation of an anymous wit: "Deduct fifty percent and assume the opposite."

2. SNOBBISHNESS

Sneering at the snob is a popular pastime providing much pleasure in exchange for a minimum of thought and effort; explaining his psychology is a more laborious procedure.

Webster calls "snob" a word of uncertain origin describing "one who blatantly imitates, fawningly admires, or vulgarly seeks association with those whom he regards as his superiors," and also supplies a corollary definition: "One who repels the advances of those whom he regards as his inferiors; one conscious of his superiority; one inclined to exclusiveness, as, an intellectual snob."

Sharper condemnation appears in European definitions. Meyer's *Lexicon,* for example, declares a snob "an uneducated, pretentious, supercilious person; a fashion ape. Snobbishness is empty pretension (*eitle Vornehmtuerei*)."

The snob has a bad press; people react to him with contempt and enmity. What about his psychological beginnings?

Different observers have repeatedly stressed the fact that snobs construct and adhere to false and artificial standards. In an article entitled "An Anatomy of Snobbery," in his book, *The Trail of the Dinosaur,* Arthur Koestler cites the case of a promiscuous girl, connected with a publishing firm, who slept with every author of a book that had sold more than twenty thousand copies. She defended her conduct by explaining that she was "sleeping with history," and as her final argument asked, "Who would blame Marie Walewska for surrendering to Napoleon? Everything one does with a famous man is redeemed from sinfulness by becoming an Historical Anecdote." Koestler also writes of another girl to whom a shy admirer had presented an original drawing by Picasso. Assuming that the picture was a reproduction, the girl hung it over the stairs. Later she discovered its value and promptly promoted it to the place of honor above her fireplace. She defended her actions with an aesthetic "doublethink": "The frame of reference has changed." Obviously she did not recognize her own snobbishness. Koestler traces the change in her attitude to "sympathetic magic" and "primitive fetishism."—"The contact with the Master's hand has imbued it (the picture) with a magic quality."

In Koestler's opinion, snobbery as an attitude arises from an area of confusion between two systems of value: that on which human judgments are officially based, such as standards of taste, beauty, and "intrinsic human qualities," and the distorting influences arising from the attractions of titles, power, personal fetishes, and so on. Snobbery, he believes, represents the psychological fusion of these systems, which are in actuality independent of each other, though people cannot apply them separately.

Many of his observations are valid and excellent; his explanations, however, are inadequate.

A snob is an inner defeatist who settles for the proximity of "the great" after having unconsciously despaired of becoming "great" himself. He is akin to the impostor though without the impostor's activity; he is a child without patience. He accepts the act of looking at other people's greatness as a substitute for his own success.

Snobbery consists of a peculiar make-believe, achieved by

means of identification, plus an even more strongly marked element of submissiveness. Rubbing elbows with "the great"—even when the "great" do not know whose elbows they inadvertently graze in the crowd—becomes an acceptable replacement for action. Fantasy is paramount in the snob; his daydream lasts twenty-four hours.

What prevents productive action? The identical masochistic submissiveness (only partially and defensively counteracted by pseudo-aggressive contempt for the "less fortunate") which pushes the child in the adult snob into his ludicrous—if not pathetic—idolatry.

Moreover, imitation of "the great" by no means reflects a simple continuance of the homage and awe accorded the father in the Oedipal situation. On the contrary, the entire attitude expresses a desperate attempt to avoid the masochistic feeling of being excluded. The snob wards off the feeling of being "out" by accepting his own invitation to join the exclusive group of "the great"—by rubbing elbows with them.

It is not even exact to say that the snob "identifies" with the famous and illustrious. The apparent identification is false, since it stops at externals. A true internal identification extends into the spheres of work and action; identification which is no more than outer mimicry ends in daydreams and inactivity. Long ago I learned this rule of thumb in analysis: *Children who continue to brag about their future achievements after reaching the age of eight or nine* (bragging is typical and unavoidable in children between three and five) *without doing preparatory and extracurricular work such as independent reading and studying and development of mechanical skills, become daydreamers and snobs.* Instead of imitating or surpassing their models, they are "crushed" by their models, because they want to be crushed. They then take the typical way out: masochistic complaints or snobbery.

It is interesting to note that the snob is never aware of the obvious fact that his mimicry-identifications are unproductive and his goals empty. He holds on for dear life to his "compass which always points in the wrong direction," simply because the inner defense mechanism of snobbery protects him from a greater danger: that of being left without a defense when his inner tyrant accuses him of emptiness and ineffectuality.

Are parental attitudes responsible for the emergence of snobbery? Decidedly not. Even when the parents themselves are snobs, automatic identification with this trait does not occur. The child's inner needs make counteridentification just as likely. Moreover, the inner reasons for snobbery (megalomania, masochistically elaborated and unaccompanied by real effort at achievement) have intimate connections with the inner, not the outer, situation that confronts the child.

3-4. TWO EXAMPLES OF FAULTY ELABORATION OF THE "VISUAL DRIVE"—BLUSHING AND SHYNESS

Psychiatric psychoanalytic investigations, so far, have largely neglected the neurotic symptoms and sublimations connected with peeping (voyeurism) and displaying oneself (exhibitionism). The visual drive, which covers both subdivisions, does not seem to fit into the usual layers but rather to live a life of its own. My studies on the visual drive, published at various times during the last quarter century, are brought together and summarized in *Curable and Incurable Neurotics* (Liveright, New York, 1961).

Freud originally described peeping and exhibitionism as partial drives. They are on an equal basis. He added that each contains an affinity to elements of the other, since a flow of unconscious identification always links the two. While exhibiting, the exhibitionist also identifies with the viewer who peeps (or is forced to peep); the opposite is also true, since the peeper identifies with the exhibitor.

My experience has been that the *parity* between voyeurism and exhibitionism is spurious. Voyeurism alone is an original drive; exhibitionism is a later defense, used when voyeurism is strongly forbidden.

Exhibitionism is not only a mere inner defense, but it is one with a marked specificity. It contains "confessional elements," the admission that one has actually passively seen (or imagined seeing, or wished to see) what one now—in active repetition—exhibitionistically repeats, frequently in an exaggerated caricature and on one's own substitutive organs.

These confessional elements in exhibitionism are paradoxical. On the one hand, they serve as guilt-diminishing factors; since they imply that imitation is involved, others (the imitated, active models) bear the responsibility. On the other hand, they do embody the admission that something has been seen, and this makes it difficult for some children to effect the transition to defensive exhibitionistic self-assertion. These children become shy.

Shyness may be unproductive and masochistic, or it may encourage autarchic imagination and thus become productive. The latter result is seen in creative individuals in all fields who are externally shy. Individuals who reach the former solution try to find the same way out, but they are sterile.

The big question is whether or not the ego can convince the superego. Of course the inner tyrant is inhospitable to the guilt-diminishing excuse of imitation, and stresses the forbidden early peeping.

Why should early peeping be defensively transformed into late exhibitionism? The history of infantile peeping provides the answer. The beginning is self-observation. All babies, when they are a few months old, become fascinated by their own toes, fingers, and so on. Later this process of fascinated inspection includes the mother's body, and especially her nutritional apparatus. This is true regardless of whether the baby is fed by breast or bottle, for every time the mother takes the baby in her arms he is in close proximity to the breast. When the child grows older, both self-voyeurism and voyeurism with the mother as the object are forbidden: self-voyeurism because it in time extends to "playing" with the child's own sex organs, peeping at the mother because cultural standards of decency must be taught. The result of both these visual defeats is defiant exhibitionism: "Who wants to look at your ugly udder? I want to display myself!"

There is another complication. At the infantile crossroads

where peeping is exchanged for exhibitionism, there can also be (under unfavorable circumstances, when the ego is too weak and the superego too strong) a meeting point with advancing psychic masochism. The transition can be accomplished normally; it is then accompanied by spitefulness. It can also be accomplished masochistically and half-heartedly; under these neurotic conditions peeping becomes a proof that this very activity has been forbidden and is a way of masochistically exploiting the taboo. This is especially visible in perverted voyeurs. These are not people who simply have a stronger voyeuristic drive than is usual but sick individuals who, under the disguise of wanting to see a woman undressing or naked, enjoy the masochistically tinged proof that she is denying them the privilege.

Generally, one can state that every neurosis connected with the visual drive and its defensive derivatives is based on masochistic elaboration of an early infantile peeping conflict.

When peeping (at breast, body) is denied, two elaborations become possible: exhibitionistic defense and flight into imagination.

1. *Exhibitionistic Defense.*

a. The normal transitory solution: spiteful refusal to look, which leads to increased exhibitionism (see above, and case of photographer described below).

b. The half-neurotic, and therefore frequent solution: Peeping is partially maintained in combination with an exhibitionistic defense, but it is elaborated in the "masochistic allure of the forbidden," so that a half-expectation of punishment is included. In consequence, the average man is a surreptitious peeper at innuendos of the half-concealed female body. This tendency can be studied in the male attitude towards female fashions. Women do not attract men by their clothes but by the way in which clothing or the relative lack of it hints at parts of the naked body. (This was elaborated on in my book, *Fashion and the Unconscious,* 1953.)

c. The masochistic grievance solution: This leads to partial attempts at reparation in the exhibitionistic defense, accompanying the seeming maintenance of the peeping "wish." But that "wish" is not identical with the original impulse to peep; it is masochistically inundated. The perverted voyeur mentioned above is an example of this solution.

2. *Imagination as Flight from the Voyeuristic Dependency Dilemma.*

Imagination is an attempt at visual self-sufficiency; the individual creates his own peeping objects and thus excludes the real, original object, which has been denied him. More than a century ago the 19th century French moralist Joubert called imagination "the eye of the soul." Heine gave a revealing and unconventional answer to a conventional query about how he had been spending his time when he said, "I gave audience to my fantasies." Herbert Spencer went one step further and defined reading as "seeing by proxy" in *The Study of Sociology*.

Retirement into undisturbed fantasy leads to the following solutions:

a. Subjectively creative fantasies. These include daydreams of erotic, aggressive or narcissistic character, pleasure in thinking, connecting of facts, etc.

b. Objectively creative fantasies: literary, artistic or scientific fantasies leading to sublimations.

c. Creation of fears and imagining of impending disaster. This is totally unproductive but unconsciously enjoyed masochistically.

All these solutions overlap and can be encountered in the same person, though in different quantities, different subsectors of the personality, and at different times.

The visual drive plays an important part in certain neuroses and certain sublimations. The neurotic sector contains the following manifestations: shyness, blushing, fear of confined places, street fear, fear of heights, fear of examinations, jealousy, pathological curiosity and logorrhea (over-garrulity), writer's block (painter's, composer's, sculptor's block), inability to function in scientific, photographic or journalistic endeavors, depersonalization, stage fright, boredom, "negative exhibitionism," lack of imagination in perception of external phenomena and lack of "business acumen," temper tantrums, general inhibition of the ability to reproduce verbally or graphically what has been seen or heard, coprophemia (predilection for obscene words), "demonstration character" in neurotic and psychosomatic manifestations, perversion voyeurism and perversion exhibitionism.

In the normal sublimatory sector, visual derivatives are important to all inventive, imaginative, and creative endeavors. They are operative in scientific, artistic, engineering, and architectural work, in all forms of professional entertainment, in fashion creation, speechmaking, success in business, etc.

Further details in the visual sphere cannot be discussed here, for instance the connections between activity and passivity. But it should be pointed out that the transition from peeping to exhibitionism represents the historical aspect of the visual drive (the genetic picture). After the exchange mechanism becomes established there are secondary defenses that can actually be observed in behavior (the clinical picture); exhibitionism can be warded off with voyeurism, and vice versa.

After these short introductory remarks, which of necessity simplify one of the most complex problems in psychopathology, one can approach the specific topic of shyness and blushing. These two phenomena are especially illustrative in discussing parental influence, because parents of shy children and of blushers are often accused of having "intimidated" their children. Clinical experience frequently proves this accusation to be unjustified, uncovering the unconscious reasons for the child's resort to shyness and blushing. An ironic postscript is the fact that parents sometimes suffer more from these manifestations than the child. Such parents try vainly to remedy the situation by correcting their allegedly or actually overbearing attitudes.

Blushing represents "more than meets the eye" (this common phrase has seldom been more apt) and has, psychologically speaking, little connection with popular notions. The traditional, conventional view of blushing in young people can be summed up in a few sentences: "The blush is a charming trait in young girls and children; it testifies to shyness and innocence. It often means that a person wants to remain in the background, unnoticed; he or she becomes confused when brought into prominence or praised. People "redden with shame,' too; this means that they feel guilt when their wrong-doing—which they had hoped to conceal—becomes known."

This is about as far from actual psychological reality as casual, folklore interpretation can go.

The psychological investigations into the phenomenon of fear of blushing (technically, "erythrophobia") have naturally had to do with pathological blushing, in which the trait is carried to an embarrassing and uncomfortable extreme. As in all neurotic symptoms the degree is the test. There is nothing abnormal about an occasional blush, yet the unconscious meaning is exactly the same as when blushing becomes pathological.

The most important aspect of blushing deals with the question of whether the blusher really wants to remain in the background or to call attention to himself. Analysis answered this question half a century ago: the blusher is unconsciously exhibiting.

A patient suffering from pathological blushing recalled how distressed he had been as a child to have to share a bedroom with his mother. Even at the age of three and a half he had felt ashamed. As the side of his bed, made of netting, faced his mother's bed, he would always drape his covers over it. Officially this was proof that he was not watching his mother undress; by inference it was also assurance that he was not watching parental intercourse. But lying in bed half-naked, he was, of course, exhibiting himself. This illustrates the original drive, peeping, and the negation of the drive by means of exhibitionism. The third-line defense, which ensured that guilt should be attached to the alibi of exhibitionism rather than the original crime of peeping, was visible in the shame he felt when his mother covered him in the morning.

Another patient with the trait of blushing told of seeing a woman he thought he knew while at a mountain cottage. Suddenly it occurred to him that she might be a patient he had often seen leaving my office. He found this possibility distressing and looked away from her. In the next few minutes he behaved in a very exhibitionistic way. He spoke in a loud voice, started singing, opened his shirt and put on another sweater. The woman actually was my patient, and she reported that he "behaved as if he wanted to attract attention, although at the same time he was rather embarrassed and quite red." Here again the primary desire to stare gave way to the defensive alibi of exhibitionism, and then exhibitionism itself was warded off with guilt.

The blusher's exhibitionism is thus not genuine but defensive, covering more deeply repressed peeping experiences. In a paper read at the XV International Psychoanalytic Convention in Paris in August, 1938 (*The Psychoanalytic Quarterly,* 13:43-59), I pointed out that what appears to be hysterical conversion has a pre-Oedipal basis: the reddened cheeks do not symbolically denote the sex organs, as scores of investigators had assumed, but the breast. The pseudo-paranoic ideas of pathological blushers correspond to an inner defense: "Other people peep; I don't." This defense clothes their voyeuristic pleasure in a moral alibi, and enables them to use other people as mirrors in which they can look at themselves with a clear conscience. Also, the spiteful defensive aggression unconsciously included in this defensive exhibitionism is masochistically elaborated and cannot be taken at face value. An example was furnished in a detailed case history, in which the pronounced exhibitionism of the female patient also showed an unconscious allusion to an ironic caricature and imitation of her coquettish mother. The caricature symbolizes a whining and masochistic reproach: "You show yourself to strange men without restraint but not to your own child."

This paper also adduced examples of the voyeuristic-exhibitionistic exchange mechanism.

In "Further Contributions to the Problem of Blushing" (*The Psychoanalytic Review,* 44: 452-456, 1957), I pointed out additional facets in the neurotic symptom of blushing. One of these dealt with the peculiar *anticipation tendency* of punishment in pathological blushers.

In my original publication, I had stated that the "organ defensively displayed (in blushing) is the entire body, but particularly the penis, the cheeks, and the buttocks." Subsequently I concluded that buttocks exhibitionism should be more strongly stressed in this unconscious sequence of shifts, since the child unconsciously uses his buttocks to negate his lack of breasts and symbolizes the equating of buttocks and cheeks in the act of blushing. The "red cheeks . . . are a masochistic demonstration of how unjustly the child has been treated, for the buttocks are red after a beating, and he shifts this alleged 'proof' upward, to his symbolic equivalent, the cheeks. A precise description of the blush, therefore, would be 'demonstration of reddened buttocks after a beating.'"

This symbolism does not necessarily pertain to actual beatings administered to the child. In children and adults bent on punishment for the sake of masochistic pleasure, an "anticipation tendency" sets in: defeat or humiliation is so eagerly desired that it becomes psychologically a fact before it has actually materialized. Here are some examples.

During my summer vacation a former patient, an author cured of writer's block, wrote to me asking my opinion on a specific problem. His analysis, a few years earlier, had lasted eight months. After four months he had begun to write again. In the next four months his short stories earned for him $1000 more than the cost of therapy. He considered this a major triumph, could not be convinced that certain aspects of his psychic masochism were still unresolved, and discontinued treatment.

This was the problem he consulted me about: He had now written a short novel about the institution where he had been employed part time (a convenient and lucrative arrangement) for twelve years. Publishing the piece, which he considered his best work, might possibly mean the end of his job. Would I read the novel and give him my candid opinion? The letter ended "Sincerely," a closing he had never used in previous letters.

The story confirmed the obvious suspicion. Publication of this venomous attack would invite dismissal. The man wanted his salary *and* his right to attack—a clear-cut masochistic attitude. It was evident too that he was aware of this; otherwise he would not have asked for my "opinion."

In reconstructing his psychic situation before writing the letter, it can be assumed that he knew exactly what I would reply:

that it was out of the question to keep his job and publish his story too. Any attempt to delude himself, therefore, had to be a preparatory masochistic action leading to an even more masochistically satisfying climax.

As for the "Sincerely"—which some time later he did not remember and actually denied using—its superficial meaning was clear; it was an unconscious aggression against me, since it meant, "You are not my friend but rather an enemy under the disguise of a representative of the 'reality principle.' "

In a deeper layer the "Sincerely" pertained to the letter of resignation he would have to write to the institution. He anticipated punishment by preferring an imaginary resignation to the renunciation of his masochistic aim.

A woman patient came to her appointment much puzzled by a peculiar case of "mishearing." She and her husband had been discussing, in a detached way, the marriage of a couple they knew (the man happened to be the patient's lover). Shortly afterwards they left for the theater. As her husband opened the door of their car she seemed to hear him say, "Get out." Actually, of course, he had said "Get in." She retorted sharply, "What do you mean?" Naturally her husband looked surprised. In thinking about the scene later she definitely excluded the possibility that he might have said "Get out." Her "mishearing" anticipated a good deal: "My husband will find out about the affair and tell me to get out!"

Masochistic neurotics such as these patients cannot wait until punishment strikes; in their eagerness they act it out in anticipation. This seems typical of the blusher. Unable to wait for the mistreatment he wants, he exhibits its results—reddened buttocks —beforehand. His exhibition includes, of course, an accusation against his elders, who allegedly treated him so unjustly.

The following case shows another aspect of the over-all picture of the blusher.

A remarkably pretty girl of twenty-two with "tendencies towards blushing," entered analysis because of chronic headaches for which a host of diagnosticians and neurologists could find no reason. When questioned about her sex life, she used a good deal of circumlocution until it became clear that she was somewhere on the verge of nymphomania of a specific type: she remained completely cold during the act, deriving her pleasure from disparaging the man. When after some time in treatment she became more outspoken, she confessed that her favorite remarks during intercourse were "You are just a flop like all the others"; "Give me a cigarette to kill time"; and "How long is all this silly jumping around going to go on?" Two things transpired, one mentioned by the patient and the other observed by me.

The patient said: "I *always* have my headache, except when I give one of these fools who want to impress me with their sex technique a piece of my mind."

"What do you conclude from that?"

"Apparently my headaches mean that not enough anger is discharged."

"You consider yourself a hyper-aggressive person?"

"Could be."

"A few facts contradict this assumption. First, your sex routine is completely self-damaging. Second, in your appointments, every time you repeat one of the derogatory remarks you have made in a one-night stand, you rub your cheek, just as if you had been slapped in the face. Just observe what you're doing right now."

She was shocked and for a moment unable to reply. She then regained her poise and said: "That doesn't mean anything."

"On the contrary, it could mean a great deal. I suspect that you provoke these men only to be slapped."

"Nobody's done it so far!"

"Too bad for you. And here is the connection with your headaches: you suffer from an accumulation of too much undischarged psychic masochism and not, as you believe, too much undischarged aggression."

"Why don't I have headaches when I abuse a man?"

"You are taking the blame for the lesser crime at these times. You are trying to convince your inner conscience that you are the opposite of a masochist, namely, a highly aggressive person. Since you present your proof under self-degrading conditions, the bargain is accepted—for the duration of your self-degradation. One lesser form of masochism exchanged for the other, bigger one."

After the headaches gradually and "mysteriously" disappeared, and nymphomania was given up (the change took months, of course, with the usual ups and downs), the girl consented to analysis of the infantile precursors, and received the explanations with some measure of understanding. Previously she had refused to "fall for that trap," as she expressed it. The story was banal; beating fantasies were behind it.

Generally speaking, the pre-Oedipal basis of beating fantasies has not been included in the scientific literature on the subject. The fact is that they arise from an unsolved conflict involving the mother's breast. Secondarily, this is masochistically elaborated and shifted to the child's own buttocks. In the meantime, the execution of these "cruelties" on the unconsciously willing victim has been shifted from the mother to the father.

In the case of a French-Canadian woman, in whom blushing, depersonalization, writer's block, and drinking were combined, the following came to the fore:

She had very vague recollections of being beaten by her father which, as the analysis continued, became clearer: she remembered her father using a leather strap, a cane, or a broom. Naturally she recalled these beatings as painful; the alluring pleasure was fully repressed. A small incident convinced her that pleasure had indeed been involved. Her favorite easy chair was made of rattan. She could not explain exactly how that chair (which had belonged to her mother-in-law) had escaped her frequent redecorating furies.

During analysis she toyed with an "unexplainable word"—*ratatouille*. After some time she recalled that this "meaningless" word was French slang for *ragout grossier,* coarse stew. She pronounced it "ratatue," which was reminiscent of *tuer,* the French word for "kill." I asked whether she could possibly have created a word from "rattan" and "tuer" and also whether she knew what her father's cane had been made of. It had been rattan-bamboo. Thus *ratatouille* meant: "The beating kills me." In toying with this word, therefore, she was accusing her mother ("bad stew") *and* her father!

Sitting with her buttocks in her favorite chair, she exposed herself to the hated and loved rattan-bamboo, and to an undercurrent of associations with Chinese torture techniques and beating methods.

One can adduce another tendency: that of blushing when "caught red-handed." It is a familiar observation that some people blush when proved guilty, or even when listening to a discourse or sermon dealing in a general way with their real or fantasied "misdeeds." An excellent example of this was provided by the son of a minister, who would blush in church when his father preached against sin.

These people anticipate punishment and misuse the beating not yet administered by turning it into a masochistic demonstration of the parents' injustice; they exhibit their "buttocks reddened by beating." This amounts to a defensive "negative exhibitionism"—demonstration of a "bleeding wound."

Shyness represents a specific neurotic trait denoting the inability to use the typical infantile mechanism of "stubborn reparation," which conveys the message, "I do not wish to peep but to display myself exhibitionistically." The difficulty lies in the "confessional element" in the mechanism. In his imitative exhibitionism, the child admits that he has seen the tabooed breast. What does this mean?

The child attempts to solve his problem of dependence on breast or bottle by using narcissistic-autarchic means; he thus denies his early dependence and the deprivation that follows at weaning time. In this technique the possession of a substitute organ is declared to be full reparation: "I cannot have been deprived of the disappointing breast (bottle) because I have one on my own body." In this way the grotesque identification of breast (bottle) and male organ is established. Both organs are pendulous; both "produce" a fluid. This infantile reasoning overlooks a series of anatomical, histological, physiological, and inner-secretory facts, but the baby, of course, does not know or care. Beggars and babies in need of consolation and narcissistic reparation cannot be choosers. The identification takes place, even though it seems idiotic from an adult's superior vantage point. The distressing (to elders) tendency towards penis exhibitionism has its emotional beginning at this point. For anatomical reasons the problem of the baby girl is more complex. (For elaboration, see *Counterfeit Sex,* Part II. Grune and Stratton, New York, 1958.)

This typical process does not work satisfactorily with the shy child for two reasons. First, penis exhibitionism includes the confession that one has seen the tabooed breast. The shy child falters and cannot bring himself to this confession. Second, the shy boy never overcomes the painful fact that there is a marked discrepancy between the size of the breast, the original object, and the size of the organ he is exhibiting in substitution. In consequence he acquires "the complex of the small penis."

To my mind, the classical proof that it is not parents but the whole fabric of infantile fears and misconceptions (plus biological factors) that makes for neurotic difficulties is to be found in this mechanism.

The complex of the small penis plagues millions of men. It was first scientifically described, but never sufficiently explained, by Sandor Ferenczi and has not received much analytic attention. Earlier assumptions connected it with Oedipal castration fear. I believe, however, that it all begins before the child reaches the Oedipal period, and that the starting point is the comparison of the child's penis with the maternal breast (bottle). The unavoidable comparison has its emotional basis in the narcissistic wound inevitably inflicted upon the child in weaning, an offense to his illusion of omnipotence. In attempted reparation he consoles himself by declaring that he has lost nothing since he possesses the perfect substitute on his own body.

The boy loses in his competition with the mother's breast or bottle, and to him this is tragic. One could, of course, ask why all men do not acquire the complex of the small penis, since the facts leading to that infantile fantasy are universal. The question is less facetious than it seems; every man unconsciously bears some scars acquired at this time. The elaboration of the experience may be normal or neurotic. When the complex is maintained, it indicates neurosis; carried one step further, it leads to complete abandonment of the female sex and resort to homosexuality. The normal solution is visible in the psychological superstructure of the biologically conditioned sex act in adult males; in a tour de force, the old standby of repetition in reverse is invoked. The child's first experience is that of having a pendulous organ containing fluid (breast, bottle) *actively* pushed into his *passive* mouth. In intercourse, the roles are reversed. By unconsciously identifying penis and breast, vagina and mouth, sperm and milk, he accomplishes an active repetition of a passive experience which was an offense to narcissism in infancy. Another remnant of this early fantasy is the "penis pride" of the boy, which covers the more deeply repressed "breast envy." Finally, despite all bragging, every man retains some remnants of those early disappointments, and no man is as sure of his sexual prowess as he pretends to be.

Every educational system must of necessity inhibit the child's penis exhibitionism. Unavoidable educational measures, as he grows older, make things even more difficult for his attempt at reparation. And he is too young to understand cultural yardsticks. When his mother reproves him for exhibiting, he takes her attitude as proof that she is rejecting his attempts at narcissistic reparation.

The irony of the situation becomes more acute if one takes another reality factor into account. The boy's later comparisons between penis and breast (bottle) are based on the size of the non-erect penis. This is no indication of its size in erection. Moreover, the usable length of the vagina is no more than two and a half to three inches, and the average length of the typical erect penis is nearly double that size.

If one thinks this problem through, one comes to the conclusion that parents do not have the power to help the child in this tragic struggle. Whatever they do is misinterpreted by the immature boy.

Neurotic shyness takes innumerable forms. A few of these will be described.

Self-Display Fully Inhibited. A French photographer, famous in his day, was partially analyzed by me in Vienna many years ago—only partially, because he repeatedly interrupted treatment. Whenever this man had to appear in public to deliver a lecture or participate in a social occasion, he would protest. After this rationalization was reduced to absurdity, he did concede that he was better informed on his own subject than his listeners could be, but still insisted that he "simply couldn't do it." He feared invitations.

Analysis revealed a massive layer of exhibitionism, which he was able to use only in substitution: in his work, in his alliances with strikingly attractive women, in the splendor of his studio. Personally he was extremely retiring. He always seemed to be apologizing for his existence.

Along with his shyness, however, went an appetite for experiment. He was always looking for "a new angle." This was a tremendous advantage in his work, where his innovations were admired, but it made for constant and severe personal difficulties. These, combined with masochistically self-arranged trouble with women, pushed him into treatment.

As already mentioned, exhibitionism, psychologically speaking, represents a defense against the more deeply rooted wish to peep. In this patient the defense itself was inhibited and could operate only through an agent or representative. Since the man was a photographer, his "agent" was usually the model who posed for his pictures, or the picture itself. It was the model who "exhibited," he could unconsciously declare, not he. Without this cover he was helpless.

Undoubtedly the kind of work he did satisfied a good deal of his need to peep. This peeping was permitted by his inner tyrant, partly because it took a socially approved form and thus represented a sublimation. But he had found another defense as well, which convincingly stated that infantile peeping was not involved. This alibi was interesting and complicated.

To begin with, it negated the element of passive dependence

so prominent in infantile peeping at the mother. Instead of display as the result of another's decision, it was the result of his command. He therefore actively reversed a situation of infantile passivity; he manipulated his models, and "forced" them to exhibit themselves.

Second, his models, as he posed them, were his "creations" and therefore in a sense himself. Peeping at them was peeping at himself. In a roundabout way he thus managed to re-establish the first goal of infantile peeping—self-examination.

Third, the very nature of his work provided an excellent unconscious excuse: "I am not peeping at the model; she is exhibiting and thus forcing me to peep!"

These three subterfuges, plus the world's approval of his work, made it possible for him to indulge his need to peep. In his exhibitionistic defense, however, he ran into trouble, since obviously he had not been unconsciously able to accept exhibitionism as the full equal of peeping.

The stumbling-block here goes back to a very early stage of development. One of the inevitable results of early experiences— a result fortified by subsequent peeping—is envy of the mother for her possession of the bountiful breast. The success of the peeping-exhibiting exchange depends largely on whether the boy can convince himself that his penis is equivalent in value to the longed-for breast. If he does not accept the shift, or only partly accepts it, he becomes masochistically attached to the enshrined mother image. The result is a pattern of injustice collecting, with its typical defense mask of false aggression.

The photographer made his pseudo-aggressive defenses quite clear. He treated the women who posed for him with contempt, often making them into caricatures. He had a way, for instance, of "depriving" them of their breasts by angling the lens of the camera.

Decisive proof that he was still trying to escape the disappointing living object of peeping—his mother—was found in his poorly developed ability to photograph mass scenes. For him any photograph including more than two people was "a crowd scene." He was unable to manipulate crowds, to turn them into his instrument. Thus, his inner alibi no longer applied and his work suffered. In his compulsion to experiment there were rational factors, of course, but underneath was the old reproach: "Mother didn't show every part of her body, everything there was to look at." This was shifted to: "I haven't created anything new!"

To a large extent this man treated his models as though they were inanimate objects. This diminished fear, since it negated the existence of the mother whom they symbolically represented. At the same time it corrected another childhood disappointment; now his models "held still" at command, instead of permitting him only quick, furtive glances.

It was this elaborate network of unconscious compensations that made this man a great photographer—within the limits that were also set by unconscious defenses.

Curiously enough, there were occasions when he did not mind exhibiting himself. At times he would take the stage for a witty description of an amusing experience. His alibi then ran: "I'm only joking; don't take me seriously."

Self-Display Performed only when Prodded by Severe Fear. The peeping-exhibiting elements in this type of shy person are identical with those mentioned above: people who do respond under conditions of fear are less tense than those totally incapable of self-display. They pay for their ability to exhibit by experiencing profound fear.

Fear arises from the psychic masochistic pattern; it represents both terror and guilt. The terror is aroused by the threatening inner tyrant and then shifted to the external world. The guilt is shifted from the real crime, psychic masochism, to its standard defense of pseudo-aggression, which takes the form of overstepping educational commands. This combination alibi is the strongest argument the inner lawyer has to offer when the department of punishment launches one of its attacks.

Sometimes the result is a peculiar compromise. Exhibiting becomes possible, but only on condition that no emotional content reaches the surface. The exhibitor is cold, frozen, and lifeless.

I once analyzed a man of this type; amusingly enough, he was a politician. His partisans worried about the lack of warmth in his speeches and anxiously urged him to come alive, to use more "oomph," at least to use more gestures. This recommendation brought up the fact that as a practicing lawyer, in the days before he had run for office, he had made use of one habitual gesture. He would raise his right hand, with the second and third fingers spread apart, and point the empty space between these fingers at the imagined enemy. Analysis uncovered the precedent for this gesture. He had borrowed it from a mathematics teacher, a man of rather shady reputation who had been tried for fraud and acquitted only because of insufficient evidence. The second finger of the teacher's right hand had been amputated as the result of an accident. The patient remembered the first occasion on which, to his own amazement, he had used this gesture—although innocent, he had fearfully anticipated being accused of embezzling a client's funds. The gesture, therefore, meant a partial admission combined with a defense—the teacher, after all, had been acquitted. Unfortunately its defensive aspects were outnumbered by compromising ones; the empty space between the fingers, for example, symbolized castration. In time, therefore, the man had to drop the gesture; it became too threatening and revealing. Without it he had no way of deflecting his fears. (All of this interpretation, of course, emerged only in the course of his analytical treatment.)

Patients of this type are never free from the fear that the inner tyrant will see through their defensive disguise of exhibitionism and uncover the real peeping desire. They shift this feat to the outside and see themselves as "afraid of the limelight."

Self-Display Made Possible by Specific "Impossible" Conditions. An extreme example of this type was provided by a patient who was so "shy" that he had to assume someone else's personality in order to perform intercourse successfully. He had worked out a technique of "incognito intercourse": during the sex act the girl would have to tell him a detailed story of her sexual performance with another man. This would have to include quoted conversation, a description of the girl's sensations, and so on. The story enabled him to identify with the other man and assume his personality. Without the story, having to perform "as himself," the patient was impotent.

Hyper-exhibitionism as Defense. The protoype here is the professional model or the actor. The unconscious accusations, defenses, and retorts which end with a socially accepted compromise can be summed up in a few sentences. The cycle begins with a peeping wish—the child wishes to peep at his parents, and later at parental intimacies. This wish is vetoed by the department of punishment; defensively the inner lawyer then presents the alibi of the opposite, maintaining that the child wishes to exhibit and not to peep. But there is a parental taboo on exhibiting also, and the inner tyrant makes that plain. A final alibi is then constructed: "I don't want to peep, and I don't want to break educational rules by exhibiting. But I want to be good, and it gives other people pleasure when I exhibit."

I would like to conclude this chapter with an example showing how careful one must be in evaluating imitative traits in children and in the adults they become. Scientifically, imitations can always be traced to unconscious "identifications," either permanent or temporary, either "leading"—meaning genuine and deeply rooted, or "misleading"—meaning superficial only and defensive in purpose. Because of this, imitative traits explain nothing unless the inner conflict that sets the stage of identification is clarified.

The life of Victor Hugo, as interpreted in a popular biography, illustrates the futility of mechanically hunting down a person's identifications in the hope of thus "explaining" him. But from the facts and events given, and certain imitative repetitions in the life pattern of the greatest of French poets, the analytically informed reader can detect his inner identifications.

One of the recurring themes has to do with marriage. Hugo's parents had a peculiar marriage. After they had spent only a few years together, his mother refused to fulfill her marital duties. From then on she and his father lived apart, although they were never divorced. Madame Hugo took a lover, Colonel Lahorie, a

man whose political opposition to Napoleon made him a perpetual refugee. Sheltered by Madame Hugo, Lahorie managed to
survive until after Napoleon's Russian campaign; the secret police
then caught up with him and he was executed. In the meantime,
Hugo's father lived for two decades with his sweetheart, Catherine Thomas.

Hugo himself married Adèle Foucher. A few years later she,
like his mother, refused to fulfill her marital duties and took a
lover, the critic Sainte-Beuve. Again there was no divorce. For
fifty years Hugo lived with his mistress, Juliette Drouet. In both
marriages the frigid wife refused sex because she was annoyed by
her husband's hyperpotency.

Another recurring pattern concerned Hugo's political views.
As a child he hated Napoleon, undoubtedly taking his cue from
his mother's lover, Lahorie, and his mother herself. When Napoleon III first appeared on the horizon some fifty years later,
Hugo's attitude was one of friendliness; this reflected his father's
support of the Napoleonic dynasty. But by the time Napoleon
III became Emperor, friendliness had shifted to bitter opposition.
Lahorie's view triumphed in the end, for Hugo imitated that
perpetual fugitive by becoming one himself, spending nineteen
years in exile on the island of Guernsey, unwilling to modify his
position or accept an amnesty.

Unlike these two repetitive themes, Hugo's relationship with
his long-time mistress differed in significant ways from his
father's apparently similar arrangement. Hugo's father married
Catherine Thomas shortly after Madame Hugo died, thus "re-
warding" the girl for her eighteen years of "servitude." The death
of Victor Hugo's wife changed Juliette Drouet's status in only
one respect—she took charge of his household. The association
had by that time lasted nearly fifty years, but there was no
marriage.

This break in the repetitive scheme is what shows up the fallacy of a mechanical approach to the problem of identification.
The inner meaning of the relationship was not the same for the
two men, nor was the personality structure of the two women.
Catherine was an aggressive shrew; she kept the elder Hugo

permanently under her thumb. Juliette was a deeply masochistic and self-sacrificing woman. Weak men reward female tyrants and tend to punish submissiveness by giving rein to their own defensive cruelty when dealing with *weak* women.

Of course one could adduce a more banal argument: Catherine was still a young woman when Madame Hugo died, while the same turning point in Victor Hugo's life came when Juliette was old. The argument evaporates in the light of the fact that Victor Hugo's debt of gratitude was immeasurably the greater of the two. Juliette had saved his life during the *coup d'etat* of 1851. He sent her a flowery message on their fiftieth anniversary, but he did not marry her.

Even masochism, however, has its limits. Juliette at length became embittered by Hugo's continual affairs (these went on until his death at the age of eighty-three) and by his tasteless exhibition of poems written to another woman.

The streak of defensive cruelty in Hugo's dealings with a person who had sacrificed her life for him can only be clarified by taking the poet's "leading" identification into consideration. This deeply rooted identification always pertains to the end result of the original infantile conflict; in Hugo, as in all writers, the solution was masochistic submission to the image of the mother of earliest childhood. His "leading" identification, therefore, was with the masochistically mistreated. His mother's lover was therefore an ideal model; as a perpetual fugitive he was certainly "mistreated," and his relationship with Madame Hugo provided the young Victor with an Oedipal camouflage as well. (He could convincingly retort to his inner tyrant: "How can I be masochistically attached to my mother if I model myself on her lover?")

Hugo's novels, the reader will recall, testify to his complete identification with the underdog. All his life Hugo sympathized with the poverty-stricken and the maltreated. Unconsciously this amounted to approval of masochism and necessitated a defensive show of activity and aggression; he provided this defense by furiously attacking injustice.

Unless one disentangles this "leading" theme from the many "misleading" and therefore defensive identifications visible in

Hugo's history, his life remains incomprehensible. One can neither understand the endless masochistic suffering materialized in his wife's rejecting attitude nor decipher his cruelty towards poor Juliette. The irony of the situation lies in the fact that Juliette's most heroic deed—saving Hugo's life in 1851—was unconsciously seized upon by Hugo as "the pseudo-moral connotation" that justified his failure to marry her. By rescuing Hugo, Juliette became (intrapsychically) Hugo's mother—the woman who had sheltered and protected Napoleon's opponent Lahorie. Isn't it moral to abstain from incest?

Parental influence is merely one of the threads the child works with in weaving his own individual pattern of life. *The parents teach, lead, forbid, reward, punish, and pronounce. The child listens, forgets, interprets, misinterprets, twists, and inflates—all at the dictation of his own unconscious needs.*

The area of pre-school education which modern parents invariably approach with care and due consideration is that of sexual enlightenment. In this area at least, they have been led to expect, the correct approach can be counted on to produce satisfactory results. Even here there is a hitch, and good intentions must too often serve as their own reward. The child accepts, *inwardly,* only those facts that correspond to the specific misconceptions he holds at the moment.

Freud had a very pertinent comment to make on this tendency. He referred to it while discussing the emotional involvement that can occur when one is reading analytic literature and one's own acute conflicts are touched upon. He then went on to state:

> I believe one can cite similar experiences in connection with giving sexual information to children. I am by no means claiming that giving children sexual information is a damaging or superfluous procedure. But the preventive results of that liberal policy have obviously been greatly overrated. Once they have received this information, the children know facts they did not know before, but they do nothing with the knowledge newly acquired. One is led to conclude that these children are by no means ready to sacrifice their self-created sexual theories in order to make way for their new information. They created their

theories to fit their own unfinished organization of libido; they have their own ideas about the part played by the stork, about what constitutes sexual contact, about what constitutes child-birth. For a long time after they have been given sexual infor-mation these children behave like the primitive peoples upon whom Christianity was thrust and who in secrecy continued to venerate their old pagan gods.

CHAPTER 3

LOVE AND UNDERSTANDING AS THE APPROACH TO CHILD REARING: THEIR POWER AND THEIR LIMITATIONS

"THE CHILD needs love" is a frequently quoted modern slogan. He does, but nobody explains why. And even the best of parents cannot turn themselves into tenderness machines, always functioning at par.

The child needs love for many different reasons. The completely helpless infant needs constant care to keep him from dying of hunger and exposure, though during the first months of life he is oblivious of the loving care that surrounds him. The newcomer to this "cold accretion," as Thomas Hardy called the world, believes that he himself is autarchic and omnipotent. This fantasy is gradually destroyed under the impact of reality. The baby goes through a transitory phase in which he sees the giantess of the nursery as a mere prolongation and instrument of his own omnipotence. He then learns that this convenient illusion is, like his earliest one, untenable and at last accepts the fact of his dependence. But it is by no means a friendly acceptance. The controlling element in it is fear, an extreme of fear. Dependence means being totally at the mercy of an uncanny power, capable of perpetrating every conceivable evil. The "septet of baby fears" described in Chapter I, grotesque as it may sound to the adult, has full reality value to the helpless baby. It is at this point that one can discern the beginning of masochistic distortion of feelings. This tragic process is concluded before the end of the second year of life.

The constant presence of maternal love in this early stage is emotionally essential to the child; it counteracts his inner and irrational fears. This explains the insatiability of infantile demands. Freud once commented on the custom prevailing in some South Sea Island tribes which decrees that any child, of any age, is entitled to be breast fed, upon his request, by any suckling mother, not merely his own. Freud ironically added that if these South Sea Island children were analyzed, as adults, one would probably uncover the repressed complaint that they did not get enough milk.

This insatiability is in direct proportion to inner fears. Love is the reliable antidote, the nest egg of security stored away for a rainy day filled with terror.

One should add that parental love does the work of rescue in quiet, not-too-masochistic periods. Once psychic masochism has reared its ugly head, however, no amount of kindness, benevolence, love, or permissiveness can help. And this is not simply a situation in which the usual antidote fails to work. When the child is masochistically tense, an offering of parental love merely produces an ascending spiral of demands, mounting until the demands pass beyond parental endurance.

A patient of mine, a young mother, decided to outsmart her three-year-old boy's provocative masochism by giving in to all his wishes. Practically every evening, between nine and ten o'clock, the boy would wake up, screaming that he was hungry and that his mother "never gave him anything to eat." In line with her policy, she would ask him in a friendly way what he would like to eat. "You tell me what you have," the boy would answer. She would then recite a long list of delicacies, all of which he would reject, repeating, "You never give me anything to eat!" Still in a friendly tone she would point out that he could not be very hungry so short a time after his dinner; the boy would ignore the remark and go on bitterly complaining of "starvation," and demanding frog's legs, caviar, snails, and other exotic foods which he had heard of though never tasted. (The boy was very clever, which may have been some consolation to the mother during these painful evenings.)

Invariably these scenes ended in copious tears: the boy crying because his mother was "mean" to him; the mother crying because of the boy's "ingratitude." The problem was eventually solved—or at least shifted—by the father. In his desperation he gave the boy a severe thrashing and laid down a new law: no demands for food between supper and breakfast. The most surprising result, as far as the young mother was concerned, was the boy's friendly acceptance of this decree. He showed no resentment against the father who had, against her wishes, treated the child "so brutally." Quite obviously the boy had wanted a beating—and persisted in his provocation until he got one.

In quiet—meaning not-too-masochistic—times, maternal and paternal love is an important stabilizer, relieving the weight of the child's inner fears.

This too is important: every child has a fine intuitive understanding of whether or not parental kindness bordering on love, or love bordering on kindness, is genuine. Walter Scott was right when he said, in *The Lady of the Lake,* "Children know, Instinctive taught, the friend and foe." This is clinically exemplified in analysis after analysis. Here is an illustration:

An engineer, aged thirty-four and the owner of his quite successful firm, came to me "in desperation." As he saw it, his problem was not his homosexuality but his wife's discovery of it, and the "hysterical and overbearing" attitude which she adopted after this discovery. Very early in our first interview he revealed the series of false moves which had made his wife aware of his homosexuality and gave me other evidence of the masochistic substructure upon which both his perversion and his general pattern of injustice collecting rested. (All homosexuals are inveterate psychic masochists.) He revealed too that he had come to me at his wife's insistence, and that his purpose was purely that of buying domestic peace. In spite of the absence of any evidence that he wanted to change his homosexuality, I accepted him as a patient—on a trial basis and at his own risk.

His analysis, which began three months after our first meeting, did not promise well. At his wife's stern urging he had read one of my books on homosexuality, and impressed by the explanation of masochism he found there, he hoped that analysis would remove his self-damaging tendencies and leave his homosexuality untouched. He frankly admitted disbelief in the connection between psychic masochism and homosexuality. A streak of infantile megalomania also pervaded his attitude: he had triumphed over me by persuading me to accept him for treatment even though he did not meet the standards enumerated in the book.

He could take the credit for this alleged triumph—and the potential triumph over his wife—only by conveniently overlooking two important details. First, he had no assurance that his psychic masochism would be cured by treatment; second, the arrangement was for a trial treatment only, lasting a few weeks. I had the impression, however, that he was more nearly ready to give up his homosexuality than he realized.

During the first appointments the patient made it clear that he was neurotically and exaggeratedly suspicious of people's motives at all times. He was convinced, for example, that I had made some kind of deal with his wife. Actually I had never seen her, spoken to her, or corresponded with her. This trait of suspicion played an important part in his subsequent treatment.

When I asked him for a short history of his nursery past, he answered promptly:

"Nothing, but nothing, in my uneventful childhood pointed in the direction of my future troubles. Father: a shy though friendly, quiet man, a postal inspector in a small, upstate New York town. He spent most of his free time in the basement of our mortgaged house, playing with his inventions—all very minor. His idea of a great inventor wasn't Edison but the man who got the idea of the square clothespin. None of his experiments ever came to anything."

"Did your mother object?"

"She was pleasant enough. No, she was condescending with a sort of ironic kindness. She was the one who wore the pants; she decided everything."

"I asked you whether she objected to your father's hobby."

"Before I answer I would like to know why you are stressing the point."

"Hyper-suspicion again. . . . There are no hidden strings attached to the question. Your father was a tinkerer and obviously an amateur. You became a mechanical engineer, a professional. Superficially it seems as though you identified with your father and then outdid him. On the other hand, your mother treated him with ironic condescension. That didn't give you a very imposing ideal to look up to and identify with. I surmise, therefore, that behind this pseudo-identification wtih your father lies a more deeply repressed aggression of some kind, directed against your mother. If she had objected to your father's hobby—a game that consumed time and money and brought no results—then your identification with your father's only interest would appear in a different light. It would mean rebellion against your mother."

"It seems my fate to confirm your hunches and guesses. O.K. You win. Mother did object, and I mean forcefully. From time to time she would go into hysterics about it: Father never spent any time with his family, she would tell him in no uncertain terms; he spent every available cent on tools, raw material, and so on. That isn't all. I did well in high school. I was captain of the football team and in general what they call nowadays a 'big wheel on campus.' Full of confidence, I told her I wanted to study mechanical engineering. She threw up her hands in desperation and said, 'I hope you don't become like your father!' "

In a later appointment another significant glimpse of the past emerged. The patient had arrived in "a brilliant mood" which it was necessary for me to caution him about.

"The old technique again," he said. "Back I go into the Slough of Despond."

"Old technique?" I asked. "Whose old technique? What are you repeating in the transference?"

"It was my mother's technique, of course. She played cat and mouse with me too, first getting me all puffed up with pride and then smashing me down. When I was five she bought me a new suit, and I was very proud of myself. Immediately she pounced and told me that conceited boys, especially in new clothes, were disgusting. Then at high school, when they made me captain of the football team, she started out by saying she was proud of me and then gave me a lecture on how physical accomplishments mean so much less than mental ones. These are just two examples; it went on all the time."

"Why did you take it so tragically? Many mothers go in for these educational afterthoughts, and many children take it in their stride. Isn't it more likely that you selectively retained and magnified the negative connotations?"

"Why do you want to absolve my mother?"

"Because reality is only raw material. What the child does with his individual reality is his, and exclusively his, business."

This patient had used the raw material of his childhood to make sure of a steady diet of psychic masochism. Superficially he had identified himself with his father, outdoing him professionally in what had been the older man's unprofitable hobby. But even here the masochistic basis made itself evident. His mother had incessantly reproached his father for his futile experimentation; in the patient's private vocabulary "experimentation" was synonymous with "failure." That explained his assumption that I had taken him on purely as an experiment, an experiment bound to end in the failure of his analysis. It explained, too, a decision he had made some years before, when he refused to go along with his partner into a new field and thereby threw away a quarter of a million dollars. The healthy sectors of his personality were generally in command of his business attitudes, but his partner's proposal had invited him to prove, again, his favorite unconscious thesis: that his mother was a frightening giantess, a killjoy, who forbade him to score a big success. It was an invitation he could not resist.

His homosexuality, of course, reflected this same attitude. By escaping sexually from woman to man, he was attempting to counteract his fear of the "dangerous, bad, damaging" mother image. He had become interested in his wife because she was "nice" and showed that she was warmly, personally concerned with him, unlike his succession of casual boy friends. But he lost interest in her after their marriage, primarily because she was

"nice," which was by no means what he unconsciously wanted
His revelation of his homosexuality was a provocation, not an
accident, and it turned her into the "bitch" he could then identify
with his stern, critical mother.

Months of analysis succeeded in changing this patient's masochistic pattern; with the change he abandoned homosexuality.
His wife changed as well, to the "nice" person she had been when
they first met.

Once the child has discovered the unconscious profit to be
derived from injustice collecting and begun the unconscious policy of provocation, parental love cannot help. Nor can cultural
teaching, even if it is communicated in the friendliest manner.

Underneath the child's typical resistance to instructions, educational precepts, and even suggestions (as every parent knows,
the typical child goes through stages in which even consent is
expressed with a "no"), there is evident a distinct need and desire for some kind of discipline. Partially this need conforms with
the child's masochistic requirements, but it has other purposes
as well. These purposes are illustrated in childhood—and adult
—attitudes towards daily routine.

In general, daily routine has no defenders; people complain
about its boredom and monotony. Hardly anyone will admit to
liking it, but almost everyone is disturbed by an interruption in
his standard schedule. The Sunday headache is a familiar visitor
in people so inured to habit that they cannot take even a one-day
holiday. People less habit-ridden tend to become uneasy during
more protracted vacations.

Why should people take it for granted that daily routine is
"hateful," while at the same time they feel, without admitting it,
a certain sense of security which is derived from it? In short,
what are the unconscious tributaries to this attitude?

Every human being has a very active list of inner fears, which
have no connection with external events. When conscious fears
are exaggerated, they too can be discerned as irrational inner
fears, left over from the past and conveniently disguised by external reasons.

Some method of relieving these various fears is essential. One reliable means is the boring daily routine. "My glass happens to be a small one, but I am drinking from my own glass," a French poet once said. As far as he knew, he was referring to his "small talent," but without being aware of it, he was at the same time referring to his big fears.

Daily routine confirms one of the few stable qualities of life— continuity. The new is always unconsciously terrifying, and routine is, of course, the exact opposite of "new." This is not, however, the major factor in its reassuring effect.

Unconsciously daily routine reminds one of the home of one's childhood, the first place in which one learned that some activities were specific, recurring, and fixed. Home, to a child, means mother and father, who are "always there." It is the unconscious (and perhaps preconscious) connection between routine and one's early home life that gives routine its reassuring and fright-diminishing effect.

It is interesting that people who never had "a real home" should invariably be less than typically capable of enduring daily routine. For them it provides no stabilizing factor, no "plus" to offset the "minus" of monotony. This significant difference has been brought out repeatedly in the course of clinical analysis.

It would seem logical to expect exactly the opposite development in neurotics who as children were deprived of a normal home life. As adults one would think they would attempt to compensate defensively for past deprivation and accept with willingness the restrictions of routine. But defensive compensation is a normal solution; what we call normality is unfortunately not the standard means of overcoming childhood disappointments.

Amazingly enough, the security-promoting effect of home life tends to be more important than the "unhappiness" that many neurotics attribute to their childhood. In any case, the conviction of unhappiness is subjective, based on internal rather than external circumstances. Only an oversimplified view of human psychology holds that all neurotics come from unhappy homes, all normal people from happy homes. Children in both kinds of environment can elaborate neurotically on reality seen through the distortions of the infantile illusion of omnipotence, projection, and psychic masochism; in both, also, normal solutions can be reached. But once the child has fixed on a neurotic solution to his conflict, an unfavorable home life can only emphasize his neurosis. Even in such cases, *any kind of home life is better than none at all.* Every home imposes restrictions, and therefore provides a hitching post for masochistic deposits. But safety and security, the realities and routine of home life, counteract the extravagance of the child's misconceptions and reduce to some extent the burden of fear he unconsciously carries.

There is a second unconscious factor at work to make daily routine unconsciously valuable. Work, even the mechanical, light work of the usual routine, is disagreeable and therefore absorbs a good deal of unconscious self-punishment. This banal fact has been intuitively known for ages. Adam and Eve, driven from Eden, were additionally punished by having to work for their bread. Daily duties and routine pay part of one's daily debt to the inner tormenter.

Some of this debt is incurred when the department of punishment levels another of its standard reproaches—the accusation that one is capable of doing only the "stupid" job at hand. This explains why so many people, without seeing the contradiction complain in the same breath about the complexity *and* the monotony of their jobs. The complaint of complexity answers the inner accusation; the complaint of monotony represents a vindicating inner protest: "Why are you forcing me to be a drudge?"

When an adult grumbles about the boring rut he is in, his statement need not necessarily be taken at face value. It may have an unconscious defensive purpose. A child at play, guarding against the over-stern educator of his distorted fantasy, will always assume that his game will be forbidden if he shows too plainly that he is enjoying it. The adult has unconsciously not forgotten this tactic, and uses it as a defense against his inner enemy. Neurotics have other inner reasons for objecting to daily routine. They may be neurotically bored, in which case they are incapable of constructing and enjoying fantasies, an occupation which all people without a voyeuristic inhibition indulge in and which helps to make their lives pleasurable. Or they may be extreme psychic masochists bent on self-pity and determined to leave no pretext unused.

These complaints do not affect the essential fact: *daily routine provides a dependable antidote to inner fear.* Interestingly enough, some of the dependability derives from the dominance of routine in childhood, when any activity, pleasurable or threatening, could be abruptly ended by the cry, "It's time to leave!" Father had to go to his office or factory at a particular time; the child had to leave for school when the inexorable clock told him to. Routine thus took precedence over even parental power; this super authority was the real "court of last resort."

Some minor narcissistic recompenses do sweeten the otherwise unpleasant daily potion. No matter how disagreeable work and routine are, they satisfy inner needs, providing outlets for activity, opportunities for pride and self-satisfaction, methods of partially fulfilling deeply rooted unconscious fantasies.

All human attitudes, no matter how banal, have unconscious tributaries. It is easy to overlook them, but they are always present.

The behavior of parents is part of the raw material the child uses, according to his perception of it, to construct his manifold inner elaborations. Too little attention has been paid to a specific unconscious elaboration called the "magic gesture," which is observable on the surface as an apparently benevolent personality trait. It has no connection, however, with "that best portion of a good man's life, his little nameless, unremembered acts of kindness and of love" of which Wordsworth wrote in "Tintern Abbey." The magic gesture actually represents a masochist's unconscious complaint about the attitude or actions of his parents disguised by consciously inexplicable kindness towards a person of no importance to him.

When it is in operation a strange metamorphosis takes place in the benefactor. If he is ordinarily indifferent, he becomes solicitous; if a penny pincher, he becomes magnanimous; if known for his malice, he becomes well-meaning and charitable. Sometimes the propelling unconscious need to perform the gesture is so great that he ignores the environment's caustic reaction and listens with a superior smile to suggestions that he is engaged in an illicit affair, has become a homosexual, or is getting senile.

The inner structure of the magic gesture explains its individual and unvarying characteristics:

1. Unimportant people are always chosen as beneficiaries, to convey the message "You, bad Mother, did not care for your own child. I, however, care even for strangers." The more remote the benefactor's responsibility towards the beneficiary, the more forceful is the accusation against the enshrined upbringers.

2. In a further extension of this accusation, animals or even inanimate objects can be used as recipients of magic gestures.

3. Abruptly the benefactor can become an enemy, shifting to the "negative magic gesture." The beneficiary can never feel secure; his position as protégé is subject to cancellation without notice. The switch occurs in response to a veto pronounced by the inner tyrant, making it necessary for the benefactor to find a new and acceptable alibi, and he does so by reversing his role. He now impersonates the allegedly cruel parent and casts the ex-protégé in the role of his own mistreated self, thus demonstrating in caricature the offenses of his educators.

The magic gesture is one of the innumerable episodes in the "battle of the conscience"—a defense against the superego's veto of criticism of parents. Of course, psychic masochism is in the deepest layer. When the inner tyrant forbids the masochistic solution, the inner argument proceeds as follows:

The unconscious ego denies psychic masochism, at the same time admitting the lesser crime of pseudo-aggression: "I do not masochistically wish to be mistreated by my parents. In fact, I hate them for their injustice." When defensive aggression against parents is also forbidden, the ego must take a different tack: "You have misunderstood me. I don't want revenge either. All I care about is being kindly treated. I will show you in my behavior towards others how I wanted my parents to treat me when I was a child—lovingly, generously, kindly."

The reproach retained in this final alibi is heightened by the choice of an insignificant person as object. Extremes of generosity or choice (as, for instance, animals) also intensify the implied accusation. The greater the contrast between the parents' alleged coldness and the warmth of the magic gesture, the more effective it is as a defense.

Ten years ago a woman in her late fifties consulted me because of a writing block. She lived in hopeless poverty, existing on an income of twelve dollars a week earned by contributing a column to a trade magazine (undoubtedly an assignment given her for charitable reasons). Though this sum was hardly enough to cover the basic necessities of life for her, she spent most of it feeding and caring for stray cats. "I simply cannot endure to see those poor creatures suffering," she told me. "Recently I spent all my savings, seventy dollars, for a veterinarian for one stray cat."

Another patient habitually dramatized his grievance against his mother by demonstrating his inability to "discriminate against" inanimate objects. Extravagance was one of his traits; he used it to exhibit his conscious aggression against his mother, since it was she who paid his bills. Combining two alibis, he would go into expensive shops and purchase more than he needed or could use. Once he went into a shop to order three shirts. He examined hundreds of samples of material and quickly rejected all but thirty. He then found himself unable to "discriminate" further. He could not eliminate any more samples, and because "there was no other way out" ordered thirty shirts.

This man had been one of six children. As he saw it, his mother had played favorites, giving some of her children special care and neglecting the others. He had been, he believed, neglected. His extravagance and indecision were symbolic arguments. They meant: "My mother preferred some of her children, neglecting the others. I would not have been capable of that cruelty. I cannot even play favorites with indifferent objects like shirts!"

The standard magic gesture, of course, benefits people rather than stray cats or samples of expensive shirting material. Sometimes the environment accepts it at face value as a sudden attack of Christmas in July, recognizing the illogic involved but casually dismissing it with no more than a "What got into him?" At other times it is an invitation to misjudgment or active search for a motive less elevated than the pure compassion that allegedly inspires the benefactor.

There is no reason to assume that the habitual use of the magic gesture as a defense sheds any light on the real climate of the home from which the gesturer came. Indifference, neglect, cruelty can never be entirely factual judgments when applied by children to parents (or for that matter, by parents to children). If unconscious elaborations call for him to do so, a child can judge any parental attitude as inimical—even a loving kiss.

There are adult neurotics who detest kissing, maintaining (like Swift) that it is "distasteful," or lining up behind Henry Gibbons to prove that it is "senseless" by reducing it to the status of an anatomical exercise. One such patient asked whether it would not be more "hygienic" to adopt the custom of rubbing noses to express affection. At one point or another these neurotics have become blank to the emotional content of a kiss, or have transformed it so that it negates emotion. The negative connotation is visible in neurotics of a particular type who have exaggerated fears of infection. They allege that they avoid kissing because the contact transmits bacteria.

The hugs and kisses of adults, especially of the mother, are generally recognized as friendly and affectionate gestures by the child. But one cannot go so far as to say that the very young child sees them as loving, because the newborn baby finds hostility in even the harmless actions of the environment. These misconceptions provide the basis on which he builds up his "septet of baby fears." In early fantasies kissing means being "swallowed up" or "devoured"; if the child persists in such fantasies, it can be expected that trouble will develop in this particular sector in the future. At a later age, of course, an allegedly rational cover is provided for inner fears.

Once kissing has been accepted as a positive emotional gesture, it also becomes a reassurance against fear. Children who kiss a great deal are not always propelled by affection; some of them are frightened. The paradox remains that kissing, originally misconstrued as "devouring" by the child, subsequently becomes important as an assurance that he is loved or at least accepted.

It is also clear that kissing has, psychologically, some connection with friendly incorporation; the old unity of mother and child is re-established through a kiss. This can be seen in motion pictures (which in this respect, if no other, assiduously copy life), where the standard kiss begins with the boy putting his arms around the girl but becomes meaningful only when she in turn puts her arms around him. Here (from the boy's viewpoint) an active repetition of a passive infantile situation has taken place.

Since everything in this world can be misused, kisses can become tools of hypocrisy (Judas' kisses): perfunctory kisses exchanged by relatives who hate each other; meaningless kisses exchanged as conventional greetings, etc. Kisses of sexual tenderness constitute a special (non-hypocritical) subdivision. Nevertheless, the kiss remains what Robert Herrick declared it to be: "What is a kiss? Why this, as some approve: The sure, sweet cement, Glue, and Lime of Love."

Kissing as a pleasure presupposes acceptance of the other person as the "good (meaning not too dangerous) food" of infancy. Many expressions in the language illustrate the link between love and edibility, a few familiar examples being "sweetheart," "honeybunch," "sugar-pie."

Some neurotics avoid kissing because they are unconsciously perpetuating the infantile game of "bad mother does not love baby." Actively repeating the alleged rejection which they once passively endured, they reverse the roles. Once allegedly refused love by the mother, they now do the refusing themselves.

In many analyses I have encountered the identical explanation for the use of the kiss as a means of expressing rejection. The patients reasoned as follows: "My parents expected a goodnight kiss from each child. These kisses were cold and perfunctory, and I hated the whole routine." By exaggerating the criticism the kiss is ruled out, and the child in the adult demonstrates his mother's coldness in an unconscious caricature.

Neurotic aversion to kissing plays a greater role than is generally known; many marital estrangements begin with distaste for kissing or refusal to kiss. Frequently the full neuroticism of the individual shows up in these situations, especially when they are preceded by a phase of sexual intercourse without tenderness.

There is no limit—certainly none set by logic—to the ramifications and random aftereffects of infantile fantasies. Who would, for example, see them at work in an adult's attitude towards a borrowed book? Yet the connection can be decisively demonstrated.

No one who has ever lent a book is unaware that each loan is a gamble; no one who has ever borrowed one will deny this. Why do people who are otherwise passably correct in their conduct, who would never do anyone out of a few dollars (at least not openly), fall from grace when the property involved is a three or four dollar book? Why the sudden departure of all scruples? The habit of borrowing and not returning books seems to have existed for many generations. It was popular in Walter Scott's day. He wrote, "Please return this book; I find that though many of my friends are poor arithmeticians, they are nearly all good bookkeepers." Charles Lamb, too, complained furiously of "borrowers, those mutilators of collections, spoilers of the symmetry of shelves, and creators of odd volumes." There is even a record of Montaigne's reaction: "It is easier to keep a book than its contents." When one considers that the printed word is hardly rounding out its fifth century, the record of "social stealing" of books seems to be quite complete.

In studying an irrational situation one is led to a survey of infantile precursors.

For the young child all printed matter is an adult mystery, and awe-inspiring as well. A remnant of this early awe is observable in all adults. Printed matter has the stamp of authority. Even nonsense, when printed, has an emotional connotation different from that of spoken nonsense.

Printed books (not picture books) enter the child's life as a duty. (The fact that mastering the art of reading challenges his illusion of omnipotence and omniscience, and that the challenge helps him to master the skill, is another matter.) Later on, after he has learned to read, he discovers reading for pleasure—a comic or the sports page instead of his required books for school. But reading for pleasure and reading as a duty remain distinct entities.

What is the situation in which a book is borrowed? The host mentions the book, or the guest sees it on a shelf. Externally the situations seem dissimilar but they are psychologically identical. The mere presence of the book on the shelf constitutes an implied reproach: "Why don't you read?" Because of this unspoken reproach, all reading matter borrowed socially is unconsciously classified under "reading as a duty." Paradoxically, this even applies to a book which the guest *consciously* would like to read if it came into his hands under different circumstances.

As soon as a book is classed as duty reading the old childish rebellion against duty ("Why don't you do your homework?") comes back into operation. Endless procrastination results or is simulated (for a book that has been read but not returned will still count as unread in the lender's opinion). This explains why some borrowed books are retained indefinitely, with the help of the rationalization, "I'll get to it, in time."

The reason the social stealing of books leaves the pilferer with a clear conscience, although he may be a person who scrupulously places five cents on his friend's desk in exchange for a stamp, is in no way connected with ordinary correctness or incorrectness in his general dealings with people. Behind this deviation lies a very primitive, infantile, and repressed fantasy: "If you, Mother or Father, want me to read, you'll have to give me the book." Whoever heard of a child of six paying his father for schoolbooks? Or returning them, for that matter?

By applying infantile yardsticks connected with the initial misunderstanding (duty reading) to an adult situation, the borrower accentuates his "moral right" to keep the book he has borrowed. In another unconscious layer his failure to return the book is a punitive act; he is punishing the lender for having forced the book on him. Objectively, of course, the lender may not have wanted him to take the book at all. That is of no importance; his role is rewritten to fit the infantile backdrop.

One could also mention that "social stealing" is not always passed off graciously, although it does generally escape comment.

The borrower provides himself with a small helping of masochistic pleasure by incurring the lender's half-revealed indignation. On the other hand, he uses the situation to take the blame for the lesser internal crime. What he has actually done has been to repeat an infantile pattern which is half-neurotic and masochistic; he now presents it in terms of his partly aggressive defense. Both defenses are, of course, unconscious.

The lender's attitudes and reactions are hardly less curious than the borrower's. For example, one often sees the facetious bookplate: "Stolen from the library of. . . ." On the conscious level, this is a stern warning; on the unconscious level it is an open invitation. Why do owners hesitate to make a direct demand for the return of their books? Why does the characteristic temper tantrum that follows the discovery of a "missing" book invariably take place behind the perfidious borrower's back? Apparently the lender unconsciously welcomes the borrower's felony and does his best to compound it.

A patient who became eloquently furious about his friends' and acquaintances' way of "stealing" his books consoled himself, when in a sarcastic mood, with the hope that the increasing popularity of paper-bound books, some selling for as little as twenty-five cents, would eliminate the entire problem. He had too high an opinion of his friends, he said, to believe they would commit so small an offense. "More likely," I told him, "social stealing will increase. The borrower will tell himself that a few cents cannot matter. Since infantile mechanisms are involved, external circumstances can make very little difference."

"What other solution can you suggest?" asked the indignant man.

"Well, since most of your friends are young writers like yourself, there is still hope for you. Experience proves that established writers and older writers read little. And there is, perhaps, good reason for it, as Will Rogers pointed out when he said, 'In Hollywood the woods are full of people that learned to write but evidently can't read; if they could read their stuff, they'd stop writing.' "

CHAPTER 4

WHAT DO MENTAL HEALTH
AND NEUROSIS DENOTE?

IN OUR contemporary culture, most adults are familiar enough with the terms "neurosis" and "mental health" to use them, often inaccurately, to indicate external attitudes and points of view. But this is only distant acquaintanceship; understanding calls for a survey of the unconscious pattern that underlies neurosis or the relative absence of neurosis.

The almost invariable confusion here arises from the fact that both states, emotional health and neurosis, are taken as absolutes.

They are not absolutes. There are only quantitative differences between the two. For practical purposes emotional health simply denotes a state that is "not too neurotic." Moreover, every neurotic has a "normal corner," just as every emotionally healthy person has a "neurotic corner." The whole problem hinges on one question: to what extent the personality has been invaded by neurosis.

This conclusion does not at all negate the existence of clear-cut neurosis.

In my opinion, every neurosis—every evidence, in other words, of disease in the unconscious—is characterized by certain unchanging factors.

First: The unconscious conflict established in earliest childhood is subsequently made permanent. From this time on the individual unconsciously re-enacts this identical conflict, translated into new terms, in his external life. As fellow actors, he unwittingly uses innocent bystanders, who substitute for the original characters in his inner drama.

This is a Freudian axiom that meets with little scientific or popular opposition today. With the exception of Freud's discovery that the unconscious is a clinically provable, dynamically effective, therapeutically accessible fact, it is the most far-reaching of his achievements.

Using this axiom as a starting point, a practical line of reasoning is followed in studying an irrational reaction on the part of any neurotic person. The questions to be answered are: What is his original repressed conflict? Why has he unconsciously chosen exactly this moment to dramatize, for the nth time, this infantile conflict? What made him choose, as an instrument of that dramatization, the specific person he has embroiled in his repetition?

In a sense, all neurotics are emotional robots. They are incapable of achieving a new or different human relationship; all their attitudes towards other human beings have been permanently engraved in the unconscious in the first few years of life, just as a robot's abilities are permanently fixed by the way its electrical circuits have been hooked up. What is more, the neurotic never really meets a new person. Everyone he allegedly hates, loves, mistreats or is victimized by is, in his inner reality, an old acquaintance in a new disguise: a successor to and representative of some enshrined figure from his nursery past. Without consciously realizing what they are doing, all neurotics fit the newcomers in their lives into already established characterizations. This shift is technically known as "transference"; it is the only emotional link a neurotic can forge.

These endless repetitions can only be halted by successful psychiatric treatment; failing that, they persist throughout life.

Second: Every child must solve the unavoidable infantile conflict; every child eventually solves it by resorting to the psychic-masochistic solution. The neurotic child becomes "stabilized on the rejection level" and makes pleasure-in-pain his major unconscious aim. He must then construct endless defenses against his psychic masochism.

This could be stated in another way. Neurosis means that the child in the adult has not been able to free himself from the conflicts of the nursery, from his infantile illusion of omnipotence and from his forbidden and conflict-ridden wishes, whatever their individual and specific contents. All these conflicts involved his mother. The typical faulty elaboration of these is the escape to psychic masochism. As a result, the neurotic perpetually seeks and provokes alleged injustices, all of which he blames on figures who—regardless of their sex—unconsciously represent to him duplications of his infantile image of the "cruel" mother.

It should not be forgotten that psychic masochism is on the veto list of the inner department of punishment and torture, and that the neurotic must establish unconscious defenses and alibis to conceal his forbidden aim from the punitive inner conscience. These secondary defenses govern the psychic masochist's external actions, which resolve themselves into a standard, unvarying drama (the "clinical picture of psychic masochism").

This drama is important enough to be described again. In Act I the neurotic behaves in such a way as to provoke disappointment or refusal, or else seizes on an external situation that seems promising and misuses it so that he achieves the same result. Unconsciously he identifies the instrument of his defeat—individual, institution, or circumstance—with the cold, denying giantess of the nursery. In Act II the neurotic indignantly resents the "meanness" of his adversary, and becomes aggressive, apparently in self-defense ("pseudo-aggression"). Consciously he remains unaware that he has provoked his disappointment. In Act III, having achieved his self-created defeat, the neurotic bathes in conscious self-pity while unconsciously he is experiencing masochistic pleasure.

When this pattern is evident in *decisive* situations in a person's life, one can be certain that psychic masochism is at the root of all his characterological problems. It is important not to be misled by the highly convincing show of indignation put on in the second act of the conscious drama, and to conclude from it that the individual's evident neurotic problems arise from "too much aggression." It is equally important not to be misled by other neurotic signs and symptoms he may produce and conclude from these that his troubles arise from other unconscious conflicts. The key is his manipulation of a really important situation so that it ends in a resounding defeat.

One should not expect to be able to discern the individual's real unconscious wishes through his conscious actions; these are never expressed directly but always covered by defenses. The pet defense of the psychic masochist is pseudo-aggression, "pseudo" because it is not expended for the purpose of self-defense or even for the pleasure of punishing the enemy, but only to increase the anger of his opponent and to provide an inner disclaimer that he can present to his inner conscience. In pseudo-aggression the unconscious intention is to arouse the enemy to his fullest indignation, and therefore strength, in order to better the *enemy's* chance of winning.

Another of the masochist's defensive camouflages has to do with "the wish to get." Even the psychic masochist, when he was a baby, wished to get milk, attention, love. But after adopting rejection and defeat as his aim, he no longer unconsciously wishes to acquire or be given but only to be refused. The apparent wish to get, in these adults, is only a defensive neurotic disguise.

If, for example, an adult stands at the window of a candy store looking appreciatively and greedily at the display, and then reluctantly walks away although he can easily afford to indulge himself, he is acting in obedience to an unconscious aim. Without knowing what he is doing, he is repeating a childhood situation in which he was deprived of what he wanted. Consciously he wants some of the candy he saw in the window; unconsciously he puts a higher value on the opportunity to "prove" that he is being deprived. This is, of course, an over-simplified example, but it also holds true when the adult's aims substitute for chocolate.

Third: Every neurosis is merely a "rescue station" representing a partially successful escape from masochistic attachment to the mother of earliest infancy.

In their behavior, neurotics are by no means carbon copies of one another. They show many different "clinical pictures," and these pictures are clues to the phase of development during which the specific neurotic symptom arose. The pictures are therefore analytically subdivided into three classifications: oral, referring to the infantile period dominated by the wish to get and the masochistic solution; anal, referring to the age of about two; phallic (or Oedipal), referring to the period from three to five. Hysteria, for example, is a phallic neurosis; obsessional neurosis is anal.

The flaw in this classification system is one which is encountered in all research into a new field of knowledge: the first discovery becomes the pivot and remains so until enough facts have been uncovered to put each individual piece of evidence in its proper place and proportion. Freud's first discoveries came about in the course of his treatment of hysterical neurotics. In consequence he unearthed the Oedipus complex, which propels hysterically regressed persons; subsequently, the anal and oral phases were investigated. Historically, therefore, psychoanalysis began at the peak of the psychic pyramid, with the last of the three formative periods in the child's growth, and then continued down to its base, the broad plane upon which all else is built. The sequence of the child's development is, of course, the exact reverse.

Until recently, different neurotic diseases were viewed as separate entities, each related to its specific level of regression with comparatively little attention paid to the manner in which one phase, reformulated, melts into and influences its successor. Although it was recognized that remnants of one phase were often carried into the next, no basic interconnections were established. However, as more analysts noticed these remnants, the originally devised subdivisions of neurosis became rather shaky and more obviously in need of revision. Karl Menninger suggested classifying neuroses according to the particular defenses used. Personally, I believe that the great variety of defenses used by neurotics represents a superficial layer, that there is only *one basic neurosis*, built on masochistic vicissitudes and going back to the oral stage, and that the subsequent stages are merely "rescue stations"

—defenses designed to cover up the crime of crimes: psychic masochism (for elaboration see *The Basic Neurosis*, 1949).

In my opinion, the persistence of remnants cannot be scientifically noted and dismissed, as in physiology one notes and then dismisses that useless organ, the appendix. The later development of the human being cannot be understood unless they are taken into account. The effects of the first phase of development never disappear; they remain powerfully operative in later life, in spite of the individual's desperate attempts in the anal and Oedipal stages to rescue himself from masochistic attachment to the mother of earliest infancy. This does not mean, of course, that physical growth and biological necessity do not force certain changes in emphasis. But the psychological superstructure still represents only a series of escape measures.

The course of the child's development proves the point. The oral, "I wish to get," phase is basically a period of passivity, relieved only by a few aggressive defenses. The scales do not balance by any means: on the one hand, there is almost absolute dependence; on the other, such ineffectual protests as crying, spitting, vomiting.

The next, the "anal" phase, continues this picture of passivity. As its name indicates, in the anal phase the emphasis has shifted to the organs of evacuation. The child no longer protests at being passively "penetrated" by nipple or bottle but instead directs his protest at the unknown but irresistible force that compels him to expel "parts of his body." Here again some aggressive measures are taken against the mysterious enemy: the child constructs aggressive fantasies, or retains his stool. The prevailing mood is still passivity.

Even in the third phase, when the child attempts to shake off the domination of the mother by borrowing strength from the father, passivity remains the ruler of the scene, for it is fear of the father's punishment that forces the boy to give up his Oedipal ambitions towards the mother.

This long history of weak counteraction opposing enforced passivity has its clearest expression in one transitory and typical phase—the so-called negative Oedipus. This stage has puzzled many observers; it is still the source of a great deal of confusion. In 1908 Freud pointed out that all children pass through both positive and negative stages of the Oedipal conflict. In the positive stage, as is well known, "the boy desires his mother sexually and hates his father as his competitor." In the comparatively neglected negative stage, a third ingredient is added to the boy's hatred and resentment of his father. The boy also wants to be loved by him, as the mother is. In this wish the boy unconsciously identifies with his mother. In the negative Oedipus the wish is in itself passive, but because of the child's misconception, this passivity is tinged with masochism. It seems to me probable that the masochistic passivity of the negative Oedipus is only a continuation of the masochistic passivity of the earliest stage of development.

In short, the growing child engages from birth in a frantic and largely unsuccessful fight to escape from passivity. A formidable barrier bars the way—the barrier of psychic masochism.

Fourth: Every neurotic symptom has a five-layer structure.

In less technical language this means that there are five separate steps to be gone through before a neurotic wish can work its way past the locked doors and detours of the unconscious and into some external expression. Elsewhere I have traced this process in "psychic microscopies" of more than fifty neurotic attitudes chosen at random; these summarize the succession of vetos and alibis from the deepest unconscious layer to the final conscious manifestation. As an example, here is a psychic microscopy of that prototype of all neurotic manifestations, psychic masochism:

Layer I: End result of the infantile conflict; stabilization on the rejection level (genetic picture).

Layer II: First veto of the superego, because of the pleasure gain involved.

Layer III: First defense of the unconscious ego: angry disclaimer (alibi) in the form of an "objective fact"—the promptly provoked outer world's injustice.

Layer IV: Second veto of the superego, pointing to the self-created mess.

Layer V: Second defense of the unconscious ego: to prove the opposite, the psychic masochist increases anger to furious pseudo-aggression, seemingly used in self-defense. This is accompanied by righteous indignation. After his inevitable defeat —which was intended—he consciously pities himself for his dreary fate. He declares himself an innocent victim of the outer world's malice, unconsciously smuggling in traces of attenuated masochistic pleasure. He pays "conscience money" in the form of conscious suffering and extensive self-damage. The "pseudo-moral connotation" is included: his show of pseudo-aggression at the wrong time and place also represents a hypocritical misuse of the educational precept: "Didn't you, parents, teach me to fight back when attacked?"

Summary: Psychic masochism (clinical picture) is a defense against a defense.

Comparing this summary with the clinical picture of psychic masochism which describes the psychic masochist's *external* drama of rejection, it is clear that only the secondary defenses against the original wish are in any way reflected in surface conduct. (Although, strictly speaking, psychic masochism is not an original wish but an inner defense against the superego's cruelty, it subsequently acquires, for all practical purposes, the valency of an unconscious wish.) The real propelling wish remains securely buried in the unconscious.

This fact has an important bearing on therapy. In the past it was scientifically assumed that the neurotic symptom represented a compromise between unconscious wish and unconscious prohibition. The unconscious wish was therefore deduced directly from the externally visible compromise, and guilt was ascribed accordingly. Since analysis fights against neurosis by using guilt feelings, this meant that the analyst's efforts were concentrated on demolishing a mere defense—which could easily be exchanged for a substitute, while the real guilt was left undisturbed and undetected. In these cases the defensive alibi constructed to delude the inner tyrant succeeded in hoodwinking the therapist as well.

Unless it is recognized that only secondary defenses against unconscious wishes become visible in external behavior, the therapist is shooting at the wrong target.

Fifth: All neurotic aggression is no more than pseudo-aggression. This point has already been touched on. To clarify it, here is a table illustrating the differences between normal and false aggression.

Normal Aggression	*Pseudo-Aggression* (False, spurious aggression)
1. Used only in self-defense.	1. Used indiscriminately, when an infantile pattern is repeated with an innocent bystander.
2. Object of aggression is real enemy.	2. Object of aggression is an artificially created enemy.
3. No accompanying unconscious feeling of guilt.	3. Feeling of guilt always present.
4. Amount of aggression discharged corresponds to provocation.	4. Least provocation—greatest aggression.
5. Aggression always used to harm enemy.	5. Pseudo-aggression often used as prelude to masochistic pleasure expected from enemy's retaliation.
6. Timing: ability to wait until enemy is vulnerable.	6. Timing: inability to wait, since show of pseudo-aggression is needed as a defense against inner reproach of psychic masochism.
7. Not easily provoked.	7. Easily provoked.
8. Element of infantile game absent; no combination with masochistic-pseudo-sadistic tendencies.	8. Element of infantile game present, combined with masochistic-pseudo-sadistic excitement.
9. Success expected.	9. Defeat unconsciously expected.

Either the one or the other set of opposing aims and unconscious elaborations invariably characterizes an aggressive action. If it is an action dominated by the normal sector of the personality, it will be true aggression; if it has been set in motion by a neurotic sector, it will be false aggression. Even the so-called normal individual has some streaks of neurosis; even the highly neurotic one has some undiseased areas. But the neurotic's healthy sectors are comparatively small. They tend to lose all their influence in a crisis, when they are submerged under a flood of neurotic aims. A neurotic aim is never served by any but false aggression. This is not at all surprising in view of the fact that psychic masochism is at the root of all neurotic signs and symptoms, and that the standard defense against an inner accusation of psychic masochism is an outer show of alleged aggression.

Sixth: The neurotic always has a double set of unconscious identifications; one of these is "leading" and the other "misleading."

The distinction between genuine and smoke screen unconscious identifications has been mentioned before; the tendency ties in with the fact that external appearances are built out of a succession of inner defenses.

The main purpose of an unconscious identification is to diminish the individual's guilt. When the inner tyrant charges that some misdeed has been committed, the reply is put in these terms: "But what about X? He does what is forbidden too." The inner identification provides a shield against inner reproaches.

To begin with, this human shield is chosen to correspond to the end result of the infantile conflict (leading identification), secondarily to correspond to the secondary defensive cover (misleading identification). Every human being resorts, simultaneously, to both types of identification, and both are unconscious. The misleading identification, since it pertains to a defense, is the more superficial of the two, and it is superimposed on the other.

Seventh: The neurotic is characterized by an overabundance of inner fear.

There is a vast difference between reality fear and neurotic fear. The former is a protective device that comes into play when an external danger threatens. The latter is a warning sign against inner dangers. But because the neurotic victim must find a fixed point to which he can attach his unconscious fears, he secondarily shifts them to the outer world and finds there a "cause" which purports to explain why they arose. In other words, one of the ways in which he fights against his inner fear is to make it appear rational, as a reality fear is.

In my opinion, neurotic fear pertains basically and exclusively to repressed psychic masochism. It comes into play when inner tension passes the point of tolerance for the specific individual. It is a signal which says: "Take it easy; danger ahead." The danger here refers to the likelihood of a new and powerful attack on the part of the department of punishment.

The best the individual can do defensively after being warned by the presence of fear is to register a denial of psychic masochism by some act of pseudo-aggression, at the same time "perceiving" some danger in the outer world to which he can fix his fear. This is a double trick: the accusation has now been changed so that the victim is charged with the lesser crime of pseudo-aggression instead of the major crime of masochism, and the inner danger—against which he could not fight—has been disguised as an external threat.

This is the unconscious history of neurotic fear: It begins with psychic masochism and the pattern of finding unconscious pleasure in conscious pain and humiliation, and at the same time it pertains to repeated blows delivered to the infantile illusion of omnipotence. In the next step punishment is accepted, but for the lesser crime of pseudo-aggression, and the show of alleged aggression which makes this defense possible is also used to repair the narcissistic damage. The projection of the inner fear outwards is also accomplished at this time. In the final stage the inner tormenter accepts the lesser crime as the real crime, tempted into the deal by an artificial increase of guilt. (This is a clever tactic, since it is aimed at the inner tyrant's tendency to accept bribes in the form of suffering.) But the presence of so much guilt, artificial or not, means that the circuit is overloaded. As a result, the anxiety signal sounds again.

In this outline of the unconscious origin of anxiety, it is assumed that fear actually pertains to deeply rooted psychic masochism and is secondarily shifted to the defensive aggression for which inner blame is accepted. On the surface, therefore, the fear seems to belong to the pseudo-aggressive act. It is clear from this formulation, too, that the extent of the forbidden masochistic wish cannot be gauged from the amount of fear showing on the surface. This evident fear is artificially augmented in order to strengthen the unconscious alibi. The whole battle of anxiety is fought on a spurious front.

Anxiety, in general, is a defense resorted to on many occasions, of which the following are the most common:

When a dramatic demonstration of sincerity and good intention is required to placate the department of punishment. On these occasions a stage of depression precedes anxiety. If depression is not enough to convince, anxiety follows.

When narcissism, or self-love, is so conspicuous in the personality that passivity is a constant source of inner reproach, and the need to pursue masochistic—and therefore passive—aims becomes a torment. The counteraction consists of admitting to an aggressive act or intention. This is an example of the unconscious repetition compulsion, in which the wound inflicted by enforced passivity is healed by actively repeating the passive situation.

When the pseudo-aggression produced as an unconscious defense becomes too pronounced, two opposing and irreconcilable unconscious conditions must be met: the defensive alibi must be continued and the needed low tension must be maintained. Apparently, the older mechanism of keeping tension within safe limits wins out, and the nearly automatic signal of anxiety is given.

Eighth: All neurotic symptoms illustrate the inner mechanism of admitting to the lesser crime.

The shift from the decisive inner conflict to the spurious one (as in the shift from psychic masochism to pseudo-aggression and seemingly libidinous aims) and acceptance of guilt for the alibi crime are indispensable parts of the picture of what every neurotic does unconsciously. If this double maneuver is ignored, the neurotic's actions cannot be understood, nor can his real motivations be uncovered.

Ninth and last: Neurosis is a progressive and not a self-limiting disease. Every untreated neurosis testifies to this tragic fact, for the best the neurotic can do for himself without professional help is to exchange one neurotic symptom for another as the inner defense it represents wears out. In the meantime, the sum total of neurosis increases.

As for the antithesis of neurosis, the most commonly encountered analytical definition of emotional health declares it to consist of "the ability to work and to love." This is a somewhat limited explanation; it is profitable to extend it, as I suggested in my book, *Divorce Won't Help Neurotics*. The ability to work should include the ability to sublimate deep-lying wishes and to transform them into satisfying, productive, and approved occupations and hobbies. The ability to love should be understood as the ability to love tenderly, with normal potency retained. Another provision should be added: emotional health calls for the capacity to have normal social contacts and interests and to enjoy leisure.

Even with this extension, two essential points are not covered. The healthy person must come to terms with his disappointments without passing through a period of giving full rein to his psychic masochism. And he should be able to construct the illusions and fantasies that make life tolerable. These two might even be combined, since the ability to keep one's propensity for injustice collecting within safe limits is closely intertwined with the capacity to build harmless castles in the air. This requirement might then be expressed as "coming to terms with disappointments without any break in the flow of illusions."

The need to comfort oneself with harmless illusions and fantasies has nothing to do with the illusions of adult psychotics, who can no longer perceive reality. The ability to create and hang on to changing illusions is a mark of normality. When the illusion eventually collapses, a suitable period of mourning follows. This postpones but does not permanently prevent construction of a new illusion. Like its predecessor, the new illusion will in time collapse.

When these fantasies and illusions are scientifically investigated, they prove to be defense mechanisms of varying importance and effect. One of the most familiar of these defensive fantasies arises from the claim that every psychic masochist puts forward at one time or another, the claim that his deepest need is to be "really" loved by a kind, giving woman. In inner reality his deepest need is to find a steady source of mistreatment, and in pursuit of that hunger he may marry a woman who can be counted on to subject him to an unvarying diet of tirades and reproaches. He complains, of course, but unconsciously enjoys it. His fantasy of "real love" is the defense that helps him to save face and provides him with some temporary respite from the attacks of the inner tormenter. (The same routine is followed by the masochistic woman.)

It is illuminating to contrast this fantasy with the also familiar face-saving fantasy of the writer whose contemporaries ignore or scorn his works. Rejected or not, he has no doubt that posterity will be on his side. Not too often, but more often than a critic, if not a reader, would believe, the author's illusion eventually becomes a reality, as it did in the famous case of Stendhal. But the fantasy does not arise from the fact that the author's literary standards are more or less reliable and knowing than the critic's. It grows as a defensive response to the reproaches of the inner tyrant, which gloatingly points to the author's failure in his chosen field and attempts to exact penance. Against this defense, the inner tyrant's best retort takes the form of irony. One unrecognized writer, a patient who made his living teaching psychology, caught himself thinking: "Sure, you will become famous; you will become a scarecrow for pupils in 2040 A.D., when some poor college boy will curse you!" This was the inner tyrant at work, debunking a comforting illusion.

Broadly speaking, it is justifiable to call the writer's fantasy normal and the psychic masochist's fantasy neurotic. This is true despite the common origin of the two as constructions erected under pressure of the inner department of punishment.

The differentiation rests on a single, but singularly significant rule of thumb: How much injustice collecting pervades the fantasy? This same rule of thumb can be used in judging any personality traits; whether or not they are *too* neurotic boils down to the question of whether or not they are *too* masochistic. The more psychic energy a person devotes to injustice collecting, to creating and cashing in on defeat and humiliation, the more neurotic he is. On the other hand, since nobody is entirely free from a tinge of psychic masochism, nobody is immune to a fall from grace into the slough of injustice collecting. The very real difference between the emotionally healthy and the emotionally diseased is essentially a matter of quantity.

And yet the quantitative difference eventually develops into a qualitative one. Each individual has his own personal budget of psychic energy; in the case of the inveterate psychic masochist, his pursuit of self-injury exhausts his emotional budget. The fantasies he creates fall into two restricted categories: they either relive one of the injustices he has created or constructed by misusing reality factors, or they present futile pictures of pseudo-aggressive revenge. Both types are designed to disarm the inner tyrant by carrying the placating messages: "See how unjust the real world is" and "It's not true that I always take it on the chin; see how I dish it out!"

The not-so-neurotic, or so-called normal person adds an important variation to this technique. The purpose is still defense, but the defense includes a constructive and imaginative element. Like the psychic masochist he must and does accept defeat; who goes through life garnering an unbroken succession of brilliant victories? But he manages to shift the focus of inner attention so that he concentrates his interest on an ever new trifle that is uncontaminated by defeat.

This does not at all mean that normality represents resignation. It means only that the normal person, although he too feels that a defeat is a blow at his infantile (but still unconsciously alive) illusion of omnipotence, uses his ability to construct fantasies to cushion and nullify that blow.

The psychic masochist exhausts his energy in unconsciously proving that defeat has left his infantile megalomania untouched because he himself engineered his defeat: "*My* provocations," he insists, "prompted the bad mother (the outer world) to punish me!"

The not-too-neurotic individual, in contrast, retires from the disappointments of reality and constructs illusions for his own sake.

In other words, the neurotic's sole purpose is to convince the inner tyrant that he is not as guilty as the tyrant charges, while the comparatively healthy individual has paid the price of disappointment and wants to amuse himself, inwardly.

This brings us to another outstanding distinction between normality and neurosis. The inner tyrant inhabiting the unconscious of the neurotic is a much more formidable opponent than that of the comparatively healthy person. The neurotic's ability to silence his department of punishment is pitifully limited; generally the best he can do is offer it a bribe in the hope of sidetracking it into imposing punishment for a lesser crime. Like blackmail, protracted bribery strengthens the enemy. The comparatively normal person is more fortunate; in addition to tabooed wishes, his list of unconscious aims includes some that are so fully approved by the outside world (sublimations) that the inner tyrant is forced into tacit approval as well. The comparatively normal person is capable of tender love, an experience which deprives the department of torture of its surest weapon and for a time bestows immunity from punishment on the score of unfulfilled promises of achievement.

Most important, the normal person's inner tyrant has not been corrupted by bribery. To the normal person an unconscious veto pronounced against an infantile and forbidden wish calls for acquiescence, not the tricky bargaining which the neurotic embarks on in order to rescue a watered-down remnant of the tabooed wish. Once the forbidden wish has been driven back into the storehouse of the unconscious, it ceases to be a troublemaker; it emerges only in dreams, or in waking life after having been transformed into a socially approved function (sublimated).

One could say that in normality the unconscious remains in a state of armed truce, while in neurosis it is always the scene of a pitched and bitter battle. The enemy is the same in both cases and still remains an enemy even after a carefully limited armistice has been agreed on. But—to continue the metaphor—the payment of tribute entitles the normal person to a certain degree of freedom from attack.

No matter how free from neurosis the individual is, he is still vulnerable to reproaches and accusations on the part of his inner department of punishment. Normality is no guarantee of "happiness," in the romantic sense of the word. Every human being has, in the first years of life, created his own inner barrier to happiness, if by happiness is understood a state in which one's cherished wishes can be fulfilled. From then on, all one can expect is fulfillment of defenses against one's real wishes, or sublimations of them. In comparatively normal human beings, this is enough for contentment and a satisfyingly productive life, if not for happiness.

Every neurotic stubbornly maintains that a direct connection exists between his neurosis and his parents' attitudes during his childhood. This affirmation of parental "guilt" I have called the neurotic's "basic fallacy"; clinical observation shows that the puncturing of this fallacy is so dreaded by neurotics that they go to enormous lengths to preserve it.

It is a banality in psychoanalysis to state that every neurotic unconsciously fights with every means at his disposal to preserve his neurosis. Consciously, and in good faith, all neurotics will declare that they hate their neurosis and will sacrifice "anything" to get rid of it; unconsciously, at the same time, they will resist the analytic attempt to destroy or even modify it. Analysts are fully aware of the difficulty of contending with their tenacious unconscious wishes, defenses, and inner guilt feelings.

When psychoanalysis undertakes to remove or reduce neurosis, a major problem becomes evident. The entire edifice of neurotic symptoms and signs rests on a single foundation: the individual's basic unconscious fallacy. Typically this consists of an erroneous conviction regarding the way the neurotic was treated in childhood, or else of careful and cunning misuse of a really unfavorable childhood situation. When this crutch is taken away, the neurosis itself becomes shaky. It goes without saying that the crutch does not disappear as the result of a single therapeutic move. Rather, it is withdrawn little by little, under the impact of a thousand incidents in the protracted process of "working through."

The basic neurotic fallacy holds that neurosis is the direct outcome of environmental circumstances. Every neurotic drags his family skeleton into analytic discussions, revealing that his father was "cruel," his mother preferred his brother to him, his sister was mean to him, the whole family was "half-crazy," and on top of it all, the brother of a neighbor seduced him (or her). Nobody claims that environment plays no part at all in coloring the unconscious attitudes of a child. On the other hand, there is no doubt that the child sees reality through the spectacles of his own projections, which means that at least *some* misconceptions are inevitable. One can only conclude that the environment's effect upon the child's development is a process in which the child himself participates significantly and selectively. If this were not so, it would be impossible to understand why two children can react so differently to the same climate of love, hatred, attention, and so on. This is a phenomenon frequently met with: two brothers or two sisters, brought up under identical conditions, acquire different neuroses or take the widely differing paths that lead on the one hand to comparative normality and on the other to neurosis. As far as this point goes, the standard refutation declares that no two siblings can have the same childhood experiences since the parents react differently to each child. This argument is much overrated; it overlooks the fact that essential attitudes can differ only in detail. No parent has a multiple personality.

It is this basic fallacy concerning past experiences that psychoanalysis must dispose of in every analysis. It may be true, in a specific case, that the patient's mother actually did reject him.

But what prevented the boy, when he became an adult, from creating a situation in life in which a woman would love him dearly and thus compensate him for the deprivation of childhood? Even if this hypothetical patient does not elaborate masochistically on the fact that he remains unloved as an adult, his direct repetition of the situation of rejection by a woman reduces itself to an alibi for psychic masochism. He is conveniently shifting responsibility—which is the defense embedded in his basic fallacy.

Even if the alleged rejection by the mother is factually substantiated (more often, the patient has distorted facts to an amazing degree), this does not of itself explain the whole neurotic process. It is merely one—overstressed—facet of the entire procedure. The psyche is more than a collection of conditioned reflexes. A witty patient once said: "Your formula for the patient seems to be, 'So what?' Even if he is right about the facts of his childhood, he is wrong anyhow!"

When therapy approaches the danger zone and threatens the security of the patient's basic fallacy, it is typical for him to engage in ingenious, and highly unscrupulous, delaying and distractionary actions. He is not deterred by the absurdity of some of his mental acrobatics nor appalled by the most blatant of prevarications. Here are a few examples from the analyses of writers whom I have treated.

Patient DD., a woman, saw me as the "devouring mother" during the transference period, when the analyst is invariably endowed with the qualities unconsciously associated with some revered childhood figure. She found a core of personal malice in everything I did or failed to do, in every harmless or helpful remark I made. Violently and belligerently she fought back against my alleged "malice"; this was not difficult since, like all psychic masochists, she possessed an ample store of pseudo-aggression. For weeks I concentrated on showing her the real facts but without making any impression. One day she came into the appointment room carrying a miniature picket sign reading "SANE." This heralded a short interlude of comparative peace, after which she resumed her pseudo-aggressive tirades.

Though she had consulted me because of my publications on writers and my successful treatment of authors suffering from writer's block, and constantly assured me that she had "great confidence" in my theories, she made a sharp distinction between my "brain" and my "personality." Her approval of me was limited to my "brain"; in her opinion my personality was an accumulation of cruelty and malice. For a long time she rejected the idea that this assessment was a projection and that she was endowing me with the contents of her fantasy of the cruel, malicious mother of childhood. During the high point of one of her conflicts, she exclaimed furiously and with all the signs of righteous indignation: "You have never given me any consideration, kindness, or reassurance; in short, never anything. You are just interested in money."

It is important to refute accusations such as these. I told her, first, that she was repeating an infantile situation. I then reminded her that I had spent approximately eighty hours, during evenings and weekends, reading her books, manuscripts, and memoirs. She had, of course, not been charged for this time. If I had really been "interested only in money," I could have adhered to the strict letter of the law and asked her to read this material to me during her appointment hours. I then asked her to figure out in dollars and cents, at the rate of my fee, the amount I had in this way "given" her. "How can you reconcile that with your accusations?" I asked. "Well, that's true, and it was very nice of you" was her rather ashamed reply.

Two minutes later the familiar tirade was again under way. "You have never shown me any kindness," she complained, with undiminished conviction.

Patient EE., a writer with personality difficulties, made it clear at a certain point in his analysis that he did not believe the "atrocity stories" circulated about the Nazis. In his opinion they were propaganda tales on a level with the atrocity stories circulated about the Germans in the First World War and subsequently disproved. Rather ironically, he ended his disquisition with the comment: "Of course you believe them all because you hate the Nazis." There was no point in discussing the question for its own sake, but it did have a relationship to the analytic transference, and this was pointed out to him. His raising the point also illustrated another of his traits—his tendency to be "contrary" on principle and to reject automatically any view approved by public opinion. Public opinion, of course, symbolically represented his mother.

His defense of the Nazis had another interesting unconscious meaning. His mother came from old American pioneer stock, while his father was a second-generation German. He was in this way, therefore, placing all the blame for his neurosis on his mother, and exonerating his father. This alibi would have been shaken if he had permitted himself to believe the undeniable facts. I pointed this out but without making any impression on the patient. Unshaken in his conviction, he teased me for my naïveté in believing "newspaper stories."

This analysis took place towards the end of the War. The patient was still rejecting the facts of his own situation as well as the facts about the Nazis when the American army occupied the concentration camp at Buchenwald in April, 1945. In the following weeks detailed descriptions of the camp and revelations about the treatment of concentration camp victims appeared in the press. Shortly after the first of these descriptions was printed, the patient fell into discussion of the atrocities with a stranger. The discussion depressed him deeply, and the next day he admitted to me that he had had to abandon his protective technique of ignoring these stories by not reading them. In other words, one of the crutches that supported his basic fallacy was in danger of collapsing; this accounted for his depression.

Patient FF., a man of thirty-eight, maintained that all his neurotic troubles stemmed from one cause—his father's alleged cruelty. His bitterest complaints had to do with his father's "attitude of refusal," but he varied this reproach with a long list of other accusations. One of these dealt with a visit his father had paid him shortly before an acute attack of anxiety propelled him into treatment. On this visit his father had watched the patient's baby for a while and had then promised that he would help the couple financially if they wished to have another. This offer had astonished the patient, he said; his father as a "giving" person was "new" to him. (His father had supported him for thirty years.) Astonishment shortly gave way to a feeling of deep depression. Obviously the offer had shaken one of his crutches—the fantasy of the bad father. His inner tyrant took immediate advantage of the temporary collapse, jeering: "Father is not so bad after all!" The next step was a break in his defense, allowing his latent neurosis to become manifest.

Later in the analysis it became clear that the patient's conflict with his father was merely a camouflage, covering the deeper conflict with his mother. His mother, too, had offered him financial help.

In the later stages of analysis patients sometimes recognize that they are maintaining the precarious balance of their neurosis only by artificially bolstering up their basic fallacy. Patient GG., a woman masochistically attached to the image of the mother of earliest childhood, wrote me the following letter during such a phase:

> You don't get too many compliments in your profession! *Whatever I may think of you at some future time,* my feeling now is that I would never have been "congratulated" by the three most venomous critics in New York if it weren't for your work with me. Do not think that there are not flaws and corrections in the story. I will tell you about that Friday. Art is long! But I have never been able to learn until this moment. I was too confused.

The next day was the Friday mentioned in her letter, and the patient appeared ten minutes early. She asked: "Am I early?" I replied: "Yes, you are." Since the patient scheduled for that hour had been detained by an important business conference, I then added: "I have free time. Come right in." Rather brusquely, she said: "O.K." I suggested analyzing both her letter and her supercilious, condescending "O.K."

"What about them?" she asked sharply.

I started to explain that both the letter, which contained a half-hidden aggression, and the response, an obvious aggression, had the purpose of provoking me into some form of retaliation. "You are incapable of giving," I went on. "If you can't help yourself and must give, as you had to give me a factual report on the success you achieved through analysis, you still manage to make me into the bad, refusing mother."

After some discussion the patient admitted her provocation. She then said: "As long as we fight I feel safe."

This was a very revealing remark. It meant that as long as she could maintain the fantasy that I was the "bad mother," she felt that there was no danger threatening her unconscious conviction that her mother had been unjust to her. This fantasy of the bad mother of earliest childhood was the cornerstone of all her unconscious attitudes; it was so important to her to keep it intact that she saw an attack even in analytic interpretations, impersonally given and therapeutically intended.

Not every patient safely passes the danger zone during which the basic fallacy collapses. Patient DD. could not take it; she abandoned treatment and became a chronic crusader against the "cruelty" of her analyst in particular and analysis in general, always hoping to find sympathetic listeners, even among analysts. The three other patients mentioned here did overcome this difficulty; for them it became at least possible to work out their problems. One could say that the stage in which the basic fallacy of the neurotic is attacked is the turning point of every analysis.

The part played by the inner conscience in the process of destroying or diminishing the basic fallacy—and especially its masochistic elaboration—has a special interest. Obviously the existence of the basic fallacy is the prerequisite for the maintenance of the neurotic structure as a whole. In the cases of patients DD., EE. and GG., the basic fallacy consisted of the thesis "Mother is cruel." Patient FF. projected the same fantasy upon his father, in a superficial camouflage. Without this assumption, none of these patients could have embarked upon their habitual drama of injustice collecting. The inner department of punishment accepts or at least tolerates this fundamental assumption; its tolerance is part of the inner system of bargains and compromises. The tyrant is well paid for its temporary permissiveness; payment is the victim's conscious unhappiness.

Under specific conditions, however, this tolerance vanishes. This occurs when the amount of conscious unhappiness sinks below a certain level, and the inner tyrant perceives that its bargain was not such a bargain after all. Always ready to break the unconscious agreement and enter upon a new one specifying terms more favorable to itself, the inner tyrant acts promptly when external factors contradict too tellingly the erroneous assumption embedded in the basic fallacy. This is what happened in the case of patient FF. When his father offered to contribute to the support of his grandchild, the unexpected, unconsciously undesired offer precipitated an inner crisis. In the other cases, the breaking point occurred during analysis, as the result of working through these patients' neurotic projections.

The first result is always a deep sense of depression; the next step takes the form of a temporary heightening of neurotic symptoms. As a patient put it: "The department of punishment renews its lease, but at a higher rent." The third step may take different forms. Sometimes, as patient DD. did, the patient runs away from analysis. Sometimes the patient remains in treatment but redoubles his efforts to provoke his analyst in the transference situation, hoping against hope to prove that the basic fallacy is no fallacy at all. In the end, after long exposure to the working-through process, the fallacy does collapse. Then, and then only, is the basis of the neurosis destroyed.

CHAPTER 5

A CLINICAL EXAMINATION
OF "PARENTAL INFLUENCE"
IN THE DEVELOPMENT OF NEUROSIS
IN TWENTY CURED CASES

THE thesis that neurosis is an *inner* process, based on unfavorable elaboration of *inner* and therefore unconscious factors in the life of the child, can best be proved by adducing actual clinical material. In the course of more than three decades of psychoanalytic work, I have published hundreds of excerpts from the histories of analyzed cases. In the following pages, I am singling out twenty examples drawn from this already published material. The advantage here is that these case histories were written years ago and for a completely different purpose. This material is, so to speak, impartial.

All these examples have been shortened. For more extensive details the reader is referred to the original versions.

TEN EXAMPLES OF INFANTILE BACKGROUND MATERIAL
IN CASES OF HOMOSEXUALITY

In *Homosexuality: Disease or Way of Life?* and *One Thousand Homosexuals* (Hill and Wang, N.Y. 1956, and Pageant Books, Paterson, N.J., 1959), long case histories are described. The abbreviated versions of ten of these case histories given below emphasize the infantile backgrounds involved. (Cases I-V are taken from the first book, Cases VI-X from the second. The initials used in the second group are the same as those in the original publication.)

Three facts are decisive for the genesis of male homosexuality. First, the homosexual has a fantastic fear of women, masochistically imbued and so strong that he runs away from the dangerous female sex entirely. Second, the homosexual retains his early masochistic attachment to the image of the mother but lives it out by recourse to his rescue station, man. Third, he employs a specific "reduplication of his own defense mechanism."

To see the homosexual clearly one would have to imagine a man who for some mysterious reason unconsciously wants to be mistreated by a woman, though consciously unaware of this wish. One would have to imagine, further, that this person inwardly fears his own wish but instead of giving up the wish itself gives up its alleged or imagined central figure, woman. Since there are only two sexes, this leaves him with only one alternative in his frantic flight: man. Officially, and as a defense against his real inner wish, he turns to man in order to find peace, quiet, love, understanding, safety. But underneath these official aims his real, compelling need remains the need to be mistreated. His retreat to "another continent" does not alter the old, unofficial conflict. Sooner or later (and sooner rather than later) he will feel that the man with whom he has sought refuge mistreats him, misunderstands him, fails to do him justice, deliberately tortures him by arousing his jealousy. Moreover, his flight has in no way affected his sex glands. Since they are still working, it is inevitable that man, his antidote against the feared sex, will secondarily be elevated to the status of a sexual attraction.

To put the same story into more scientific terms: The homosexual is unconsciously a masochistic injustice collector who has shifted the "power to mistreat" from woman to man. His brother under the skin is the Caspar Milquetoast who (unconsciously on purpose) marries a shrew who soundly mistreats him. Consciously he complains bitterly, but his apparent resentment and dissatisfaction do not affect his actions. Death, not divorce, will part him from his torturer. The Milquetoast is not a heroic figure, but at least he compares creditably with the homosexual; he does not run to "another continent" to escape his fear.

Under the disguise of a bad imitation (which frequently becomes a caricature) of woman, the homosexual acts out what seems to be the Oedipal game. This half-conscious imitation has given rise to the erroneous opinion that all homosexuals are "inwardly women." The opinion is fallacious, simply because every "feminine" homosexual is matched by a "masculine" one. Moreover, analysis proves that this Oedipal camouflage hides a deeper layer in which homosexuals act out the drama of "bad mother mistreats the innocently tantalized baby." The active, "masculine" homosexual unconsciously plays the role of "cruel mother," while the passive, "feminine" homosexual is the "mistreated" baby.

The homosexual is so deeply attached to the image of his individual giantess of the nursery that he also acts out—unconsciously, to be sure—a specific defense in a fearful though reassuring manner.

Every child has to cope with the problem of weaning. This far-reaching disappointment is a universal childhood dilemma; every child must overcome and adjust to the loss of the breast or the bottle. Typically the infant boy comforts himself in this crisis with the discovery that he, too, possesses a magic apparatus capable of providing a liquid. It does not matter, he reasons, that one does not possess a breast as long as one has an equivalent—and even superior—organ, the penis. This line of reasoning leaves narcissism triumphant and prepares the boy for the full restitution of adult sex, where he unconsciously plays the role of active and giving "mother" with a woman whom he unconsciously sees as the passive and receptive "baby." (Such familiar terms of adult endearment as "baby" and the outmoded but still persistent "little woman" are psychologically meaningful.)

The future homosexual is so unsure of this substitution, which amounts to a defense mechanism, that he must constantly bolster his confidence in it by *duplicating* it. The penis of his partner denotes to him both the lost breast and the reassuring defense, his own penis. (I have suggested that this inner technique be called "reduplication of one's own defense mechanism.")

CASE I

A wealthy, middle-aged stockbroker came into treatment in a state of extreme depression. The latest in the succession of young "Greek gods" who were his love objects had callously and casually "played him for a sucker." He showed no eagerness to change his homosexuality; his approach towards treatment was one of resignation. Its motif ran: "What have I got to lose?" His chances of a successful analysis were poor, and I told him so.

He described his childhood as a lonely one. The household atmosphere was cold; his parents showed him little affection and asked for little in return. He solaced himself with daydreams about the future, when he would be loved, admired, and "somebody." His mother channeled her charitable impulses to causes and persons outside the home, and the boy resented this. "I was determined to show her up," he told me. His idea was that he could do so by proving to her that other women—especially women she would look down on—would be willing to give him the love she withheld. But there were no women within his immediate orbit who could be used for this purpose; his "cold" mother chose only "cold" servants. "And you know," he added, "that snobs as servants are worse snobs than their masters."

"Aren't you yourself still using snobbish expressions?" I asked.

"Meaning I'm a snob, too? That amuses me. My contacts later in life prove the opposite."

"There could be different reasons for that."

"Such as?"

"Using your own phrase, such as 'showing your mother up.' In short, pseudo-aggression tinged with self-damage. . . . By the way, in your caricatures of the members of your household you omitted your father. Was there a father?"

"Technically, yes; practically, no. He was seldom at home. First I admired him; later I had contempt for him, seeing how much he catered to my mother's so-called opinions. As an adult

I realized that he couldn't win, and so he made his life outside our home."

"So you were lonely and had heterosexual dreams of glory. At least you haven't told me the usual sentimental tale of the homosexual—that he was always interested in playing he was a girl."

"I wasn't."

"But you do run true to form in another way: you deny that you were afraid of women. You mention only shyness. What about fears? . . . What frightened you?"

"As I told you, there were only women around me. Women and adults were synonymous."

"You said that you were curious. What did you observe that frightened you?"

"Now you are bringing up that worn-out analytic red herring called castration."

"You have obviously misunderstood what you have read about the castration complex. There is, of course, phallic castration fear. But it is just the summary and late expression of many precursors. Admittedly fantastic precursors. There's a good example in the fairy tale of Hansel and Gretel. The tale is about being starved, bitten, eaten, about cruelty and meanness—and it's all the fault of women. This story has parallels in all cultures. These are the fears I'm referring to—fantasies of 'oral' castration."

"I know nothing about it. I do have a silly fear of dogs, though I personally never had any bad experiences with dogs."

"When did this fear start?"

"Very early. Every time I was dressed to be taken for a walk I cried bitterly, expecting that dogs would harm me."

"What's the dog's technique of harming?"

"Biting. O.K.—long live Hansel and Gretel!"

"With or without irony, isn't it likely that you transposed your fears of servants and governesses and other mother substitutes into a fear of harmless animals?"

"Does this ever happen?"

"Very frequently. All irrational animal phobias are based on this shift, which, of course, is unconscious."

This patient's psychic masochism, so explicit in his description of his adult life, was implicit in every detail he gave of his childhood history. In his opinion this proved that he was his parents' "victim," and he took it for granted that I agreed.

"Nothing of the sort," I told him. "Reality is only the raw material." In his case, I explained, he could have made up for his parents' coldness by compensating for it in later life, marrying a loving woman who would have given him the warmth denied him in childhood. The other possibility was to perpetuate the wrong masochistically, either by marrying a cold woman or by seeking mistreatment within the framework of homosexuality. The question to be decided was whether or not he was addicted to self-created suffering. I asked him whether his last disappointing homosexual experience was typical. He was reticent about this part of his history, and for good reason. When the recital of his past experiences finally came it proved that the recent tragedy ran true to form.

The "Greek god" in one guise or another had appeared at regular intervals in his life. He was always an expensive and narcissistic deity. Ashamed to make outright payments, the stockbroker would pay these young men for their interest in him by taking them into partnership on stock deals. Repeatedly he would be asked by his so-called partner for a premature settlement of accounts and would have to confess that the investment was imaginary. This was countered by a threat to sue for damages. He would then pay and pay and pay again in order to avert a scandal.

I said: "As I piece your information together, this is the picture. You have always paid for your sex; you were always taken advantage of; you always felt unjustly treated."

This summary shocked the patient into silence. Some days later he revealed why it had hit him so painfully. On a few occasions he had speculated with clients' funds, sometimes barely escaping discovery. Remembering the risks he had taken, it had suddenly occurred to him that I might be right about his masochism. This realization also gave him some insight into the unconscious changes that take place during analysis of homosexuality. What happens eventually in a successful analysis is that the patient no longer uses homosexuality as his main means for expressing psychic masochism.

In the next stage of treatment we concentrated on finding out why his original heterosexual interest in sex had died out. He recalled his discovery, while watching a maid undress, that women do not possess the male organ. After this he had developed a series of hypochondriacal symptons connected with the penis.

"Was this at the period of your dog phobia?" I asked.

"More or less."

"The question, then, is: whom does the frightening animal represent? Since you have repeatedly stressed the fact that women were predominant in your childhood as educators and punishers, isn't it likely that the dog derived his 'biting power' from one of these women?"

"Even shrews don't bite."

"No. But the suspicion arises that observing 'castrated' women revived earlier, repressed fears connected with them. I mean baby fears. Biting and being bitten figure largely in these fears."

"Why?"

"Because the mouth is the baby's only effective weapon. When he is angry he bites the breast, the bottle, or anything that is put into his mouth. Later, seeing the negative reaction of adults to this, he becomes frightened—perhaps precursors of guilt are already involved—and shifts the process projectively. The story then reads, 'I don't want to bite; my bad mother (or mother substitute) wants to devour me.' "

My suspicion was fully borne out, not only by the evidence of the patient's dog phobia but also by examination of his eating habits. He was a finicky eater with many food idiosyncrasies. His food habits proved to be hypochondriacal remnants of another baby fear: "Bad mother wants to poison me!"

Eventually the analysis uncovered the starting point for the patient's switch from hetero- to homosexual interests, and for his admiration for "Greek gods."

"Why this emphasis on beauty?" I asked during one appointment. "Were you told that you were ugly as a child?"

With great fury the patient repeated a remark his mother had made decades earlier: "Be glad you're not a girl; with your looks you couldn't get a man." On another occasion she had told him that people whose hair grew low on their foreheads were likely to become criminals.

"So you proved her prediction wrong on both counts. You got your 'man,' in fact a troop of them, and as for criminality, you were never detected."

"So?"

"On the other hand, if your mother were here she would undoubtedly point out that you always paid your men, and that you were lucky in not being detected."

"Why rub it in?"

"To rouse a little opposition—via identification—to your masochism. Or shall I say your previous masochism?"

"You can do that."

"Well, let's go on about your switch to homosexuality. Isn't it likely that under the pressure of phallic fears and revived baby fears of 'nobody loves me' and 'I'm ugly,' you reverted to the only person who seemed to love you—yourself? Aren't your 'Greek gods' beautified editions of yourself?"

"The last part of the sentence I can accept."

"Well, let's put your acceptance of masochism to the test. I suspect that by always paying your friends you denied yourself the chance of finding someone who would be selflessly attached to you. Doesn't this prove that you have used the self-degrading technique of 'Nobody loves me; I have to pay for love?' And doesn't it also confirm your mother's statement, 'You couldn't get a man?' And isn't this all deeply masochistic?"

Little by little, analysis undermined the basis for his homosexuality. Eventually, despite the unfavorable portents that had made treatment seem no more than a doubtful experiment, he was cured. Faced with the evidence that he had not been the victim either of an imaginary biological imperative or of the atmosphere of his parents' household, but instead had himself chosen to perpetuate his grievances for the sake of masochistic pleasure, his psychic masochism diminished and his homosexuality disappeared.

Comment: Since the human being is more than a sum of conditioned reflexes, the *selectivity* in the inner elaboration is decisive. The patient described above could have taken different ways out: he could have repaired his early disappointments or he could have perpetuated them masochistically. Both possibilities did exist. Inwardly he chose the latter. The fact that in childhood he was surrounded by women could just as well have led to his selection of a loving woman in later life. This did not happen because he ran away from the frightening sex altogether. Did the rescue station, man, compensate? It did not, because even (and especially) with men he acted out a continuation of his drama of mistreatment. He was always on the receiving end, because unconsciously he wanted to be.

CASE II

A prominent industrialist in his late thirties came to me for treatment of his homosexuality after having spent six years in unsuccessful analysis, two years with each of three psychiatrists. The diagnosis in each case was "feminine identification"; analysis on this basis made no progress. Having read my writings on homesexuality, he decided to give analysis one more chance. I consented to a trial treatment of four weeks; his previous analyses made it likely that he did not actually wish to change his homosexuality but persisted with treatment to provide himself with an alibi. As I pointed out to him, a "reasonable person would have terminated those various treatments much earlier than you did." Clearly he had used them as a means of collecting injustices. Also, since he had not become an overt homosexual until he was actually in his first analysis and had then followed the typical development of an untreated homosexual, it could be concluded that his masochistic propensities were monumental. What he had to learn to recognize was that the role of victim that he played with his former analysts was merely a continuation of a role he had played all his life. To show how this single theme pervaded his entire history we went back to his childhood. He said: "I am a living example of the fallacy of the theory that a homosexual develops only in families where the mother is dominant and the father a weakling, or absent altogether."

"For your information, the theory is outdated," I replied. "It was constructed at a time when homosexuality was considered an aberration of the Oedipus complex. Faced with the question, why the boy doesn't identify with the father, the theorists took the convenient way out: When a strong mother dominates the home there is no model for such identification, since the father is a weakling. Today, we know the question is a sham. The homosexual's conflict pertains to the unresolved masochistic relationship with the earliest image of the mother (pre-Oedipal); the complex itself, since it is a much later development, is without basic importance in homosexuals. Another proof of this is the fact that homosexuals use pseudo-Oedipal traits as camouflaging defenses. In rare, comparatively durable affairs they often act the roles of husband and wife. Since the unconscious *is* unconscious, a consciously approved camouflage cannot be 'the real thing.' "

"I'm glad to hear that. In my family my father was a shouting tyrant; my mother was a subdued, meek female-ette. Of course, this opens up a new contradiction. How could such a meek and submissive person have been elevated to the role of the witch, which I understand is the part ascribed to the 'giantess of the nursery'?"

"You are mixing up your chronology. Your opinion of your mother's submissiveness was formed at a later period, a period you remember. The image of the giantess belongs to a period that is repressed and cannot be remembered. No recollections that can be verbalized go back as far as the first eighteen months of life. This period can be reconstructed only from later actions."

"Strangely enough, most of my father's yelling at my mother started with a complaint about food. He was ridiculously particular about food. . . . If it wasn't just so, there was a terrible outburst. Since he was highly inconsistent in his preferences it was impossible to please him."

"How did he treat you?"

"With pompous neglect. . . . My younger sister and I were nonentities for him. Fortunately children annoyed him, so I was shunted off early to a military school."

The patient's use of the word "pompous" had not been limited to the sentence quoted above. He had recalled his father's general manner as "pompous" also, and he had found "pompousness" in one of my remarks. The picture he had formed of my character, however (this picture is part of the transference and as such becomes an important part of every analysis), bore no relation to this quality, and he himself suggested that his connecting it with me represented the projection of the father image in the transference.

In substance this conclusion was correct, but it needed enlargement. I told him: "I doubt whether your projections in the transference are totally traits and attitudes pertaining to your father. Superficially they are. But in a deeper layer, I believe, will be found some masochistic reproach directed at your mother. True, your father's noisy, pompous, tyrannical attitude conveniently provided the possibility of shifting pre-Oedipal attitudes to the Oedipal blind. If I understand you correctly, you simply hated his guts. However, your relation to your mother was more complex. Despite her weakness, her complete dependence on your father, you were constantly putting her to the test: did she really defend you against your father? That accounts for your hyper-suspicious attitude. I also suspect that your statement that you would like to see me 'cringe' was mother and not father transference. The same goes for your ironic, exasperated, injustice-collecting attitude in our first interview. That was more closely related to the masochistic infant than to the defensively aggressive boy."

He spent a weekend thinking about this interpretation and then confirmed its important points, giving many examples of his "open defiance" and complete rejection of his father. As for his wish to make me cringe, he had checked the word in the dictionary and discovered that the definition exactly described his mother's attitude towards his father.

"But I'm stuck at this point," he went on. "When I said I wanted you to cringe, I was playing the part of Father and reducing you to my mother's passive image. How does this prove *my* passivity?"

"Well, you're overlooking a point. Your bullying is superficially a father identification. Therefore you have to make people cringe. For example, you incessantly threatened your three previous therapists. But beneath this superficial and pseudo-aggressive defense is your identification with the victim."

"This is even more confusing, because it's identical with the feminine identification theory that was unsuccessfully served me in my other analyses."

"No, you misunderstand. The feminine identification is in itself a defense—it's the admission of the lesser crime. What you are warding off so frantically is your deep masochism."

"Passivity of any sort is passivity."

There was a radical difference, I told him, between the harmless passivity of feminine identification and the poisonous passivity of masochistic attachment to the earliest image of the mother. To prove this, we examined his history of homosexual attachments, the nature of his homosexual affairs, and the details of the marriage he had made when he thought that marriage could "cure" homosexuality.

He had no recollection of heterosexual wishes in childhood; as a child and as a mature man his sexual interests had consisted exclusively of a kind of gloating violence. He was not interested in being touched by his partners; he derived his pleasure from a rape-like attack on the partner's sex organs.

He had welcomed the interpretation of "feminine identification" presented by his first therapist; it meant to him that at bottom he was a kind and unaggressive person. Against this therapist's specific advice, he had married. He was impotent in his marriage and, what was worse, his presumably "nice" wife had reacted most unpleasantly to the discovery. As she saw it, his impotence proved that he was homosexual. She threatened a "dirty divorce," and at great financial sacrifice he "got rid of her." After this he returned to therapy and to his furtive homosexual escapades, always afraid that his violence would get him into serious trouble.

"Let's summarize," I proposed. "Superficially, you identify yourself with your bullying father; your partner is the masochistically mistreated mother. Obviously your exaggerated cruelty toward your partners is the only way you have of rescuing yourself from your over-dimensional masochism. Experience proves that sadism in adults (not in children) is merely an inner defense. All this is compartively superficial. In a deeper layer, you are identifying yourself with the victim. Proof: what excites you is the danger of getting into trouble. This being the case, a question remains to be answered. Why do you choose homosexual and not heterosexual objects? . . . If a woman had a penis, you would be heterosexual. Your cruelty—am I correct?—is directed exclusively against that organ."

"Exclusively is correct. I don't even look at these fellows; their bodies are of no importance."

"That means you are acting out these roles in the inner drama: first, in your father's guise you play the giantess in relation to yourself—you are the mistreated partner. Second, still in your father's guise, you reverse the roles, and the giantess's 'udder' is mistreated—."

The patient interrupted, greatly excited. "What makes you use the word udder?"

"Did I hit something?"

"Once one of these boys—my boys, you understand—nearly hit me because I referred to his organ as 'an ugly udder.' He took offense, God knows why."

"Not much of a mystery. Unconsciously, behind every homosexual's search for the male sex organ is hidden the search for the breast. With your remark you endangered the fellow's repressions. That explains his fury."

At his next appointment the patient presented a significant confirming fact dating back to the period before he first entered analysis. He had then been thinking of buying a dairy farm.

"What excited me sexually was the idea of milking cows, but roughly, to the point of cruelty. There you are—make the most of it. I had forgotten all that nonsense till you used the word 'udder.' Are you really so smart, or was the choice of the word just an accident?"

"The identification of breast and male sex organ in the unconscious fantasies of homosexuals is a clinically established fact."

"But why couldn't I become simply a sadist, torturing women?"

"Because of the extent of your compensatory hatred and fear. Women, even in degradation, reminded you too insistently of the 'torturer' of infancy. You had to run, to retreat as far as you could—to men."

"And the recollection of the breast is completely repressed? I feel a distaste for these organs."

"So deeply repressed that only in the narcissistic disguise of reduplication of your reassuring organ—the organ of your partner—can it be tolerated, if only to be mistreated."

After eight months the patient's heterosexuality was established; analysis had finally enabled him to make the necessary unconscious adjustment to a situation that had arisen when he was still in the nursery.

Comment: This case is interesting because it disproves the so frequently promoted opinion that the absence of a strong father and the presence of a domineering mother provides the basis for homosexuality. In this instance, there was a strong father and a weak, loving mother, but still it was the unsolved masochistic conflicts from the first eighteen months that determined the outcome. The patient found these facts astonishing and unbelievable because his mother appeared as a kind person in all his recollections. *No direct congruity* between educational and emotional facts and later development could be discovered. The child's selectivity of the raw material presented was decisive.

CASE III

The Oedipal camouflage, in which a male homosexual adopts the manner and attitudes of a woman as part of his unconscious defensive pattern, is a familiar stereotype. But it appears less often than one would expect as part of the equipment of homosexuals seen in a psychiatrist's office. Most homosexuals cannot be externally distinguished from heterosexuals. The patient in this case, however, fitted the pattern. His feminine masquerade was so careful, pronounced, and detailed that on first meeting him I was not actually certain of his sex. He assured me that anatomically ("unfortunately") he was male, that he was "meant to be" a woman and would prefer to be one, but that under the unpleasant pressures of this brutal world he had decided he wanted to change his homosexuality. A minimum of questioning brought out the real reason for his visit. A wealthy uncle, appalled and angered by his nephew's "vice," had offered him a tempting bribe to abandon his homosexuality. If the nephew successfully underwent analysis (at the uncle's expense), married, and produced a child within three years, he would become the sole heir to the uncle's considerable fortune.

The patient had his own opinion of the basis for his homosexuality. "Both my parents were six-footers," he explained. "I was the oldest child, small, sickly, and more girlish than a boy is supposed to be. Disappointed by my size, they produced a second child, a giant girl who grew fast. They loved my sister. I identified myself with her. That's all."

The trouble with this solution was that it omitted entirely any consideration of the unconscious. My matter-of-fact explanation was received with the standard response of a mid-Victorian heroine of cheap fiction: with tears and a plaintive "You brute!" This old fashioned expression suggested a possible clue, and I asked him who had been the "brute" in his childhood environment. "Everybody!" he answered. "They made fun of me, had no understanding of the fine feminine structure in me."

This "fine feminine structure" referred to the assortment of poses which the patient used instead of genuine reactions. He was all pose, from the stereotypes of feminine attitudes that served him as emotions to the borrowed esthetic and intellectual judgments that he consistently parroted.

I told him: "Isn't it remarkable how uncomfortable you are if one deprives you of your esthetic-girlish phoney props?"

"You mean I'm nothing?"

"A collection of phonograph records, played *ad nauseam.*"

"What am I? I must be something."

"A bitter, disappointed, deeply masochistic child with silly defenses."

"I'm not bitter! I'm not disappointed!"

"You are. Let's uncover this part of your past."

Reluctantly the patient went into detail about the "brutes" in his family circle. He had been rejected by his parents and repeatedly humiliated by their frankly disparaging remarks. They had bewailed his microscopic size, his movements, his facial expressions, even the size of his sexual organs. His father had loved sports and prided himself on his athletic ability; he had not known what to do with a boy who showed neither interest in nor aptitude for his favorite hobbies. His mother had echoed his father's attitudes. In contrast, both parents pampered his younger sister.

"You'll admit," the patient concluded, "that my environment forced me into my fate."

"I don't. Your home life was unhappy, of course. What you did with it, how you elaborated it inwardly, is your own contribution."

The masochistic purposes which prompted this patient's poses and attitudes were hardly hidden. His intellectual imitativeness provided bitter confirmation of his father's disparaging assessment of him. "This boy amounts to nothing," the father had said, and the boy made every effort later on masochistically to prove his father correct. His unnatural thinness (he kept himself on a starvation diet "to look slim, as a girl should") also amounted to a dramatization of a parental criticism. This was not a reproach, as might have been expected. Very often eccentric food habits mean "bad mother is starving or poisoning poor helpless child." On the theory that large food intake would help the child to grow, his parents had unceasingly urged him to eat. But their naive hopes had proved futile and the patient recalled his mother disgustedly saying to his father: "Don't waste your energy. The shrimp can eat and nothing shows!" His food habits in adult life served the unconscious purpose of proving that he was, as his parents had concluded, nothing but a "poor shrimp." Undoubtedly they also embodied an inner reproach against the parents: if the food had been "better," perhaps he would have grown.

In everything that he did his masochism prevailed, yet it had, curiously enough, failed to provide an impediment to his analysis. The bribe offered by his uncle, although it threatened his neurotic balance, could not be refused because it reinforced his major unconscious alibi against masochism: the assertion that he did not wish to be deprived but wished "to get." Conscious wishes—nobody consciously wants to refuse a generous gift— and unconscious necessity happened to coincide, and the way was cleared for treatment.

At the root of this patient's homosexual alibi was his deep inner fear of women. His two greatest enemies in childhood had been his mother and his sister. In identifying with them and masquerading as a woman, he had acted like a person chronically afraid of police who solves his problem with the anti-fear solution and becomes a policeman himself. Living in the largest city in the world and addicted to quoting the most sophisticated literature of his time, he proved to be entirely ignorant of female anatomy which could only be accounted for by overwhelming fear. He added one enlightening detail to this revelation: he "detested female breasts" and in his masquerades had never imitated them.

"There you are," I said. "The original enemy."

"Enemy?"

"Nutritional enemy. Have you forgotten that you were stuffed with food, to no avail? Doesn't this also lead to the fantasy, 'Mother pretends to feed me, but she really starves me because the food doesn't suit me?' Have you a nervous stomach?"

"Very much so."

In spite of my skepticism, I saw that analysis was gradually having its effect on the patient. He became less of an imitator in his profession and shifted to a new and better-paid job. Then, without warning, his millionaire uncle died, and it was discovered that poor investments had so whittled away at his fortune that the patient received less than $50,000—the remains of a special fund his uncle had established in his name and from which he had paid his analytic bills. By this time, however, the patient really wanted to be cured, and he took his financial disappointment calmly. He was cured, has become successful in his profession, and is successfully married.

Comment: Total rejection in childhood (by mother, father, sister) characterized this case. The child was a pariah. However, this did not explain why he could not store away his "wish to be loved" and subsequently, as an adult, create a situation in which that universal fantasy could be materialized. Instead, he unconsciously identified with his "main enemies," his mother and sister. What is more, he faithfully perpetuated his masochistic propensity in homosexuality. His pronounced, rather ridiculous feminine attitude also provoked the open contempt of his environment. This was the contempt and ridicule he had inwardly loved as a child.

CASE IV

A man of thirty-six with an independent income, which permitted him to devote himself to intellectual interests without testing his abilities in the job market, consulted me, ostensibly to ask me about some "work difficulties." During our first interview it became clear that this was a mere pretext; he wanted me to guess his real reason for seeking analytic help. Evasions and general suspiciousness gave me the clue and I made the correct deduction: his problem was homosexuality.

He was the only child of a marriage dominated by the mother. The instrument through which she ruled was an unending flow of words. The father was a reticent person who defended himself by ignoring his wife. At first the boy had admired his father for his "strength"; later, he had concluded that the older man was merely a martyr "with cold poise." The boy had been unhappy. Reacting against his mother's chatter, he had hated noise. As he grew older, he found all sounds—"even music"—offensive.

"I was a very lonely child," he recalled. "I was kept in such seclusion that I didn't even have any playmates. If I did play with other children, I usually gave up fast and went home; I couldn't hold my own against more aggressive children. Later, I had to train myself to be assertive. I took jujitsu lessons and became quite an expert in self-defense. My mother died when I was twenty and my father two years later. When I liquidated my father's business, the assets were considerable. My inheritance from my mother was even larger. I managed both estates myself. I studied, was bored. I had a few transitory affairs with girls. Sometimes I was half-potent, sometimes not. Then, when I was around twenty-five, I met some homosexuals and decided that I must be one. Unfortunately the material at one's disposal is poor. I'm disgusted with three-minute affairs, and it's practically impossible to live with a homosexual for any length of time— there's more quarreling than fun. Not to mention the parasitic tendencies. In short, no good. That's why I decided to change."

"Why didn't you give me this information immediately?"

"Suspicion and caution are part of my personality."

"Let's start with this trait of hyper-suspicion . . . Was your mother in the habit of turning things around, extracting information from you and then making a case out of it?"

"She was; how did you know?"

"That's obvious; you promptly repeated your suspicious attitude with me. Here you have a good illustration of how a pattern unconsciously built up as an individual defense in childhood is automatically repeated, even if neither the person nor the occasion fits."

This had been a typical transference repetition. Ascribing to the analyst the traits he had most resented in his mother, the patient had "defended" himself by withholding information. In this curious and self-defeating way he was preventing his "mother" from using this information against him and at the same time rebuking "her" for her inquisitiveness. In later stages of the analysis, it was no longer so easy for the patient to confuse the real person of the analyst with his infantile projections.

An important part of this analysis had to do with a series of repetitive dreams during the early stage of treatment. They fell into the category I have suggested calling the "refutation dream"—a direct response to an analytic interpretation, *if it is correct*. An accurate interpretation presents the punitive inner torturer with fresh and sure torture material, and the tyrant loses no time in basing new reproaches on it. These reproaches, leveled during sleep, are alibis and denials in the form of dramatized situations proving that the interpretation is wrong.

This patient's refutation dreams (which, as I explained to him, enabled him to check on the accuracy of my interpretation) concerned his attitude towards women. He had maintained that they were all like his mother, garrulous, overbearing, cruel, and altogether intolerable. When I pointed out that this was not so, he produced a series of dreams centering around the wife of a friend, a woman who happened to be overbearing, cruel, and altogether intolerable.

In time he realized the important role this woman was playing in his unconscious defense. I asked him:

"Don't you think she is so necessary for you that if she hadn't been handy, you would have had to invent her?"

"I still believe she is no worse than any other woman."

"If you were to say, no worse than any other wife chosen by a masochistic man, I would agree."

"I could give you a list of dozens of dangerous, man-eating bitches."

"Do you deny that nice women do exist?"

"I've never met one."

"Of course not; you would give her a wide berth. By the way, you are misstating your problem. It isn't true that you protect yourself against bitches, as you graciously call women, in self-defense. You are masochistically attached to women; your avoidance of them is merely secondary, and its purpose is to prevent the full bloom of your masochistic propensities."

"That's fantastic!"

"Is it really? Who repeatedly used the phrase 'man-eating women?' Let's not be naive. Unless we make the assumption that there is a deep masochistic attachment to the distorted image of what you imagined your mother to be, your flight into homosexuality is inexplicable."

"Believe me, Mother was worse than my description."

"Let's grant that. It doesn't follow that you couldn't have built up the image of a nice woman to compensate for all the evil in the type represented by your mother. What did you do instead? You ran to Ultima Thule, to the end of the world inhabited by womankind, to rescue yourself. You fled frantically from your own masochism, centered on your mother, and where did you land? In a worse mess—with disappointing homosexuals. There's no percentage in it."

Gradually his deep masochism was worked out and he began to accept women on a more or less conventional basis. Gradually, too, his personality became more amiable, although the absence of a sense of humor prevented it from being really attractive. One day I asked him: "Are you willing to analyze your slightly ridiculous and funereal hyper-seriousness?"

He made no objection, and I went on: "I suspect that your hyper-seriousness and sourness are only defensive weapons from the arsenal used in your anachronistic fight with your mother. Obviously, she was a self-willed person—."

"You can say that again."

"Like all self-willed mothers—and theirs is a highly mistaken policy, of course—she wanted to inflict her own wishes on her child. This can flow over into some very petty details, such as forbidding the child to play a game that interests him at the moment in order to force upon him her idea of fun. Some neurotic children react with hyper-solemnity: 'Try whatever you like as a substitute; I won't be amused.' "

The patient found a number of recollections to confirm this deduction.

His humorlessness had two other advantages, I told him. "You use your own sour mood to prove you're an innocent victim of suffering—that's handy when the inner conscience is about to ferret out the masochistic pleasure. And in your case sourness meant identification with your poor father's martyrdom, which you attributed entirely to your mother."

"Was I wrong?"

"Of course. Have you forgotten that he chose her?"

The analysis was a success and the patient married a kind and loving girl.

Comment: This patient had to deal with a disagreeable mother, but he masochistically mismanaged the situation. In his case the defense of hyper-suspicion was justified in childhood; however, he did not discard it when no longer needed. In the same way he clung to the masochistic attitude built up as a child. The reality situation of the early days was not the decisive point for him; his neurotic elaboration *was*.

CASE V

The problem of the female homosexual—the Lesbian—tends to receive much less attention than that of the male homosexual, and for a very simple reason. Concealment and camouflage are easier for her and are resorted to more often and more successfully. The fact is that homosexuality is also widespread among women. The underlying causes stem from exactly the same root, unsolved masochistic attachment to the mother of earliest infancy, and the unconscious alibis involved differ in only one respect. Lacking a penis, the girl cannot use the previously mentioned "reduplication of one's own defense mechanism." Where the male homosexual asserts that he does not masochistically love the image of the giantess of the nursery but rejects and hates her and all women, the Lesbian must go one step further, denying both masochistic attachment and hatred by asserting sexual love. The key is still masochism; the alleged sexual object is still a defensive ally.

The patient to be described below was a Lesbian in her mid-forties, the publicized type of Lesbian—over-assertive, over-aggressive, nearly masculine. As she put it herself, she was "the perpetual boss," both in her successful business life and in her relationships with a steady succession of "sweet girls."

She wanted analysis, she began by saying, because of a depression which "she could not understand." This explanation I easily recognized as an excuse since I happened to have treated and cured one of her "sweet girls." Her depression began when this former patient told her of her analysis and cure and left her domination to get married. Since I also knew the details of the stormy scene which followed that dramatic confession, I was able to deduce the aftereffects. This "perpetual boss" was by no means the boss of her inner conscience, which had undoubtedly taken advantage of the opportunity to point out that she too could be cured by analysis, and she had had to buy herself off for her crime by paying the price of guilt and absence of pleasure in her subsequent affairs. Then, when she decided on analysis, she took the curious step of consulting the particular analyst who had unwittingly been responsible for the breach in her defenses. More peculiarly, she chose to introduce her problem in a deliberately deceptive way, when even a casual review of the sequence of events would have reminded her that I knew the facts and could point them out. There was only one possible explanation for this conduct. Masochistically, she had hoped the interview would end in deep humiliation. To some extent it did; she had been caught in a series of lies. These she accepted meekly, revealing a side of her personality which would not have been recognized by her office associates or her "sweet girls."

She summed up her life history in a few sentences. Her parents had lived a stodgy, unexciting life. They had both been "weak dreamers"; the extreme of fantasy for them was to be found in the pages of the Sears-Roebuck catalogue. She was the only child. At sixteen, despising their lack of ambition, she had left home. Now she had achieved success and at forty-five was "the envy of all."

This was not sufficient a foundation to build an analysis on, and I told her so. I asked her why she had always avoided men;

she gave vague answers and admitted she could not understand why she was "contemptuous" of weak men and interested in "weak girls." Throughout this discussion she remained mild, meek, and polite—an attitude which did not seem natural. I pointed out that this studied politeness was as false as her well-publicized harshness and that her inability to find a half-way attitude, somewhere between the extremes of pseudo-aggression and false meekness, probably provided a clue to one of her important problems.

"O.K.," she answered. "What would you say I'm after in life?"

"The proof—the constant proof—that you and passivity do not even know each other."

"If that's so, I've proved it!"

"No, you haven't. By attaching yourself sexually to the sweet-girl type, you just walled off the part of you that is allured by passivity."

I explained that to her, "sweet girl" meant "masochistic girl," and masochism both allured and terrified her. Among the unconscious identifications that took place in her Lesbian relationships, she was able to acknowledge and enjoy her own hidden masochistic wishes. Not unexpectedly the patient denied the validity of this but found herself confirming it a few minutes later with a sudden recollection from her adolescence. She said in surprise:

"I believe I owe you an apology. I just remembered a thought from my early teens, when I was fighting desperately against my parents' contented, passive, immobile, unchangeable rut. I thought: 'There must be something unbelievably pleasant in the acceptance of being nothing.' I also remember that once or twice I had a similar idea when in the company of these little nobodies of passive homosexual girls. Imagine that!"

Aside from this one concession, the analysis did not move quickly. The patient was reluctant to go into the details of her childhood; the descriptions that came out when she was urged consisted mainly of rhetorical enlargements on the general outlines already given. But a few enlightening facts found their way into her editorials. Her father, she said, had been "hopeless"; she remembered him as "a man with a pipe, a dog, a half-contented, resigned face." Once she had shouted at him: "If I were only a man, I would show them." Her thumbnail sketch of her mother presented her as "the cow, the lamb, the eternally resigned domestic." Her mother had borne the brunt of her reproaches; she had blamed "the eternally resigned domestic" for her failure to spur her father on to success.

I said: "here is part of the explanation for your disparaging attitude towards men. They are patterned on your father, hopelessly passive in attitude, or you assume that there is a hidden weakness somewhere and only you can discover it."

"Perhaps."

"But this leaves the most important question unanswered. Why did you turn to sweet girls?"

So far, no clue to this key detail had emerged. It was clear that the sweet girl always represented a hidden part of her personality. The puzzle was why she had chosen these girls instead of passive men. I decided to approach the problem from another angle and went back to the events of our first interview, when the patient had so transparently plotted to be humiliated and rejected.

"In your fantasy there must have been someone in your family who kicked you," I reasoned aloud. "Your description of the personalities of your parents doesn't fit the picture. There is a catch somewhere."

"I'm still listening."

"The power of the helpless! Invulnerable passivity, as accumulated in your parents, represents fantastic strength to the active child who wants to penetrate this barrier. Now we have the missing link explaining your homosexuality. You did not turn to passive men because your real revenge belonged to your mother. Didn't you say that you wrote your father off as hopeless and kept all your violence for your reproaches against your mother? It is clear that you must have considered her the real malefactor."

I continued: "As a defensive reaction against your father's passivity, you built up the image of the ambitious, energetic man —that was the role you acted later in life. As a defensive reaction to your mother's sweetness and resignation, you built up the image of revenge and executed it on your long list of sweet girls. Both of these are defensive actions. What is more real is the passive-masochistic allure."

This explained her stunned reaction to the news that one of her sweet girls had been cured by analysis. The news had undermined her most valuable defense—the defense of pseudo-aggression.

Gradually and reluctantly she moved towards normality. She never became very cooperative, but she did make some valuable admissions. The point about "the power of the helpless" had evidently made a deep impression on her, and she volunteered the fact that she had found her mother's "sweetness" extremely irritating. Evidently her mother had been the original model for her "sweet girls." The mixture of aggression, detachment, and condescending love with which she treated these girls represented the three stages in the unconscious formula of the Lesbian: "I'm masochistically attached to mother; no, I hate her; no, I love her sexually."

It took a long time, but the patient eventually became a reasonably pleasant human being, the satisfied companion of "a reasonable man."

Comment: The childhood situation in this case was ideal. Both parents were kind, loving, devoted to each other and to the child. Nevertheless, the effect of this abundance of sweetness and love was far from what one is led to expect: the child hated both parents for exactly that love.

Once more, the facts defeat any attempt to construct a direct connection between the parents' behavior and the child's reactions.

CASE VI

Mr. L. was a homosexual who "emotionally refused to acknowledge" his perversion. The basis for his refusal lay in the fact that his homosexual contacts had occurred in fantasy only; what had shaken his conviction was the definition of a homosexual found in one of my books.

He was twenty-four years old and a member of a very wealthy family. Their status provided him with another reason for seeking treatment; as representative of "a dynasty," he knew he would be expected to marry. Moreover, he dreaded the consequences of homosexuality and the possible shame of discovery.

His fear of exposure was concentrated on keeping his inclinations secret from his parents and especially from his father, described as "something of a tyrant." We agreed in our first interview that there was no need for his father to know anything about his analysis. Upon leaving, he made this illogical request: "Please don't tell my father why I'm really here." Clearly he had purposely cast the analyst in the role of betrayer even before the analysis had begun, an eloquent testimonial to the amount of masochism in his make-up.

This attitude came through again during the first analytic session, largely devoted to an explanation of the ABC's of analysis. He listened to my brief exposition with conspicuous impatience, the identical impatience he had shown when his parents delivered their habitual "long discourses," as I discovered later on. He could not detach himself from his fiction of the perpetually preaching, tyrannous older person, even for the purpose of absorbing some useful information.

I asked him to describe his parents, first as they had appeared to him in childhood and then as they appeared today. In neither version was he particularly laudatory. His father had taken innumerable business trips; in between, he had been a noisy tyrant. His mother, seeing herself as a *grande dame,* had given him very little of her time. He was left to the mercies of a series of "disagreeable governesses."

The "disagreeable governesses" were important, and we spent some time on those he remembered. One, a handsome girl who had taken care of him when he was four or five, had disliked him in general and had reproved him severely for proudly calling her attention to his sex organ in his bath one evening.

"So nobody really appreciated you," I said, "and you had to love yourself."

"Strange that you say that. I am, people tell me, good-looking. I never thought so myself."

Mr. L.'s sexual fantasies always involved a boy between nine and twelve. He was very specific about this dream figure: he had to have a beautiful body, either naked or clothed in tight trunks. The setting was always a beach, to make the absence of clothing logical. The boy's hair was worn in a crew cut; he always had well-shaped, high-arched feet.

"What was wrong with your hair and feet?" I asked. I then explained my deduction: that the boy of his fantasies represented an improved edition of his former self.

"Your deduction floors me," he said. "I had flat feet and for years I had to wear high shoes that made me conspicuous, I thought, and certainly ridiculous. And the hair? It was too wavy and there was too much of it, and I was forced to display it."

"Wouldn't you say that you masochistically abandoned, very early, the hope of being loved by others? Isn't the reasoning 'Nobody loves me, therefore I must love myself' rather defeatist?"

At a later appointment Mr. L. brought this theme up again in connection with an experience in Rome two years earlier. A boy —not of his "type" but one he found decidedly unattractive— had solicited him on the street. He had said "no" and walked on, but then he turned back and asked the boy what had made him into a male prostitute. At this moment he noticed two suspicious-looking men watching him from the other side of the street, immediately concluded that the scene was the preliminary to blackmail and took the quickest way back to his hotel. He had been genuinely frightened by the thought of a scandal and thoroughly repelled by the personality and appearance of the boy. Nevertheless, this scene repeatedly recurred in his masturbation fantasies, and he had never understood why.

"Under the disguise of a sexual scene," I told him, "you are living out a masochistic fantasy. You are attracted to the situation of danger, as represented by the two unsavory characters on the other side of the street."

Other confirming material proved this interpretation accurate. Mr. L. recalled two significant childhood incidents, one dating from his thirteenth year. Fascinated by a hypodermic syringe he found in his mother's room, he took it to his own room and began experimenting. First he pretended to inject himself. Then, having found a spot on his side that was comparatively insensitive, he half-filled the syringe with alcohol and gave himself an actual injection. The second incident had occurred a year before the syringe experiment. While on a vacation trip to the Orient with his mother, a man had invited him to "go for a walk." He refused the invitation. Immediately afterwards he ran to his mother and told her about it. She alerted the hotel employees and they called the police. Before taking the man into custody, the police gave him a severe beating. For weeks the child had relived in fantasy the pain he imagined the man experienced when beaten.

With these clues to follow it became possible to explore this question: why had L. chosen to hide his masochistic propensities behind a mask of homosexuality?

The scene in which L.'s governess had reproved him for penis exhibitionism was helpful here. As already mentioned, male homosexuality represents one means of solving that universal problem, the tragedy of weaning. Instead of the normal process of reparation for loss of the breast, the homosexual is so unsure of the value of his substitute that he perpetually looks for an ally. The unconscious reasoning runs: "One isn't enough, but two will turn the trick." That is why the male homosexual looks for a duplication of the breast substitute in the penis of his partner.

Mr. L. interpreted this explanation from his own point of view. The severe and rejecting attitude of the governess, he concluded, must have damaged him.

"I would not say that," I answered. "I have seen cases in which the boy's exhibitionism was checked in the friendliest way and severe aftereffects developed; I have seen other cases in which the parents interfered brutally and there were no deleterious effects. It all boils down to the child himself: how does he accept the unavoidable?"

This subject was not yet exhausted. Mr. L. had casually mentioned that he derived sexual excitement from a certain style of sandal worn by men and especially boys at the beach. Actually, the attraction of these sandals came from their prominent display of the big toe, which he saw as a symbolic penis. His old grievance—his flat feet—contributed to this attraction; he could not have applied this symbolism personally, since his feet had given him "nothing to brag about." No wonder his fantasy boy always possessed beautiful, high-arched feet.

"I don't understand," the patient said. "On the one hand you claim that I created my improved Narcissus type in order to be loved. On the other hand, as the Roman blackmail episode shows, you claim that I derive my real pleasure from my masochistic enjoyment of danger. Which is which?"

"There is a contradiction between your two types of homosexual fantasies, but it is a contradiction you implanted yourself, and it is spurious. Every homosexual declares that he wants 'love.' Yet he conducts his love affairs in such a manner that masochism comes out on top."

Masochism as a covert aim was not limited to L.'s love affairs, I reminded him. In his analysis he had used hyper-suspicion as a weapon, constantly managing to see himself as the innocent victim of the analyst's sinister designs. As for the combination of masochism and sexuality, this had been visible even in adolescence. The episode of the syringe, for example, demonstrated this clearly.

I asked him: "Why did you fill the symbolic syringe with a fluid and apply it—in spite of the pain—passively against yourself? Why didn't you experiment on, say, a dog or a cat, playing the active part yourself?"

"I don't know."

"Both choices did exist."

"That's true. I never thought of that."

"That was your mother's syringe you found; therefore you were acting as her representative. Your game meant: 'Mother inflicts pain—and that's sex.' Is it surprising that you should run away from that 'torturing monster'?"

Mr. L.'s homosexuality, it appeared, was an unconscious alibi that took two forms: a masochistic fantasy and a romantic, narcissistic one. These were the "safety islands" to which he retreated for temporary relief from passivity and fear. He was still attempting to repair the narcissistic humiliation of infancy, still basing his attitudes on the masochistic and defeatist conviction that nobody loved him. In all this he was acting upon conclusions reached during earliest infancy; he was still fighting the giantess of the nursery, whom he himself had endowed with mysterious powers and inexplicable malevolence.

Analysis succeeded in Mr. L.'s case. His homosexual fantasies disappeared. He lost his fear of women, embarked on and enjoyed heterosexual experiences.

Comment: This patient could not explain why he had retired into a "narcissistic retreat" consisting of self-love and self-duplication in his imaginary partner. His parents and governesses had been distant and even cold, it is true, but the solution was still his own. If his wish to be loved had been genuine, he would have clung to it and seen to it that it was satisfied in later life. What he did cling to, and what was genuine, was the masochistic elaboration; this was visible in the Roman episode and in the other facts of his adult life.

CASE VII

Mr. Y. chose to be known by a pseudonym throughout long stretches of his analysis. He was a middle-aged lawyer with a notably funereal expression. Solemnity and judicious detachment marked his entire attitude. He viewed his problem, homosexuality, in this way, explaining "I enjoyed homosexuality but I do not feel comfortable about being a homosexual. Don't ask me why, because I do not know. I abhor loose ends and unsolved questions. That is why I am here."

As he described his life, it was a model of careful organization. He had arranged for an appearance of propriety by marrying and begetting two sons; he was active in the affairs of his college, depending upon its student body to provide him with a steady flow of young homosexual contacts; he was untroubled by moral scruples, the puzzle of "biological inadequacies," or religious considerations. The only flaw in this well-balanced pattern was the intrusive presence of a certain uneasiness—which he would not acknowledge to be guilt. It impelled him into analysis. Whether or not he wanted to change his homosexuality was a matter, he said, on which he would have to "reserve opinion."

The description of his life history was as formal as a legal brief.

"The direction of my life was determined before I was conceived. I was to be a corporation lawyer and to enter the firm which for generations had borne my family name. I was to uphold the family honor, marry, produce at least an heir, and commit no nuisances."

In the same style, occasionally relieved by a ponderous joke, he presented a picture of a cold, bleak family atmosphere in which a mild and only surreptitiously rebellious boy found it best to be the "Yes, sir" type. In puberty he began to resent the grayness of the existence he had known. He dated many pretty girls and encountered another taboo, this one pronounced by his mother. He was cautioned to remember his station in life, and concentrate his attention only on girls made eligible by breeding, not physical appearance. Obediently he looked her candidates over and found them dull and unattractive. At nineteen he entered upon a secret engagement to "a warm-hearted scatterbrain." His mother discovered the engagement and broke it up.

He experienced his first homosexual experience in college, with a boy from a background like his own. It was a stormy and uncomfortable experiment. After it ended, Mr. Y. decided he would limit himself only to transitory affairs in the future. He never broke this rule, which avoided trouble, although he complained it meant depriving himself of emotional satisfaction.

After his admission to the bar he married one of his mother's approved candidates. The marriage quickly deteriorated into a formal housekeeping arrangement. There were no mutual interests. He arranged the mechanics of his life so that he had a bachelor's freedom. Comparatively successful in his law firm, he had no objective reasons for discontent. But he was not happy. He did not know why.

Throughout his exposition, I pointed out, there was a recurring single theme: anti-woman hatred. His mother had been described as the villain in his life, interfering with his engagement to "a warm-hearted girl," urging him into a loveless marriage. But he had reacted to this alleged victimization in a suspicious way: since none of his compensations brought him happiness, it was likely that happiness was not his unconscious aim.

An explanation of psychic masochism evoked the usual incredulity. I reminded him: "You knew of your parents' social prejudices and your mother's hyper-prejudices. You must have known they would never consent to a marriage with a girl they considered beneath your station, as 'the warm-hearted girl' was. You were building a case, not a future."

I continued "Your mother rejected the girl because she was 'beneath you.' A short time afterwards you began a homosexual affair with a boy who had a background like your own. Isn't this masochistically tinged irony against your mother? Didn't your action say, 'You want me to stay in the upper crust; all right, I will'?"

"I see the hidden irony, but why do you call it 'masochistically tinged'?"

"Because homosexuality always means trouble."

Mr. Y.'s whole life, I told him, had revolved around the theme of pleasure-in-displeasure; his feeble attempts at reparation had in themselves been self-damaging in their end results.

During his analysis Mr. Y. found himself with an unexpected opportunity to test the extent of his psychic masochism. His nineteen-year-old son came to him, confessed that he was a homosexual, and asked for help. Mr. Y. took the sensible course of arranging for the boy's psychiatric treatment and balanced this action by attempting to use the boy's problem for his own masochistic purposes.

"It is not necessary to make a tragedy out of something that can be cured in a few months," I said.

"Do you really believe I am not responsible?" he asked.

"Well, your father certainly wasn't a homosexual, and the results were identical."

"That's true."

"This is another case of the boy running away from the distorted image he himself created of his mother. Of course, there might be reason to reproach yourself because yours was not a good marriage; in a good marriage your wife might not have hovered over the boy as she did. He must have misunderstood this hovering, taking it as a threat. But where would that argument lead you? Once more to your mother, who seemingly forced you into a misalliance. And you need not stop there. You could bring up your grandmother and your great-grandmother. In short, the environment and the personal responsibility of the people in it cannot explain neurosis."

The final link in the chain of evidence proving Mr. Y.'s masochistic attachment to the mother image had to do with a matter he had never considered a problem: his overweight. His attitude towards food, like that of every other human being, was colored by the adjustments he had made as an infant towards this many-faceted problem. To the very young child, food and mother are synonymous; to the slightly older child food is seen as the instrument of the mother's malevolence ("bad mother poisons or starves helpless child"). Food is also seen as the symbol of the child's dependence on the mother; the inevitable rebellion against this aspect of dependence sometimes stops at a distaste for bland foods and an eagerness for taste sensations far different from the neutral insipidity of the warm milk with which all diets begin. Almost as often, a pseudo-aggressive "extra" is added: some form of food faddism, which conceals the reproach of "bad mother poisoned me"; spasmodic or consistent greediness, which conceals the reproach of "bad mother starved me." This last was Mr. Y.'s thesis; it formed the unconscious basis for his habit of overeating.

After many months of analysis Mr. Y. abandoned his homosexuality. With this inner change came external changes of a surprising kind: he lost weight, and he lost his funereal, old-man appearance.

Comment: In this case the mother was loving and protective, although she tried to imbue the child with her own prejudices. Instead of an identification she achieved a masochistic pseudo-rebellion. The inner irony exhibited in this case is paradigmatic. The patient was separated from the "warm-hearted girl" because of her low social background, and he then attached himself to a homosexual boy from his own set. In this he acted as though the "social background" were decisive—a clear-cut case of "reducing to absurdity." Once more, reality is only the raw material; the child's future is built on his own elaborations.

CASE VIII

Mr. N. was a man of forty-eight who looked his age and more. He introduced his problem with an unusual statement of intention. He was a homosexual, he said, who wished to remain a homosexual. "But I would like to know from experience what a 'normal guy' feels."

In more than half of his preliminary interviews with prospective patients, the analyst finds it necessary to sweep away a certain amount of fog. Sometimes this amounts to unconscious evasion of painful issues; sometimes it arises from a misunderstanding of the terms on which an analysis can be undertaken and reflects the individual's unwillingness to go beyond half-measures in seeking a so-called cure. In a technique very much like that of the archeologist, the analyst must dig under the surface of what has been said and sift through every phase of the prospective patient's statements to find the pointers that will direct him to the real situation. In this case, Mr. N.'s preliminary challenge revealed several hidden factors.

It showed, to begin with, that he had no clear idea of the function of analysis. He took it for granted that his personality, like an apartment house, was divided into a series of unconnected and independent compartments, and that repairs could be made in one of these compartments without in any way affecting the others. Clearly, too, he had no accurate knowledge of the psychological basis for homosexuality; he had swallowed whole the popular myth of the "bisexual" who is equally potent and equally content with both sexes.

Combining this "statement of principles" with Mr. N.'s other remarks and the general impression he made, yielded additional —and more important—evidence. I told him my impression: it seemed to me that his real problem was how to cope with his "diminishing sexual returns." Like many aging homosexuals, he was no longer attractive to young men and had to resort to other middle-aged men as partners, or else pay for his sexual pleasures —two unsatisfying and therefore unacceptable solutions.

This deduction proved to be accurate. Bringing his problem into the spotlight changed Mr. N.'s manner and attitude; he abruptly dropped his cynical and arrogant approach and became almost pathetic. "What am I supposed to do?" he asked. "What's so wrong with wanting to switch to the opposite sex? Maybe I could find somebody in the other camp who would care for me a little bit."

Mr. N. habitually used a cynical-provocative attitude, and his moods followed this pattern. It was rather deflating for him to hear that cynicism is no proof of "superiority," since it reveals the adult as, in inner reality, a frightened child masquerading as an iconoclast and frantically seeking allies.

Mr. N.'s childhood history was not typical for his generation, he told me. He was born before the First World War, but his parents' educational methods resembled the "progressive" and "permissive" theories of the 1930's. "My mother's upbringing had been cruelly strict; she had sworn a solemn oath to treat her own children differently. I was the oldest; in fact, I was the only child until I was eight. When my sister and brother finally appeared on the scene, the age differences were so great that there was no chance of 'sibling rivalry.' You could almost say there were no 'siblings.' For all practical purposes, I did as I pleased. My mother never punished; my father fell in with her ideas. I wasn't even scolded or lectured. When I behaved badly I was called into 'conferences' and my mother would explain—using adult logic, of course—why my behavior was impractical or undesirable."

These facts tied in with evidence already uncovered in the analysis. During an earlier appointment Mr. N. had characterized an observation of mine as "a reproach," which is an example of the extreme to which a masochistic child in an over-permissive atmosphere will go in looking for evidence of "mistreatment." One can justifiably assume, as well, that such a child will do his best to provoke punishment if punishment is not part of the educational program. It was so in Mr. N.'s case; he turned into "an intolerable brat," he explained.

As he grew older, these family conferences grew more frequent and lasted longer. "Whenever I was with my parents," he remembered, "I would catch them exchanging exasperated looks. Then, finally, we had a big scene—provoked, of course, by me. I stole a few dimes from my mother's purse. This was too much even for her: she smacked me. . . . I was highly indignant, and for a little while quite good. It seems that at the age of seven—that's how old I was at the time—I had already learned to hit below the belt. Every time I showed up Mother's educational methods she was deeply hurt. Of course I knew other kids were beaten, and even severely beaten. I don't remember envying them but maybe I did. My favorite homosexual game makes me wonder." (Mr. N.'s favorite homosexual game was being beaten by his partner.)

I asked him whether his mother, aside from her principles, had not been essentially a stern person. I had seen many women like her in analysis—women who were raised strictly and were rearing their own children with determined mildness but who were strongly tempted to repeat their own past experiences, making their children the victims. The result is surface kindness with inescapable severity showing through.

"You are describing my mother perfectly," Mr. N. agreed. "I had exactly that feeling with her. I also freely admit I never really liked her; I believe I must have been scared by her—without reason."

Fear had undoubtedly existed and still existed unconsciously, judging from Mr. N.'s personality traits. One of these was hypocrisy, and I reminded him of an incident showing this tendency.

"Experience proves," I went on, "that hypocrites come out of families where lip-service is held to be more important than inner acceptance of the family rules. In other words, they came from authoritarian families. You describe your home life as the exact opposite. Conclusion: You must have viewed your mother, unconsciously, as an authoritarian, and therefore feared her."

Mr. N. dismissed his father as "a rather friendly nonentity" who took over his wife's educational principles without amendment. His favorite admonishing phrase had been: "Do what your mother suggested!"—"You see," commented Mr. N., "they were afraid to 'tell' me anything—they would only 'suggest.' "

Mr. N.'s earliest sex information came from his contemporaries; sex was never mentioned in his home and he had no early memories connected with sexual misconceptions or his parents' sexual relations. Trying to steer his recollections into these channels brought a result which could have been anticipated: it uncovered impressions persisting from the period of infantile fear fantasies.

"I was watching, once, while my mother was busy in the kitchen," Mr. N. said. "She was preparing some dish and she was cutting up raw meat. She must have caught a peculiar look on my face because she said, 'It is necessary.' "

Typically, Mr. N. had taken this—and undoubtedly other similar experiences—as proof that his mother, and all women, were capable of "any cruelty." The unconscious identification of the child is with the "victim," the animal that is being prepared for the table. It is this type of fear that is reflected in the homosexual's unconscious view of woman as so dangerous that she must be avoided at all cost and also, though in attenuated form, in such perversions as beating fantasies. These comparatively harmless fantasies are a denial of more deeply rooted masochistic wishes, of wishes growing more directly from the misconceptions of the septet of baby fears. They have the double advantage of being less threatening to physical well-being than, say, an evisceration wish, and they also gain plausibility by their connection with educational methods or disciplinary warnings.

Mr. N. asked: "Do you mean that sexually I'm still a baby

wanting to be treated in ways that match the septet of baby fears?"

"Yes."

"And my turning to homosexuality was the way I protected myself against the mother who was capable of such cruelties?"

"Again yes."

These were points which had been touched on, and dwelt upon, time after time in the analysis. To Mr. N.'s surprise, they suddenly penetrated and he became emotionally aware of his masochism. Some weeks later he announced that he was "through with homosexuality"; again to his surprise I told him that this did not mean that he had come to the end of the masochistic road. What we still had to explore was the unconscious reason for his sudden interest in heterosexuality. The plaintive, naive hope he had expressed in his first interview—"perhaps a woman could give him some love"—could not stand up under analytic scrutiny. The fact was that he was still pursuing the aim of punishment, just as he had in his homosexual experiences. Since he still classified women as the prime danger, his interest in heterosexuality could only mean that he was now increasing the masochistic stakes in the old game of self-punishment.

After this, the analysis went faster, and in time Mr. N. reached his goal of normal sexuality.

Comment: This case is important because the patient was educated in accordance with the most modern, permissive precepts and became a homosexual none the less. One could object that his mother had used permissive words but was "stern" in spite of them. But if the child projects his own aggression, even a lenient educator (parent) appears stern. The basic fact remains: When the child inwardly requires a masochistic hitching post, he finds it (if necessary, by constructing it himself) regardless of his real situation.

CASE IX

Mr. O. was a man of twenty-six, married and a father. His homosexual problem dated back to his college days, when he had been seduced by his roommate. Their homosexual relationship lasted for two unhappy years. The roommate was promiscuous; Mr. O. was jealous, guilty, depressed. He explained the entanglement: it had not come about in response to his spontaneous desire but partly as a result of the powerful argument implicit in the Kinsey statistics on the high incidence of homosexuality among American males. (Kinsey alleges that approximately every third male has had homosexual contacts during his adult life). This was the argument used by Mr. O.'s roommate; without it Mr. O. was certain he would have escaped this unhappy and damaging experience.

The first problem was to put his attitude towards his college experience into proper perspective. Mr. O. was of course correct in stating that Kinsey's fallacious figure of one man out of every three provided the confirmed homosexual with a persuasive talking point when approaching possible recruits. But even the "statistically induced homosexual" (a phrase he quoted from one of my books on homosexuality) must begin with some degree of vulnerability to the argument. The damaging effect of the Kinsey statistics applies to the "borderline case," the young man who has not yet taken a decisive step away from heterosexuality. The fact that the potentiality exists in him is a focal point for possible trouble.

Even more interesting and more significant was Mr. O's inability to forget this unpleasant interlude. For years his sex life had been heterosexual, yet he still approached each sex act with apprehension, "haunted" by the possibility that he was really a homosexual. The unconscious force of these torturing doubts was so great that he had even managed to increase them by misinterpreting a statement in my book on homosexuality. "Masochism *plus* is the basis of homosexuality," he had read, but he took this to mean that masochism—which he could see clearly at work in himself—led directly to the homosexual solution. To reach this conclusion he had to ignore another clearly stated definition: the "plus" of homosexuality, added to the virtually universal element of psychic masochism, calls for "the shift of the power to torture and harm from woman, representing the mother, to man."

Mr. O. described his parents as "quiet, rather reserved people who traveled a good deal, enjoying their wealth." He was their only child. The home atmosphere was one of kindness and consideration. No attempt had been made to influence his personality or ambitions, but every one had taken it for granted that he would eventually go to work for the family firm. The future seemed secure, and the prospect contented him.

The trouble with this description was that it was suitable for an official biography but not for an analysis. The only detail that was at all revelatory had emerged in negative form; he told me that references to sex had been taboo in his home. He refused to enlarge on this point and gave only vague answers to other questions. He could not remember his dreams. The real facts began to come through only after I questioned him about his subdued and invariably serious manner. He seemed to have neither a sense of humor, nor a capacity for gaiety. I asked him to tell me his favorite joke; it concerned a young ostrich who returned home to find his entire family standing around with their heads buried in the sand. The young ostrich asks: "Is anyone home?" Favorite jokes are not favorites for frivolous reasons; they are remembered and repeated because of their links with the unconscious. In this case the joke expressed an unconscious accusation against his family; it meant, "You are unwilling to face facts."

This glimpse under Mr. O.'s surface led to an important deduction. His subdued, invariably correct manner, coupled with his often used phrase, "That isn't done in our family," were indications that he was acting out a negative magic gesture, which unconsciously demonstrated how he did *not* want to be treated in childhood. I told him: "I believe that your extreme seriousness is an ironic way of reducing your parents' quiet, subdued manner to absurdity. The bitter accusation—'See what you did to me!'—comes through at the same time."

After thinking this over, Mr. O. said, "The family tradition really consists of one rule: be reticent, don't let your feelings show, keep a stiff upper lip. I fell into step without any trouble; it seemed natural to act that way. But I acted quite differently on at least two occasions. During my homosexual affair I showed violent jealousy. I felt more than I showed, of course. And when that was over, when I began to fear that I would never recover from the damage, I was nearly hysterical, though again I covered up and suffered in silence. I may seem to others to be lifeless, but these examples show that I'm not. I don't understand myself."

"Why not simply accept the fact that you are carrying over grievances from your childhood—a lot of grievances? You cover up your inward tears with outward detachment and a pretense of equanimity."

"But what is true and what is pseudo?"

"Your masochistic propensities, your 'inward tears,' are the end result of your individual infantile conflict. The stiff-upper-lip attitude is a secondary defense."

Gradually Mr. O. recalled that there had been a time when he was not content to do "what was done in his family." In early childhood he had resented and criticized "the dead house" in which he lived with his parents. "So I was 'alive' then!" he exclaimed.

"Who taught you the stiff-upper-lip attitude?" I asked.

"No one. But some atmospheres drag you down. It was like that at home."

"In short, instead of rebelling against the environment you used two very damaging defenses. You repressed your feelings, which led to the use of the negative magic gesture, and you defied your parents' teachings by taking up pseudo-homosexuality."

The pattern of quiet conformity which began after Mr. O. reconciled himself to his "dead house" had been broken in the homosexual affair. Was the violent jealousy he exhibited then a part of his general masochistic technique, or did it tie in with some episode in his childhood? This jealousy might have been a new edition of an old story; he could very well have felt shunted aside and rejected when his parents went on one of their trips.

"Who took care of you when your parents were absent?" I asked.

"Usually I went to camp; sometimes I stayed home with my governess."

"Did you resent that?"

"No."

"I can't believe that your conscious recollections are precise."

Eventually they proved not to have been. A clear memory emerged after a seemingly irrelevant discussion of statistics, a subject which had fascinated and impressed Mr. O. for a long time. Some time before entering analysis he read the book, *How to Lie with Statistics,* and reacted with fury and indignation to the facts in it. Why statistics fascinated him, to begin with, he could not understand; why he had become furious upon reading a debunking book about them puzzled him even more, since the star argument in his homosexual "seduction" was statistical in nature—Kinsey's statistics. Then came a recollection which clarified the puzzle.

He did not accompany his parents when they traveled. The usual routine was planned for his eighth summer. This time he threw a tantrum and demanded to be taken along. His parents explained why he could not go; the main point of their argument was a statistic showing that a large percentage of the boys in his age group went to camp if their parents could afford to send them. Years later Mr. O. turned this type of argument—the statistical average—against his parents, reasoning: "If the statistical average is decisive, Kinsey's statistical argument is irrefutable."

I told the patient: "You see that I was justified in suspecting that you bitterly resented not being taken on these trips. Of course the diabolical joke you played on your parents (turning their own argument against them) was masochistic. I once described a case in which a four-year-old was taught the alphabet by his father, a professor of technical engineering. The father constantly complained that the boy wasn't 'thorough enough' in his studies. Twenty years later, when the boy came into treatment, he was a student of technical engineering and had been refusing for two years to take his final exams. The procrastina-

tion infuriated his father. 'Take that idiotic examination,' the
father kept urging. 'I'm not thoroughly prepared—yet,' the son
always answered. This was unconscious irony. He was using the
same old stick—thoroughness—with which to beat his father.
And you did exactly the same thing, using statistics. In both cases
the unconscious irony was highly masochistic. Both the other
patient and you were damaging yourselves more than your
parents."

This discovery marked the turning point; the real work of
analyzing Mr. O.'s psychic masochism could now begin. Eventually his fear of homosexuality disappeared.

Comment: Mr. O. freely admitted that both his parents had
been kind and loving "in their quiet way." The child had misconstrued their undemonstrative manner as an indication of lack
of love—a total misconception. In the same way he had misconstrued the banal experience of being sent to camp for the summer. Having unconsciously acquired—facts or no facts—a masochistic attitude, he used the "statistical argument" to play an
inner joke on his parents. The joke damaged him more than his
parents, of course.

People who believe parents are to blame for their children's
neuroses would have a hard time proving their point if they had
to use this case as an example. Both parents were loving. Still,
the boy saw their "quiet way" as a terrible injustice.

CASE X

Mr. U. was a man of fifty who seemed to apply a shrewd prac-
ticality to all of his business and leisure hours. He had many
hobbies; he managed his inherited capital expertly; he had even
devised a complicated and rather cold-blooded technique to simplify his homosexual affairs. Nevertheless, a flaw had developed
in the latter arrangement. "A peculiar boredom with the whole
business" of homosexuality had brought him into analysis.

Mr. U. specialized in introducing young married men to
homosexuality. He would listen to their complaints about their
allegedly tyrannous wives and then capitalize on their dissatis-

faction with marriage to persuade them into a short affair. Quantity, and not quality, seemed to be the aim in these affairs. The high point of his homosexual career had been reached many years before, when he took a cross-country bus trip and slept with seven out of the eight drivers who had appeared for successive shifts.

When Mr. U. read one of my books on homosexuality, he learned that self-damaging tendencies were always connected with homosexuality, and he became worried about the possibility that his masochism would increase as he grew older and play him "new and damaging tricks." Although stinginess was one of his conspicuous traits, he decided to overlook the expense and indulge himself with an analysis.

He described his relationship with his mother as having been "favorable." This meant that he could not complain, since she had not interfered with him or denied him in any way. His dreams contradicted his conscious judgment, however. A bad, cruel woman appeared in all his dreams, menacing or at the least slighting him.

The most interesting portion of this rather routine analysis dealt with the genesis of the patient's preference for what he termed "heterosexually married homosexual virgins."

His mother had been the driving force behind the success of the family business. When he was seven years old (his mother was then forty) she initiated a new business policy. From that time on the firm featured a training program for young men just starting their careers. These young men, although nominally business apprentices, were treated like members of the owner's family. After a few years of training they were set up in independent businesses in various parts of the country, receiving enough capital to start with and helpful supervision as well. After his mother's death Mr. U. continued this "family tradition" of helpfulness to young men just starting in business. He added some variations to the established training program. Before the young men became full-fledged apprentices, he would seduce them. After they had served their apprenticeship, he would make them half-owners and managers of one of his newly established chain of retail outlets.

This maintenance of what the patient saw as a "family tradition" was directly connected with one of the deepest of his childhood defeats. Undoubtedly he must have been severely hurt by his mother's interest in an ever-changing succession of young men. The masochistic fantasies about witches that still rose to the surface in his dreams must have been present in childhood too. Consciously Mr. U. did not remember suspecting his mother of a sexual interest in these young men; the suspicion could be deduced, however, from his subsequent actions. When he took over the training program he went his mother one better. This was his unconscious reasoning: "Any woman can seduce an inexperienced boy. That's what mother did. I can do better. I will seduce heterosexuals and married men, make them into homosexuals for as long as I want them, and then contemptuously send them back to their wives. Those bitchy women will find out that their husbands will never be what they were before I worked them over!"

Mr. U. had found a complex inner solution to his problems. He escaped from the threatening "witch," his mother, by becoming a homosexual. He revenged himself, pseudo-aggressively, on this same "witch" by outdoing her as a "devourer" of young men. He even improved on her trick of exploitation by canceling the custom of setting the apprentices up in their own businesses and arranging instead to retain a half-interest in the retail stores which they managed after graduating from the training program.

Despite all these ramifications, Mr. U.'s original problem remained clearly visible. The basis for all his defenses was his masochistic attachment to and fear of his mother—a pattern which dated back to earliest childhood.

Comment: In this case, a realistic fact—the mother's training program—was unconsciously misused for purposes of "revenge." It would be naive to assume that the training program *per se* acted as "traumatic experience." On the contrary: it was the catalyst which brought to the surface an *earlier* infantile conflict. Moreover, there was no objective proof that the patient's mother actually slept with her protégés.

This point should not be overlooked: The boy's relationship to his mother was favorable; she was loving, she gave in to all his demands. Nevertheless, the child's insatiability constructed a case against her. How little reality counts in the development of a masochistic neurosis is well demonstrated in Mr. U.'s life history.

FIVE EXAMPLES OF INFANTILE BACKGROUND MATERIAL IN DIVORCE CASES

The five cases following all deal with people who came into analysis primarily because of marriage problems. All of them had been divorced or were in the process of divorce. All of them had been through this experience before, some repeatedly. All of them had taken it for granted that closing the door on an unhappy marriage would open the way for a new life, without problems and without complications. (Detailed accounts of these cases are in *Divorce Won't Help Neurotics,* Harper & Bros., New York, 1948.) The fact is, of course, that *repeated* failure in marriage testifies to the presence of a serious inner conflict, and that the marriage partner is not the cause of the trouble but merely an instrument for expressing it.

It is admitted that not every divorce is neurotic. An inexperienced boy or girl may half-neurotically choose the wrong partner and later on correct the mistake.

Neurotic divorce is characterized by an unchanging inner conflict. The second, third, and nth marriage will be a repetition of the first. Divorce does not solve neurotic conflicts; it is merely an admission of the inability to master them. Neurotics can divorce their marriage partners, but they cannot divorce their neuroses. Paradoxically, one can say that a neurotic's divorce decree is merely a renewal of the marriage license that ties him or her to neurosis.

This is what happens in a neurotic marriage: The husband or wife, who has unconsciously been chosen to fit into the require-

ments of the partner's inner conflict, is cast in the role of antagonist and torturer, although in reality the enemy is an inner
enemy, the torturer an inner torturer. (The secondary role in
these marital battles is generally a pale version of the more prominent one; neurotics tend to marry neurotics.) Without conscious
awareness of what has been done, an unbearable inner problem
has been projected outwards so that the partner becomes a part
of the neurotic's entire network of alibis and defenses.

It should be understood, to begin with, that unhappiness in
marriage is no defect to the psychic masochist. Such a marriage
begins to break up only when the inner tyrant refuses to accept
the bribe of conscious suffering in exchange for the unconsicous
masochistic pleasure supplied by external conflicts. Once the
inner tyrant rejects the bribe and points out that alleged external
unhappiness has not prevented inner pleasure, a new alibi must
be constructed. That alibi declares: "This marriage is too painful; I cannot stand it any longer." If the inner tyrant insists on
proof, the alibi goes beyond threats, and actual divorce proceedings are initiated. This means that the current marriage partner
is sacrificed in order to retain the possibility of repeating the
whole procedure with someone else.

CASE XI

A man in his early forties consulted me in order to straighten
out his marital conflict. He had been married for sixteen years.
During almost fourteen of these he had not been "sexually interested" in his wife. This meant that he had been impotent with
her, though potent with other women.

He was a successful industrialist, outwardly very sure of himself. He discussed his marital affairs without emotion but with
polite regret. After only a few remarks had been exchanged it
became clear that he did not really care about re-establishing his
marriage. He believed he was in love with another woman and
had decided to get a divorce. "It's not easy to break up a home
after sixteen years," he said. Consulting me, I also discovered,
had not been his own idea. He had done so because his wife

asked him to see a psychiatrist before taking the decisive step.

If he had really wanted a divorce, I pointed out, he would not have been so obliging. Perhaps, I suggested, this was not the first time he had "about made up his mind" to get a divorce.

This turned out to be the case. The present crisis was the fourth in fifteen years. Each previous attachment had been broken up by the lady in the case when she tired of waiting for a definite decision from him.

The man described his wife in lukewarm terms as a friendly, rather submissive person who accepted everything he said or did without comment or contradiction, "not a bad-looking" woman who unfortunately had no glamour. In none of these attributes did she resemble her four rivals. They were all sophisticated and glamorous; they wore smart clothes, and dominated their husbands.

I asked the patient if it had ever occurred to him that these women would have dominated him too, if one of his divorce plans had gone through. That had never struck him as a possibility, he said.

"What do you suspect?" he asked.

"That you are scared of your own choice of the four ladies."

"I never thought of them as being aggressive."

"That doesn't prove anything."

"Do you mean that there is trouble ahead?"

"There could be—divorce or no divorce."

This had all come out in the course of a preliminary interview. It was six weeks before treatment could actually start and we could begin exploring the patient's childhood background.

A good deal of material emerged to confirm the suspicion aroused in our preliminary interview. In childhood he had "detested" and been dominated by his completely unstable mother. In inner reality this contempt represented his defense against unconscious masochistic attachment. His mother had been an hysterical person, a hypochondriac whose days were generally spent in bed nursing her imaginary ailments. Consciously he wanted a repetition of the "scenes" of his childhood; he had chosen his wife to correspond with this defense. What he really wanted, unconsciously, was a woman as unlike his wife as possible, a woman who would not be kind, submissive, and soft, but aggressive and highly emotional. In other words, he wanted the masochistic pleasure of being mistreated.

His insistence on "glamour" could be traced back to childhood. In analysis he recalled an unusual outburst from his "weak" father. In a moment of exasperation the man had exclaimed to his wife, "Do you think you are something special and better than other people that you always act like a princess?" The second link was defensive rather than merely descriptive; it related to his mother's rather humble social background. By attaching himself to what he considered a socially elevated level, he provided himself with an alibi for use when the inner tyrant ironically charged that these four "smart" and "sophisticated" women were identical with his mother. Because of their glamour, they were *not* identical.

The interesting contradiction here was that marriage reflected and strengthened his unconscious defense; it was only after marriage that he reverted to his real interest in aggressive women. It was because of his wife's usefulness as living testimony to his defensive alibi that he could never make up his mind to divorce her. Without her he would have been submerged in passivity, as the victim of a new wife who would dominate him. But every defense has its drawbacks; he could be sexually potent only when he was being aggressively mistreated.

In an indirect way he managed to get some masochistic pleasure also from the way each of these episodes ended. When each of these glamorous sophisticates became disgusted with his "indecision" and left him, he felt that he had been unjustly victimized and rejected—an excellent excuse for unconscious pleasure-in-displeasure.

Analysis cured this man of his neurotic craving to be mistreated and he returned to his wife. This result astonished her; she was even more astonished to discover that his potency had returned.

Comment: This case is noteworthy because the patient began his marital life with a pseudo-*normal* attitude. Having had a domineering mother, he attempted to correct, instead of neurotically perpetuating, the unfavorable infantile situation. He therefore chose to marry a kind, loving woman. But—and the "but" is decisive—there was no solidity to his attempt to rescue himself from his early masochistic attachment. Soon after his marriage he reverted to his real type, the aggressive woman who could be counted on to cause him pain.

If this man's defensive efforts had been solid, not spurious, he would be an example of what has been constantly stressed in these pages: the fact that an unfavorable infantile situation can be corrected—provided the psychic masochistic "magnet" does not interfere.

CASE XII

A woman in her late twenties reported that her marriage had limped along for ten years before it finally collapsed. During that period she left her husband four times, each time because she had discovered his infidelity. Each time he promised to "be good" and she returned. The aftermath to these abortive rebellions followed a regular schedule. There would be a few weeks of armistice, after which her husband would become moody and restless. This restlessness meant that he was looking for his standard antidote, another woman. The new affair raged a few months and then collapsed. Peace and penitence would then reign until the next cycle.

The pattern was finally broken when the husband wrote his wife, while on a business trip, that a tragic experience with another woman had left him impotent and consequently he decided he was through with sex. Since he no longer needed a wife, would she give him a divorce and her best wishes? In exasperation she asked herself why she had spent ten years tolerating this kind of "nonsense." She was not without some knowledge of psychiatric literature, however, and suspected that she had not been altogether the innocent victim in the marriage. She then decided to go into treatment.

Analysis uncovered the unconscious basis for the role of willing victim she played for a decade. Instead of overcoming the disappointment of the Oedipal defeat, when she discovered that it was futile to attempt to supplant her mother in her father's affection, she used this disappointment to reinforce her already present masochistic pattern. (In treatment she admitted that both parents had been kind and loving to her in childhood.) Having summed up the situation in these terms, "Father cares only for mother; I'm left out," she unconsciously incorporated this rejection into a more general complaint: "I want to be the disappointed child, neglected by my parents, who enjoy themselves without me." This masochistic aim, of course, could not be pursued without doing some unconscious bargaining, and she paid the standard price of conscious suffering for her unconscious pleasure.

This was exactly the pattern that unconsciously prevailed in her marriage. The disappointed child, always "left out" by a husband who made it plain that he "enjoyed himself" without her, was consciously unhappy and unconsciously satisfied. When her unconscious satisfaction became too evident to her vigilant inner tyrant (superego), she would stage one of her rebellions and leave her husband. These rebellions were unconscious alibis, denying her aim of pleasure-in-displeasure; when they were accepted by the inner tyrant she would return for another installment of masochistic satisfaction.

The sympathetic but uninformed observer might conclude from the description of her husband that he was the villain in the story and she the innocent victim. Far from being a victim, she was really a collaborator. This was proven shortly after the marriage ended. Her next attachment was to a man who appeared to be an excellent prospect for a normally happy marriage. It was "sheer delight," she claimed, to be with someone who spoke so eloquently about his ideal of marital contentment. But contradictions in this man's behavior eventually made her suspicious; she discovered that he was an impostor. Her unconscious masochistic pattern had lured her to this new romance; marriage to a man of his type would have meant another installment of the conscious unhappiness she still needed. Analysis changed that unconscious tendency. Her next marriage proved successful.

Comment: This case shows that even "kind and loving" parents cannot prevent the child from developing masochistic propensities. The parents' crime here was that they loved each other and also loved their child. Obviously certain disappointments must be borne by all children, and not masochistically misused. If some children find this impossible the failure should not be blamed on the parents.

CASE XIII

A good-looking woman of French extraction, in her early forties, had been married for eighteen years. For six of these years she had known (because he had told her) that her husband, an artist, was having an affair with her best friend. For several years before the formal announcement she had become suspicious. This did not prevent her from offering the hospitality of their summer home to the other woman. (During one of these visits the friend had a miscarriage; the patient had also been aware that her husband was the father of the child.)

Her reason for consulting me, she said in her first interview, was prompted by a request her husband had just made. He wanted the "friend" to move into their apartment; for appearance sake, he suggested, she could be their "subtenant." As he saw it, only the "bourgeois" would find this suggestion shocking; he was merely proposing that lies be eliminated from their relationship.

"I just can't stand the whole thing," said the patient. "Am I wrong?"

Her husband refused to have anything to do with analysis, declaring that there was nothing to discuss. But she returned, and in later interviews it became clear that she was not primarily concerned about her submissiveness in marriage. Although she thought of herself as a martyr to her husband's cruelty, she was terrified of her own impulses towards cruelty: she was "scared to death" that she would cut off her husband's genitals while he was asleep.

I explained that she had no need to fear her revengeful impulses; since she was aware of them, they must represent defenses and not real, impelling wishes. (What appears in consciousness is never an unconscious wish directly expressed but only the multiple inner secondary defense against that wish.) Her real trouble, it was clear, was deep neurotic passivity and psychic masochism. The consciously perceived impulse towards revenge had to be a pseudo-aggressive defense. Further analysis proved that she was a rather extreme example of what psychic masochism can do to a person.

She was still repeating an unconscious pattern stenciled in earliest childhood. Her real conflict pertained to her mother, who had also "excluded" her by preferring a sister. This source of masochistic pleasure (arising from forbidden hatred followed by unconsciously enjoyed guilt feeling) was pushed into the background as she grew older, and the girl began to use her father as her primary instrument of self-torture. At an early age she knew that he was unfaithful to her mother; often she would overhear their quarrels. In her fantasies she imagined herself in the "impossible" role of his mistress. She could do this only by paying—beforehand—the intrapsychic fee of guilt and punishment. Subsequently "the impossible situation" became her emotional way of life. She could allow herself to become attached to a man—a situation which she unconsciously saw as "impossible," just as her childhood fantasies had been—only on condition that this attachment made her suffer. This explained her willing acceptance of her painful marital situation. The fantasy in which she mutilated her husband in his sleep provided her with her needed pseudo-aggressive defense. After analysis she left her husband.

Comment: This patient's conflict with her mother, who had preferred the younger sister, did not begin with a reality factor but with an attitude provoked by the patient herself. She had been so intolerant of the attention her mother paid to the new baby that she aroused her mother's anger. In short, the masochistic "injustices" were inaugurated by the patient herself; if provocations are continued long enough, even a friendly mother will become impatient. Secondarily, the impatience can be neurotically elaborated and presented as proof that "Mother is mean."

She was set on rejection, repeating the same procedure in the Oedipal phase, and later in her fantastically masochistic marriage.

CASE XIV

This patient was a woman of forty. After thirteen years of marriage her husband announced that he wanted a divorce; he was unhappy at home and had found someone he loved. As far as he was concerned the situation was clear-cut: he was in the grip of "forces he could not control," but otherwise he wished to make things as easy for his wife and son, financially, as he could. At first she was "paralyzed with fear and shock"; after the "paralysis" came convulsive weeping. She refused to get a divorce and her husband left home. Eight months later she was no less determined to deny him a divorce, and so he returned. Although they lived in the same house, he refused to talk to her and spent his evenings reading. He made no advances whatever in her direction; they had neither sexual nor friendly contacts.

Clearly an unconscious mechanism must have dictated her reaction to her husband's announcement. What explained her willingness to sacrifice pride, self-esteem, every advantage of marriage, simply for the sake of retaining the outward appearance of having a husband?

In the eyes of his family, the patient's father had been "a weak personality"; evidently this was the official euphemism used to veil the fact that he was a gambler who could not be relied upon as a breadwinner and who was "rumored" to be a woman-chaser as well. In spite of all this, however, the marriage had survived; the patient apparently thought of this as a triumphant achievement. She had been strongly attached to her father, having been his favorite child.

The generally unsatisfactory nature of her parents' marriage provided a ready-made alibi for the child to use during the high point of the Oedipal period: she could unconsciously excuse herself for competing with her mother by saying, "Father wants to leave mother anyway." As an auxiliary inner defense, she told herself that she really wanted her parents to stay together and developed a conscious attachment to her mother.

Thirty-five years later, when her husband unexpectedly asked for a divorce, the old feeling of guilt returned. The inner tyrant, the superego, seized the opportunity to reproach her for the "crime" of the past and linked it with the present by charging: "You wanted your father to abandon your mother; now your own husband wants to leave you for another woman." In this crisis she fought back with her old alibi: "I want my parents to remain together." To reinforce that alibi, she refused to give her husband a divorce.

Her entire marriage, in fact, had been a repetition of a pattern set up in childhood. The emptiness of her parents' marriage had been her justification for competing with her mother for her father's love; as an adult she punished herself by clinging to her "empty shell" of a marriage and derived unconscious satisfaction from her conscious unhappiness.

After some time in analysis she consented to a divorce. For some years she remained alone, still partially bemoaning her fate. A few years ago, to my surprise, I received a letter from her announcing that she had remarried and that "everything was going well."

Comment: The bad marriage of her parents encouraged this patient, as a child, to hope she could capture all her father's affection. This increased attachment led to increased guilt. Later in life, when her own husband wanted to leave her, she did not react to the actual realistic situation but to the old infantile conflict. That is exactly what neurosis means. That is also the exact meaning of the statement that reality is only the raw material. If the patient, as a child, had been the third party in a good instead of a bad marriage, the fact would not have lessened her conflict (see Case XII). It always boils down to this question: How does the unconscious ego elaborate on a given situation? This holds true whether the situation is favorable or unfavorable.

CASE XV

A pretty woman of forty married a man who was known among his friends as "a born bachelor." He was cold and detached, however, with some wit and charm. As a husband he was "unreliable," his wife declared when she came to me shortly after discovering her husband's secret file of love letters from other women and his replies. She reproached him; he defended himself. The atmosphere of the household became and remained highly charged. As far as the man was concerned, his wife's discovery was not disturbing. He said frankly that he did not believe in monogamy and that she knew when they married that he was not "good material" for matrimony. He asked for a divorce. She refused and became hysterically quarrelsome. She described her "attacks" to me; she would reproach her husband for his "coldness" in a completely irrational way.

She described herself as the product of an utterly impersonal and detached upbringing. Her mother, reluctantly supported by her father, had believed that cold and reserved behavior provided the best educational medium. Outwardly the child conformed to the cold manner ordained for her; inwardly she had been full of hatred. This hatred was at the bottom of the many sexual adventures she had experienced before her delayed marriage; each of these adventures unconsciously provided her with a pseudo-aggressive triumph over her puritanical family. At the same time, of course, each of these experiences fed her psychic masochism. None of them brought her happiness or contentment. Her choice of a "confirmed bachelor" as a husband fitted into her psychic-masochistic pattern. Like the cruel mother of the past, he was cold, detached, and incapable of love. In other words, he was her mother all over again.

The mother-child relationship was imitated in the patient's quarrels with her husband. In these quarrels the "mother-husband" used cruel words to victimize the helpless "child-wife." On the other hand, her husband often charged that the reproaches she leveled in her calmer moments were "cold and cruel." At these times she was playing the role of victimizing mother; it was only when she became hysterical that she played the part of the child.

These quarrels, however, were *not* exact imitations of her childhood situation. Two unconscious amendments were incorporated in her dramatization. The first took the form of a reproach: "I cannot stand your coldness, Mother; even your hatred and anger would be more pleasant." This correction became possible after her repeated hysterical outbursts had penetrated her husband's usual coldness, leaving him in despair. The second amendment had to do with her "interpretation" of the role of cruel mother. She played this role by complaining angrily and thus nullifying her mother's real coldness.

After some time the patient dissociated the infantile situation from the marital one; some kind of compromise was reached.

Comment: In this case the often encountered childhood fantasy of the "bad mother" was real and not fantasy. However, reality did not account for the subsequent neurosis. Why didn't this woman correct her early disappointment by looking for a kind, loving husband? Why did she have to perpetuate coldness? Unless one understands the masochistic elaboration, one is simply the dupe of the neurotic's "planted clues."

FIVE EXAMPLES OF INFANTILE BACKGROUND MATERIAL IN PATHOLOGICAL GAMBLING

The compulsive gambler—who must be differentiated from the person who gambles occasionally, for the fun of it or for the sake of sociability—is usually thought of as an individual who devised a scheme to make money without working for it. This is not seen as a particularly laudable aim, but certainly as a rational one, despite its risks and its setbacks.

Analytic scrutiny of the pathological gambler, however, casts a new light on precisely the point that is taken for granted and considered self-evident: the gambler's real purpose. It has been my clinical experience that the gambler is a neurotic propelled by the unconscious wish to lose. In other words, he is a psychic masochist who has chosen gambling as the major instrument through which he can obtain his needed quota of rejection and defeat.

The following excerpts briefly describe the histories of gamblers who were cured through analysis (taken from *The Psychology of Gambling,* Hill & Wang, N.Y. 1957; the initials originally used to identify the cases are retained here).

CASE XVI

My first knowledge of Mr. A., was far from promising. An appointment was made for him over the telephone by his wife; the appointment was subsequently canceled. Two weeks later a second appointment was made and canceled; again Mr. A. had refused his wife's plea that he consult me. A third appointment was made. This time Mrs. A. kept it as substitute for her husband.

Mr. A. was her fourth husband, she told me, an "impossible" person who drank, gambled, and made himself generally unpleasant. He stole money from her well-filled purse (she had inherited a good deal of money) and lately had forged her name to checks. A bystander could have classified his latest exploit as amusing. When Mrs. A. tried to safeguard herself against his forgeries by instructing her bank to hold up all checks for more than fifty dollars until they received written confirmation from her, he forged ten fifty-dollar checks in a single day. Mrs. A. was decidedly not amused. In the stormy scene that followed her discovery, tears were shed and blows exchanged. Mr. A. cynically reminded her that she could not afford a fourth divorce but was sufficiently shaken to agree "definitely" to enter analysis.

The interview then turned into a preliminary examination— of the analyst. Mr. A., his wife explained, thought highly of himself as an amateur historian who specialized in political criminology; before entering treatment he wanted to make sure that I knew enough about American political history and its connection with crime to understand him. Rather vaguely, she passed on his explanation of the link he saw between his gambling and the political picture of the past: "Crime in politics is not unusual, and gambling, being a part of the crime picture, is not unnatural.

His favorite example is Boss Tweed." Both Mrs. A. and I began to laugh, but after a moment her laughter changed to tears and we both forgot the absurdity of the situation.

As it happened, I was able to qualify as a knowing crime historian; I had read a good deal about the Tweed period and have always been interested in history. Best of all, I had written on Talleyrand, a political crook. As it turned out in the eventual analysis of Mr. A., his pleasure in learning all the facts about unsavory political events provided important clues to his unconscious processes. This is not at all unusual, of course; people do not choose their hobbies by chance or to follow the fashion, but because these activities reinforce in some way their unconscious defenses.

As guaranteed but not expected, Mr. A. did turn up the next day. He was a man of sardonic appearance, deeply depressed under his self-possessed exterior. His self-assurance extended into his remarks; he seemed cynically sure he could continue getting money from his wife and naively certain that he was bound to become a winning gambler in time, if only he had enough capital to work with. He was equally certain that analysis was futile and unnecessary. Nevertheless he thought of himself as "an analytical prisoner," delivered to the jail by his wife and left, without any choice, to go through the motions of treatment.

I told him: "This means that you want to misuse treatment for temporary appeasement of Mrs. A. and not for a real change. Either it will be possible to convince you that—unconsciously—you are well on the way to breaking your neck, or you will have to discontinue treatment because it will be hopeless. Analysis can help you only under one condition; you must understand how sick you are."

Mr. A. decided to remain in the trial analysis, largely because it provided him with an effective argument to use in his quarrels with his wife. "Analysis will change all that," he could say when she reproached him.

During his first few appointments the patient's contributions to treatment consisted largely of verbal fencing. Intuitively he realized that he could safeguard his neurosis only as long as he kept the door to his past securely closed. He repeatedly attempted to entice me into arguments on the "moral justification" of gambling. His thesis, which leaned heavily on texts borrowed from Boss Tweed and his spectacular plundering of the assets of the city of New York, was completely cynical.

I explained the psychological background of that attitude. The cynic, I told him, is a frightened child disguised as an iconoclast and frantically seeking allies. When he makes his irreverent or even blasphemous statements, he is offering himself to his audience as a model for identification, asking his listeners to admit that they secretly agree with him. When they reject him, he jeers at them for not having "a sense of humor"—couldn't they see that he was "only teasing"? This retreat offers another proof of the cynic's undigested fears.

Mr. A. abandoned Boss Tweed for the moment and returned to what he called his "main argument."

"I told you," he said, "that in playing poker one frequently nearly makes it—"

"One-inch-from-victory disappointments, so to speak?"

"Correct. Eliminate these disappointments by uninterrupted gambling—assuming that there is enough capital, and that the rule of probability still operates—and one must win in the end."

"The proposition is impossible to start with. Of course it's true that more play means more opportunities for lucky breaks. But even assuming that the chances for winning or losing are even (which is not so), there is the *inner* wish to get oneself into a mess by losing. It is exactly this unhappy-happy tension which provides the allure in gambling. . . . What you underestimate is the psychological substructure in that masochistically elaborated 'pleasure in fear.' That's the decisive point. The near misses are only the bait for further defeats, disguised as further victories."

"Don't you believe it. If it had not been for Tweed's little mistake in appointing the wrong auditor, nothing would have happened to him."

This assertion might have been accepted by Tweed's contemporaries; it has a very doubtful ring to any informed twentieth-century listener. Knowledge of the unconscious has taught us to be wary of "little mistakes," especially when they lead to large defeats. The overwhelming possibility is that these small errors are unconsciously planned by people masochistically seeking their own downfall. I explained this to Mr. A. at some length, and added: "Why do you rate Tweed so highly? Whom or what does he represent for you?"

"Well, I'm a lifelong Republican. Do you expect me to choose a Republican grafter as example?"

"Clever, cynical, and wrong. You admire Tweed. Your distinction between political parties does not apply."

"I needed the example of a near miss in the success story of a grafter; Tweed fitted. Of course you will claim that he is a 'father figure.' "

"A little knowledge is dangerous. I will not claim that, but the opposite. Tweed represents yourself, idealized, magnified, beautified."

Mr. A. had a subdued air when he came to his next appointment. He made no cynical remarks, but asked me to give him a further explanation of the psychology of cynicism. I did so, using an incident in Talleyrand's career to illustrate the points I made.

I told him: "If I were not aware that behind your interest in Tweed and Talleyrand is hidden your own problem, I would refuse to discuss them. As it is, it seems to be the first approach— tangential, to be sure—to understanding the 'weak guy' whose camouflage is pseudo-superiority."

From this point on the analysis moved more quickly. Mr. A. provided more material, first through making the complaint that analysis depressed him and made him moody (a complaint which opened the way for an explanation of the injustice-collecting pattern he was following in the transference), and later by actually talking about his childhood and family background.

He had been unhappy as a boy. "Victorian stuffiness and sour morality" had shadowed his youth. His parents were self-righteous educators and "preachers," against whom he had rebelled by playing truant and stealing pennies. "They always beat me down, first with words, later with blows, and still I continued." He provoked both the words and the blows, he conceded, but what else could he have done, having "a puritanical mother and a moralistic father?" This justification hardly obscured the child's apparent masochistic purpose: he had been deterred neither by lectures nor beatings, but instead provoked new punishment by repeating his truancies and thefts. This was not his view; he had just been "testing" his parents, hoping for "one understanding word."

In retrospect Mr. A. saw his parents' "moralistic notions" as the *bête noir* of his childhood. Early in life he had begun to hate everything remotely connected with "the moral order of things." To bring him back into line his parents had once called in his grandfather, the "grand old man of the family," as reinforcement for their views. Mr. A. dismissed the "grand old man" as a "shoddy expolitician" in describing him to me, which provided another tie-in with Boss Tweed. The patient suddenly remembered that the old man had used Tweed as a warning example in lecturing to him and had threatened him with Tweed's eventual fate. As a result, the five-year old boy had adopted Tweed as his personal hero, an identification which persisted into his adult life.

A few appointments later, I asked the patient: "Does it still sound so foolish when I assume that the time passed between perpetration of some infantile misdeed, and the expectation of punishment for that misdeed, could have been elaborated in a 'pleasurably painful tension'? And isn't the thrill of gambling identical? Just substitute the time between placing your stake and the outcome of the game."

"Not so fast, please. If you connect my gambling with my childish attacks on the moral order, I can tentatively agree. But you go further. You claim that the attack and the rebellion are fake, and they just cover the wish to fail. This part, pseudo-aggression for the purpose of receiving a masochistic kick, is what I find unacceptable."

Mr. A. continued to find this interpretation "unacceptable" for many months. In time the theory penetrated under the impact of repeated demonstrations proving the masochistic basis of his childhood attitudes and his conduct as an adult. His childhood stealing, for example, which appeared to carry out his "wish to get," actually had been a defense against the inwardly forbidden—masochistic—wish to be refused. It had been a message to the inner tyrant, saying "it is not true that I want to be refused; I wish to get." His gambling urge, as an adult, actually represented a revised version of this identical statement.

Throughout his entire life, too, Mr. A. had represented himself to be the innocent victim—first of his parents, who refused to give him "an understanding word" when he repeatedly stole and played truant, and later of his wife, who unaccountably resented his stealing from her purse and forging her name on checks. In the more impersonal world of business, Mr. A. used the same self-damaging technique with his customers; he would provoke them into quarrels and in this way lose their patronage.

After many months, Mr. A. finally realized that he was still a neurotic "child in swaddling clothes" behind his masks of gambling, amorality, and cynicism. He learned to understand the infantile aims that he was pursuing in these ways. He lost his taste for gambling and no longer found Boss Tweed fascinating or heroic. His marriage improved, as can be judged from the fact that Mrs. A. established a joint checking account with her husband.

Comment: Mr. A. is a typical example of the tendency to make ogres out of harmless, though naive parents. The trick is done by means of repeated provocations. In general, one has to be guarded about accepting at face value any person's description of his nursery years. Memories are frequently distorted. Even if they are correct, these recollections omit the self-created preamble: the child's provocations.

In Mr. A's case the masochistic solution of his infantile conflict came first, and the parental counteractions were a result. Like all psychic masochists, A. claimed that all he wanted was "love and understanding." This convenient and universal alibi has no foundation in psychic masochism. The means through which the psychic masochist achieves love prove that wish to be spurious ("counterfeit love"). Only the masochistic substructure is genuine.

CASE XVII

Mr. B. came to his first appointment with me wearing a casual, amused air. He was a man in his middle thirties, without a profession but married to a wealthy girl. He had consulted me, he indicated, because his wife thought he had problems and not because he agreed with her. After some questioning the real story emerged.

Mr. B. had met his wife when they were both at college. They had embarked on an affair that proved to be "difficult" because the girl seemed "frigid and yet insatiable." He was on the verge of giving her up when he discovered how wealthy her family was; this changed his attitude towards her and he persuaded her into an immediate marriage. They both left college and for some time merely enjoyed themselves. But more was expected of him than pursuing a life of leisure, both by his wife and by her "domineering mother." At their insistence he agreed to go into some business—but only after a year of travel. He kept this bargain, though with tongue in cheek; when his relatives bought him an interest in a business, he saw to it that they lost their investment in short order. It was at this time that he became a gambler. His idea was that he would use his mother-in-law's money to pay for his apprenticeship in gambling, and that he could support himself as a professional gambler once he had learned all the tricks of the trade.

Since that time all thought of a business career had been dropped. He and his wife lived on an allowance. His wife objected to his gambling and at one time had threatened divorce. A pregnancy had luckily intervened to change her mind. Now she had "gone on the warpath again," this time because he had complicated his life with an infidelity in addition to his gambling.

Mr. B.'s purpose in entering analysis was clear: he wanted an alibi which would enable him to continue living on his wife's money while he went on gambling and entertaining his girl friend. I told him I could not treat him, and he did his best to change my mind, putting forward a series of arguments. The arguments, which included the fact that he was impotent with his wife but not with his girl friend, reinforced my conviction that he was neurotically ill and needed treatment, but they also strengthened my impression that he was not a candidate for treatment. I did, however, consent to see Mrs. B.

Mrs. B. introduced a new element into the situation. She seemed to be living in a different world (a psychotic one). She spoke charmingly of her delusions and hallucinations, and it became clear that her mother must have had a reason for permitting her to marry a worthless and parasitic man. It had undoubtedly been a question of letting her have her way or of watching her move closer and closer to a psychiatric institution. I also had the impression that breaking off the marriage would drive her directly into the grip of her psychosis.

In speaking of her husband, however, she seemed quite rational; she described him as a scoundrel and a parasite. Because of her evident condition, I misrepresented my attitude towards Mr. B. I told her I had deliberately engaged in a delaying action to make him more amenable to treatment. Although I cautioned her that there was no way of foreseeing results, she was both grateful and hopeful; she was certain that treatment would be successful.

Mr. B's request that I see his wife had been his ace-in-the-hole argument; he had known that I would perceive her pre-psychotic state and react in a medically responsible way. Medical ethics, I told him after he had reluctantly made these admissions, had bestowed a trial treatment of four to six weeks upon him; what happened after that was entirely up to him. Without some clear indication that he wished to be helped rather than alibied, his analysis would end at that time.

Mr. B., like Mr. A., had no doubt that "enough capital" would make him a winner in the end. I asked him why he would want to continue gambling if he had that much capital, and for the first time he seemed to question the neat blueprint he had drawn for life. Allegedly, his aim in life was enjoyment and idleness. If this were his real aim, I pointed out, how did he account for the risks he was taking? His wife had threatened a divorce once; he had countered by making her pregnant, and the divorce had been forgotten. Still later, he had conducted his extramarital affair in a way that ensured his wife's discovery. (He had "ordered" his girl friend to join him and his wife in Rio.)

"What's your second point of indictment?" Mr. B. asked, indicating that there was more guilt in his unconscious than in his external manner.

There *was* another point, though Mr. B.'s use of the word "indictment" applied only to his unconscious view of himself as a "victim." This second matter had to do with his wife's psychosis. I told him that he was minimizing his wife's illness by calling it "eccentricity" so that he could establish a picture of himself as a good husband. If in the future her condition deteriorated and she had to be hospitalized, he would then be in a position to get the custody of their children and act as the trustee of his wife's estate. If this actually was his conscious aim, I concluded, he was making certain of its failure. As a known gambler and adulterer, how could he expect his wife's family to permit him to become guardian of the children and custodian of their money?

The possible problem had never occurred to Mr. B. The logical conclusion—that his conscious aim of "having a good time" was contradicted by his unconscious appetite for self-damage—was pointed out to him, but he heatedly denied its validity. The facts were against him, however, and summarizing them broke down some of his surface assurance. He became frightened, and for the first time I began to have some hope for analytic success in his case.

During the next few appointments Mr. B. attacked me as "revengeful," as a plotter who was cunningly driving him into quitting analysis, as "a sadist with ulterior motives." This marked the onset of the transference period; clearly he had assigned to me the role of the powerful enemy. This was of course a repetition of an infantile image, and I asked him: "Who was the model for this projection? Did you feel that your mother was so mean to you?"

The patient's infantile history was simple. He had felt that his mother rejected him, her oldest child, preferring his younger brothers and sisters. His father had been a nonentity, a distant figure "who did not count, even as a provider." The family had been supported by the energetic mother; she sold insurance and acted as a renting agent. A strict and often short-tempered person, she had been intolerant of gaiety and even laughter, perhaps because of her difficult life or possibly for neurotic reasons. Mr. B. became a petty thief while still very young. His thievery, when discovered, temporarily made him an outcast. This was only one of his provocative acts as a child; he rebelled against his mother in many other ways. One of his complaints against her was based on her alleged stinginess; in reality she sacrificed herself for her family. Despite her disappointment she offered to send him to college. He accepted—and kept on complaining about her.

The circumstances of his childhood, Mr. B. concluded, explained why his wife's money "opened up a new world to him."

I said: "A person who wants to correct his childhood disappointments should think twice before endangering his rule of financial security. But you seem determined, unconsciously, to perpetuate your childhood deprivations. Try to explain this logically. You cannot."

"To tell you the truth, I always felt I was something special."

"This feeling of megalomania, of being the chosen one, is a convenient blind for hitting yourself. Don't you have the same feeling when you gamble?"

"To some degree, yes. How do you explain why I'm so convinced that I'm going to win?"

"This feeling is shifted masochism. You know that your opponent is going to be 'unjust' to you by letting you lose. Your unconscious certainty that the projected mother will be proved a wrongdoer is shifted to conscious certainty that you will win. That's one of the most powerful attractions for gamblers."

Later in the appointment Mr. B. offered his own interpretation: "Didn't you tell me that gambling is a way of flouting the moral precepts of the environment? If I were you, I would say it's exclusively the continuation of my infantile rebellion."

"That's the superficial layer. Beneath it is the massive wish to be punished, masochistically embroidered."

Mr. B. remained unconvinced. His conscious hedonistic philosophy, he insisted, exactly reflected his real purposes. He maintained this position in spite of the contrary evidence of his dreams, in which he invariably appeared as the victim in flight from persecution or mistreatment. Dreams, he declared, meant nothing; analytic interpretations of them also meant nothing—except that they gave the analyst a chance to play "malicious tricks" upon the patient.

I asked him: "How do you explain the fact that your masochistic dreams coincide so well with the interpretation of your self-damaging tendencies? If you are a 'super-hedonist,' as you claim, why are your dreams painful? For the same money, to use your phrase, you could have pleasant 'success' dreams."

"I don't know, and I don't care."

"Let's single out one facet where you do care. You suffer from jealousy in your affair with your girl friend. This situation, too, was self-provoked by your choice of a flighty and aggressive girl. In any case, your conscious wish is that she be faithful to you. How do you account for your dreams about the girl, in which she is always unfaithful, disappointing, malicious?"

"I believe I shall finally fulfill your wish and leave analysis."

This remark and the short interchange that followed (in the course of which I told him that I had begun to modify my pessimistic prognosis for his case) showed that Mr. B. had reached an important crossroad. Analysis, which he had accepted as a tool he could manipulate, had begun to menace his psychopathic trends. This was a dilemma he had to solve, and he did so in a characteristically masochistic way.

He announced that he was taking a three-week vacation and would resume analysis upon his return. This was not according to standard procedure, I explained. If he wanted his appointment hours preserved, he would have to pay for the interim appointments, since they would be held for him and could not be used for another patient. Mr. B. did not want to pay for the interim appointments and argued bitterly about the "injustice" of my attitude. The irony of the situation was considerable: he did not need a vacation, to begin with, and, moreover, his wife was paying for the appointments. Finally he decided that he wanted his vacation and that he would pay for the interim appointments.

Upon Mr. B.'s return he minimized our "little misunderstanding," although he used it as the basis for another attack:

"Why should I have asked you—one of the fools who make their living by working—indirectly to finance my vacation?"

"Your contempt for work is charming. Or am I supposed to feel provoked? Is that your plan?"

"As you wish. In any case, my unreasonable demand proves one thing: I'm still a parasitic baby who wants to get. So all your deductions about my alleged craving to be refused in life, love, and gambling just collapse."

"I must say that you didn't pile up many arguments during these three weeks. What did you produce? First, pseudo-superiority. You are a 'clean' parasite who doesn't work, but I am one of 'the fools' who does. Second, a spurious argument which purports to prove that you wish to get, not to be refused. Why is the argument spurious? Obviously because you presented your wish to get in a way that made it clear you would be refused. Was it likely that I, the 'working fool,' would be refused. Was it likely that I, the 'working fool,' would finance a vacation for the 'parasitic genius'? Under the disguise of wanting to get, you wanted to be refused. Before you contradict this, let me add that the example in the transference is a perfect duplication of the gambling addiction. Here, too, you want to win—officially. But unofficially you want to lose."

Weeks of working through this material followed, with some favorable developments and many periods of depression. Mr. B. got rid of his gold-digging girl friend, and answered my "why" with another question: "Why should I make my life miserable?" Later he caught himself misreading his poker hands and between excitement and despair asked me: "Do I really want to lose?" Still later he came up with a productive idea: why shouldn't he abandon gambling and take up some "exciting" business venture instead? This could be done, I told him—if he could really abandon his unconscious wish to lose.

From this point on, things moved rapidly. Mr. B. went into

the real estate business and became so successful that his fortune overshadowed his wife's. He lost his interest in "pure gambling," and even acted correctly towards his wife. All in all, analysis achieved reasonably favorable results in this man, although the initial prognosis was so unfavorable.

Comment: Mr. B., like so many other patients, misunderstood maternal sacrifice and saw it as "malice." His poor mother sacrificed herself for her children and especially for her older son. Her reward from that son was hatred, and later, masochistic-provocative behavior.

Under the disguise of "wanting to get," Mr. B. was a masochistic spoiler of his own "hedonistic aims." This held true ("in spades," as he would have said) in his parasitic marriage, where he behaved in a manner that dangerously threatened his "security."

CASE XVIII

Mrs. C.'s husband hovered over her upon her first appearance in my office. She kept her face hidden behind her handkerchief as he explained her problems to me. She was moody and depressed, he said, and suffered from crying spells which had been officially diagnosed as "nerves." This had been going on for a year, and Mrs. C. could not explain her difficulties. He summed up the situation by stating that their marriage was "perfect," asked that his wife receive immediate treatment, and tactfully left the scene.

As soon as he was gone, Mrs. C.'s handkerchief was returned to her bag and I saw a businesslike, good-looking woman in her early thirties. Having asked for and been assured of medical secrecy, she told me her story. The "perfect" marriage was dull and her husband a "bore," which accounted for her decision to improve matters by having a few affairs. Frigid in her marriage and hardly less so in her extramarital experiments, she had concluded that whatever "plus factor" was evident in her affairs had nothing to do with the men themselves, but with the element of danger involved. In the meantime, her boring husband had become enough of a success to make her marriage more valuable to her; this fact dictated her actions when he got some inkling of her affairs and threatened divorce. Her denials were clever enough to convince him partially; to eliminate his suspicions entirely she hit upon her pose of "nervousness." She made her "spells" so convincing that she even managed to delude her physicians.

At this point, Mrs. C. asked a surprising question: "What is my problem, Doctor?"

For therapeutic reasons I did not insist upon her answering the question herself. From the clues she had given in the first part of her story (which was of course more detailed than the synopsis given above) it was possible to draw up a list of logical alternatives and eliminate others that did not apply. (The problem could not be sexual, for example, since she had readily admitted her affairs. This readiness constituted an assurance that "lasciviousness" was not her "real" crime. If it had been, she would have admitted only her defense against it.)

After excluding addiction, my conclusion was that Mrs. C. was mixed up with the criminal element in gambling, and owed more money than she could pay. This proved to be the case. Mrs. C. had lost forty thousand dollars. She covered her debt with IOU's. The gambler who held her notes had, since receiving them, treated her as a gangster would treat a girl friend, forcing her to be his hostess at his exclusive gambling club and subjecting her to other humiliations. She lived in fear of his threats and in fear of being recognized at his club. Buying him off sexually had occurred to her, but he was impotent. A lawyer had advised her to tell the story to her husband, but she had not done so.

This refusal, I told her, testified to her love of danger. She had consented to try analysis only because she dimly glimpsed her own masochism. We agreed on a trial analysis, in which these problems—as well as her frigidity, which was bound up with her masochistic craving for failure—would be discussed.

The beginning of Mrs. C.'s analysis was complicated by her external dilemma; something had to be done about her gambling debts and the blackmailer who held her notes. To gain time,

Mrs. C. suffered a "nervous breakdown" which required that she retire to Florida. This was partly on the advice of her lawyer, partly her own idea. With the cooperation of a friend in Florida, the gambler was given "proof" that the retirement was genuine, and the pressure on Mrs. C. was relieved. Except to keep her analytic appointments, she never left her house. (The grand hope that the gambler would send incriminating letters to the Florida address never materialized.)

The subject of these analytic appointments—the only subject that interested Mrs. C.—was "how much are *we* to tell my husband." The "we" illuminated another aspect of her willingness to go into treatment; she had coldbloodedly calculated on using the analyst as a protector and go-between.

This was exactly what happened. It was I who told Mr. C. of his wife's situation. He was not given the whole story; merely learning of her financial predicament was shock enough.

At home that night Mr. C. alternated between "terrible reproaches and self-humiliation." Mrs. C. remained quite calm, countering the reproaches wtih the story that she was "neurotically sick" and therefore could not be held accountable. Now that the problem was in the open, however, it was quickly cleared up. Mr. C.'s lawyer arranged for a payment of ten thousand dollars and the gambler surrendered all evidence of the debt. The terrifying blackmailer, to Mrs. C.'s surprise, proved to be quite meek as soon as legal steps were threatened.

There was a curious aftermath to these events. Mr. C., who could not decide whether or not he wanted a divorce, stopped talking to his wife and seldom appeared at meals. Mrs. C., on the other hand, felt certain that he would not leave her, and began to speak of her husband in cold, rather contemptuous terms. In general, she behaved as if she had just proved her superiority over events and people. Both her husband and the blackmailer were dismissed as "weaklings," and analysis—now that it had served her conscious purpose—was virtually dismissed as well. She began to miss appointments. When she did appear for them she acted as if she were going through a meaningless, irritating routine.

This could not, of course, go on. I tried to make Mrs. C. realize that her masochism must inevitably embroil her in situations even more serious than the one she had just escaped from. Her amazing response to this was the announcement that she was thinking of divorcing her husband, with assurance, she explained, that his masochism would guarantee a quiet divorce and a generous settlement.

Mrs. C. had learned from analysis to detect masochism in other people, but she still remained convinced that her endowment of it was merely "normal." She misunderstood her masochistic tension, which she took for boredom, and dismissed her frigidity, which was the starting point for all her trouble. Fortunately for her, a forceful discussion of her real situation penetrated to some extent, and she grudgingly began to "cooperate" with the analyst.

Mrs. C. blamed her "disappointed" mother for her unhappy childhood. There had been an air of futility in her home, arising from her mother's cold rejection of her father. She too had felt rejected by her mother. At an early age she had become disgusted with her father's "godlike submission" to his inaccessible wife. As far as she was concerned, her father too was inaccessible; he was interested only in his wife and paid no attention to the child's attempts to win his love. She hated her mother for her emotional detachment and coldness, and hated her as well for being the obstacle which blocked off an emotional relationship between father and daughter. Eventually she resigned herself to the possession of "peculiar" parents and became cynical about her life at home. But she still, at intervals, caught herself doing things "to please mother"; invariably the result was disappointing. She would then reproach her mother and burst into tears. Mrs. C. concluded this recital by commenting: "You will have to admit that only an unhappy child could emerge from this environment. Now prove to me that *I* made a masochistic mess of it."

This proof took up many analytic sessions. Often deceptively simple questions punctured the rationalizations with which Mrs. C. had concealed her real aims. Why, I asked, had she perpetuated instead of correcting her unhappy childhood situation? Why had she adopted her mother's attitude of aloofness and boredom? Why had her premarital attachments always been to cold and disagreeable men? Did this represent an unconscious reversal of the parental situation, and had she been submissively, like her father, pursuing inaccessible sexual objects, like her mother? If she was right, and her interest in these men reflected her desire for "a strong man" and not a masochistic aim of humiliation, why had she not learned from experience instead of repeating the same failure again and again? Her marriage to the "nice" Mr. C. might have meant that she had stopped using her sure formula for achieving disappointment, except that the history of her marriage proved that she had merely adopted another method for ensuring masochistic rejection.

As for her frigidity, it had been a means of proving to herself that she could never meet with anything except rejection and disappointment. This had been true of her gambling, also; her opponent in the gambling game symbolized the "bad, refusing" mother. Even in her analysis she persisted in her technique of injustice collecting.

Working through these resistances took many months. Mrs. C. gradually changed, until one day she informed me that she was no longer going to "live by the unconscious." As she had foreseen, her husband gave her a divorce and a handsome settlement. Since then she has successfully remarried. She has stopped gambling, or—as she put it—has stopped "playing with dolls filled with dynamite."

Comment: Mrs. C.'s mother had been neurotic and inaccessible. Instead of correcting her disappointment—the normal solution—Mrs. C. unconsciously chose to perpetuate it masochistically and endlessly. Her whole life thereafter was a masochistic fiesta.

Mrs. C.'s behavior also illustrates this typical masochistic technique of the neurotic: *he is submissive to a stronger person and mercilessly cruel to a weaker person.* The "strong" gangster became meek when he discovered he had to deal with a lawyer; Mrs. C. began treating her husband harshly as soon as she realized that he was not going to "throw her out," gambling debts or no gambling debts. His forbearance was construed as "weakness."

Mrs. C.'s behavior towards her inaccessible mother proves another point in the psychology of neurotic children. *They remain tied to disappointment, real or imaginary, instead of detaching themselves from it.* Mrs. C. stated specifically that in childhood she had "caught herself doing things to please Mother," only to meet with indifference. Why had she not concluded that nothing could be done? This conclusion was out of the question; the masochistic elaboration blocked it.

CASE XIX

Mr. D. was a successful lawyer in his late thirties. He consulted me because of a potency disturbance. He was not interested in his wife and regretted his marriage. Nevertheless, he conceded that she "had a case" and he was willing to "do something about it."

From his description of his recent history it was clear that he had problems in addition to his impotence. He had married— or been captured, he indicated—during a period of depression, when he had been working too hard, smoking too much, and losing money at his incessant poker games. He had not had sexual difficulties before marriage, but then he had not been much interested in sex. This was the only sector in which he considered that he needed analytic repair, although he had no objection if treatment cured him of the habit of smoking too much. As for his gambling, that was "perfectly O.K."

I corrected his compartmentalized picture of analysis and explained that analysis treated the psyche as a whole, and not in independent sections. His gambling, for example, was a tendency that, when exaggerated, could represent a neurotic symptom; as such, it would become a part of his analysis. He was confident that he could keep the forbidden subject of gambling out of our discussions. I assured him, with equal confidence, that sooner or later he would see the interconnections and bring the subject up himself.

In the meantime a trial analysis was arranged, and Mrs. D.'s request for an appointment was dealt with.

Mrs. D. came to see me the next day. Neither her appearance nor her personality impressed me as attractive. It was difficult to see why her clever husband had married her. Her attitude towards me combined self-righteousness with superciliousness—an incomprehensible approach to a person one has asked for help. The story she told, however, explained both puzzles.

Mrs. D. was by avocation a "soul-saver." She had married Mr. D. to rescue him from his addiction to gambling. Her first marriage, too, had been a crusade, but an unsuccessful one: she had not been able to cure her first husband of drunkenness. Mr. D. had been her lawyer in her divorce, and he struck her as being an eligible subject for a future campaign. Two years later, during the depression that resulted from his gambling losses, he capitulated to her argument that she was indispensable to him and married her.

Now she had had to confess defeat with him, also, and had been forced to "refer his case" to someone else. This explained the resentment that colored everything she said during our interview.

Mrs. D.'s inner motivations, which fall into a recognized category (many female psychic masochists specialize in the "rescue fantasy"), are only incidental to the story. Her conscious appraisals of her husband's problem, however, included some interesting perceptions. She saw, for example, that his gambling was the real clue to his situation. As far as his impotence was concerned, she thought it of no importance: an inadvertent admission of frigidity. Nevertheless, she had used Mr. D.'s narcissistic humiliation to push him into treatment, where, she hoped, something could be done about his gambling.

Mr. D.'s analysis did not begin propitiously. His attitude made no sense to begin with: he acted as if he were confronting a hostile witness and not a physician. Unconsciously there was a protective purpose to this procedure; his unconscious had recognized the danger signals and knew that analysis threatened his cherished neurosis. "Unmasking" the physician-witness would have been a guilt-free way of leaving treatment.

A very cursory description of Mr. D.'s family background drew a picture of a mother who "willfully" hid behind her hypochondria, a father who had been naively deceived by the mother's complaints, an older brother who was a boisterous nonentity, a younger sister who was a second edition of his mother. All his relatives, he said, were spongers who came to him with their troubles.

The patient had given me one clue to his hidden personality before I heard this sad parody of a personal history: he revealed blatant and insistent narcissism, a narcissism which had to be a flimsy product since it provided him with no protection against the blows of his environment. From this quality it was possible to deduce others. Extreme sensitivity necessarily concealed inner passivity, plus extreme guilt rising from the passivity. His injustice collecting pointed to the probability that he had unconsciously misjudged his mother's neurotic self-centeredness (which arose from her hypochrondria) as a malicious refusal of love and attention.

Mr. D. filled in the vague picture, piecemeal. To his own surprise, he produced a few recollections demonstrating his mother's coldness. He had preferred to believe that his adult judgment of her as a harmless nuisance exactly reproduced his childhood opinion. He also revealed that there had been considerable rivalry between him and his brother and sister. The brother especially was a formidable opponent, superciliously trading on his five years' seniority and excluding the younger boy from his circle of friends. His mother had been certain of her oldest son's future success and had lost no opportunity to praise him. D. now gleefully pointed out that the brother was a failure, while he had become a success. As for the younger sister, she had been the traditional rival, the infant who always captured the mother's attention.

In speaking of his father, D. had seemed to be drawing a composite picture of father and disagreeable brother. I suggested that this combination must have been a comparatively late development and that the two images remained distinct until the feeling of being excluded, which originally pertained to his parents, had shifted to the brother who kept him away from his friends.

This assumption proved to be correct. The masochistic pattern which originally pertained to the mother of earliest infancy had been repeated, in identical form, with father-brother-sister. A new element then entered the picture of masochistically tinged defeatism: the boy suffered from the comparison between his small sex organ and those of his father and brother. He solved this problem by imagining he was a woman. He would stand in front of a mirror, hiding his organ between his legs. He described this solution as having been both comforting and frightening. Fantasies of having damaged himself by masturbation (fantasies fostered by his parents) strengthened that fear. When I told him that his guilt arose from inner passivity, he promptly connected the explanation with his fear of being unmanly. In his opinion, he had certain feminine traits, and his potency troubles had reminded him of submerged feminine tendencies.

This was an important admission, although it was only a beginning. His admission revealed fragments of the "negative Oedipus complex," a stage in the life of every boy. In the hopeless competition with father for mother, the boy usually renounces the allegedly criminal organ. Psychologically, in the negative Oedipus complex, he becomes a woman, entitled to his father's love. This phase is typically short-lived, but D. had maintained it indefinitely because it could be used as "an admission of the lesser crime." Defending himself against an unconscious reproach of masochistic passivity, he denied the indictment, admitting to *feminine* passivity instead.

The importance of "feminine tendencies" as an alibi explained why Mr. D. had retained in consciousness the memory of his "negative Oedipus."

All of this he found "too painful" to believe; the complicated connection between his inner alibi and his potency disturbance he termed "fantastic." He made many attempts to argue against these deductions and confirmations. One day, triumphantly, he announced a refutation.

His passive tendencies were connected with gambling, he said, ironically adding that I would undoubtedly tell him that he gambled and lost in order to admit to the lesser crime, the wish to be overwhelmed in feminine identification, in order to deny the greater crime of psychic masochism. This was, of course, nonsense, he concluded; everybody wants to win.

Mr. D. had finally brought up the matter of gambling and he had actually figured out the correct interconnections, although he believed he had merely been ironic when he stated them. As for the gambler's wish to lose, a symbolic expression of his unconscious wish to be humiliated and deprived, I asked him to listen to a rather long explanation, think about it for a few days and then give me his opinion.

"All your ranting and shouting started the moment it dawned on you that your conscious feminine tendencies were only superficial inner defenses against more deeply repressed masochistic tendencies," I said. "Why an intelligent person should defend his assumption of a self-damaging diagnosis is understandable only on condition that this diagnosis covers something even more disagreeable.

"When did you marry?" I continued. "After your gambling losses increased in a specific period. These losses were by no means dangerous; still, you reacted with deep depression and suicidal moods. What was your cure? You married. What happened next? You proved yourself impotent; you were left saddled with a marriage you did not really want. Now, isn't the sequence of events slightly suspicious? Assume for the sake of argument that gambling is based on deepest unconscious masochistic passivity, and a potency disturbance of your type on unconscious feminine identification. Isn't it possible that this sequence of events is exactly what I suggested as interpretation—taking the blame for the lesser crime?"

I did not see Mr. D. for an entire week. When he returned he told me calmly that he thought my interpretation correct. He had been convinced by two facts which he never told me.

One concerned gambling. He had classified poker players into stronger and weaker types, types bound to win or to lose. In the period of his heavy losses he avoided weaker players, who "bored" him, and chose to play only with stronger types, though he suspected they would win. He realized now that his real aim had been masochistic satisfaction.

The other factor was a recollection that came to him that week. As a boy of four he consistently worried over whether his penis, when flaccid, would ever "grow big" again. He feared that his masturbation had damaged his penis and that it could never again become erect. At the poker table a poor hand would remind him of the "small size" of the organ; a good hand meant "not everything is lost, yet." During the week he spent arguing with himself about my interpretation, he realized that identifying a losing hand with the "small size" and a winning hand with the "big size" had been expressions, in genital terms, of a pregenital aim: the desire for masochistic self-torture.

These were excellent and encouraging deductions; they showed that much of the work of analysis had already been achieved. After a period of working through, Mr. D. was cured of both gambling and impotence. He eventually divorced his wife, whom he had married for masochistic reasons alone.

Comment: Mr. D.'s mother was self-centered and neurotic. He misinterpreted her hypochondria as personal malice, thus justifying the masochistic attachment which he faithfully repeated in the sequence father, older brother, sister.

His compensatory secondary narcissism became a covering cloak, just as his alleged femininity became an "admission of the lesser intrapsychic crime." In inner reality he was propelled by the masochistic allure of perpetual failure in gambling, marriage, career.

CASE XX

Mrs. E. came into analysis because of her increasing stage fright, but this was only one of the factors that made her miserable. In spite of modest success as an actress, she thought of her life as a series of failures. And so it was in every sector except her work. Her first unhappy marriage had been to a homosexual; in her current unhappy marriage, after two years her husband attached himself to another woman, and treated her with unrelenting "coldness and cruelty."

She was still confident that her marriage could be saved, that sooner or later her husband would tire of his "bitchy" girl friend, as he did his "bitchy" first wife, and turn again to his "real type" —the nice person, as exemplified by herself. In the meantime, she had been staying at home weeping; when weeping palled she had taken up gambling as a diversion, repeating the pattern she had followed while waiting for a divorce from her first husband.

We arranged for appointments, but Mrs. E.'s real purpose in entering analysis remained unclarified. She thought of her gambling as a minor matter; her stage fright she viewed as a chronic and expected hazard of her profession, now temporarily grown acute; her marital unhappiness, both first and second editions, she saw as a tragic fate beyond her control. She rejected entirely any thought that she was dealing with neurotic problems.

In the early stages of analysis she acted as if she were discussing matters with the head of a husband-retrieving bureau, who would give her helpful pointers on how to win back lost happiness. This was pitiful and naive; it expressed the extremes to which she would go in order to maintain her masochistic aims. She was willing to enter the "danger zone" of analysis in the hope that it would help her maintain her source of injustices.

Because of her misconception of analysis, I suggested that we begin treatment by exploring her husband's motivations in this situation. Not realizing that this approach would also cast light on her own, Mrs. E. enthusiastically agreed. My deductions— that *he* was a masochist who unconsciously preferred domineering women and had turned to the "nice" Mrs. E. to provide himself with an inner alibi and that *she* too was a masochist who used marriage as a sure road to rejection and disappointment— displeased Mrs. E. Her subsequent attitude led me to ask whether she really wanted to continue analysis. At this point the husband discovered that she was in treatment, and under pressure of his demand that she quit at once she "showed her independence" by becoming a champion of analysis. Mr. E. then requested an interview with me, which was arranged. The wife looked forward hopefully to this encounter.

Mr. E.'s external behavior and appearance astonished me: he impressed me as being a homosexual. I tabled this impression temporarily and looked for other attributes as I listened to his opening remarks, which consisted of a rather banal attack on my profession and the science which it serves. He had, I thought, the charm of an aging and faded playboy, with an air of unreliability, insincerity, and artificiality about him.

A good deal of what he told me—aside from his demand that I end his wife's analysis because it was damaging him professionally (he was a theatrical agent)—was unexpectedly interesting. It seemed that Mrs. E.'s favorite reproach against him was his homosexuality; she never mentioned this to me. As for his marriage, he had made no attempt to end it legally because he feared his wife's anger and had no wish to see his private life in newspaper headlines. He would welcome, he said, a quiet divorce. His most interesting revelation concerned his wife's gambling. "It's really dangerous," he told me. "She loses money hand over fist, faster than she makes it."

I suggested that he stop interfering with Mrs. E.'s treatment, pointing out: "It is to your own interest that the whole affair be cleaned up inconspicuously, in one way or another." We agreed on a "truce" for two months, and he went home to report our conversation to his wife.

The woman arrived for her next appointment in good spirits, elated with the "good impression" I had made on her husband. She was shocked and sobered, however, when I recited the list of omissions and misstatements in the story she had told me. For the first time she realized that analysis dealt with facts that could not be glossed over when they were unpleasant.

Now Mrs. E. amended the picture of her childhood as a paradise of love and understanding. Her mother was "a darling," yes, but so submerged in her father that the child felt excluded. A new character now entered the story: the child's uncle, a gentleman who was all charm and no virtue. The child never saw him but overheard enough to be fascinated with his history of grandiose swindling schemes; one ended with a long jail sentence. She had also seen a photograph of him, which made it easier for her to utilize him as the hero of a glorified legend and the object of libidinized girlish fantasies. This image had a double purpose: it became the basis for a reproach against her mother, who cruelly betrayed "her own flesh and blood."

Despite Mrs. E.'s happy childhood, she had unconsciously constructed a neurotic elaboration of environmental and biological factors, using her disowned uncle to symbolize and justify her own feeling that her parents excluded and neglected her. In his name she pseudo-aggressively attacked her mother and at the same time identified herself with him and his dreary fate. (It was significant that she had described him to me as "charming," the same adjective she had used in connection with her husbands. Later Mrs. E. recalled that one of the legal counts which had sent her uncle to jail had been homosexuality—another trait linking these three men.)

Mrs. E.'s fantasy of her uncle set the unconscious pattern for her unhappy marriages, and I pointed this out, giving reasons for this deduction. She was bitter, but not so resentful that she was incapable of following through and asking a reasonable question: How did her pattern of choice account for the unhappiness of her marriages?

Her preference, I explained, reflected both pseudo-aggression against her mother and masochistic attachment—both under pressure of inner guilt, which leads to self-damage. Self-damage was the aim in her marriage. Pity, which she imagined a major motivation, had been a superficial disguise, adopted both as an alibi against unconscious accusations of psychic masochism and as a means of "proving" that if her mother's attitude towards the uncle had been different, his entire life would have been changed. Unconsciously, Mrs. E.'s two husbands and her uncle represented herself.

"According to you, I have to reorient my entire emotional life," said Mrs. E. This was correct; Mrs. E. had to learn to stop seeing herself as the eternal victim and begin to build on solid —non-masochistic—foundations.

We turned now to an examination of her stage fright, which entailed a study of exhibitionistic tendencies.

Exhibitionism, Mrs. E. had to admit, was one of her prominent traits; she used it productively in her acting and masochistically in advertising her marital problems. Exhibitionism is the child's standard unconscious defense against guilt-laden peeping. "Who wants to peep?" the alibi runs. "I want to display myself." Since many forms of exhibitionism are fostered and applauded by the environment, the alibi is an excellent one.

Mrs. E. confirmed this deduction by producing a long-forgotten (repressed) incident. At three and a half she peeped through a keyhole and saw the intimacies of a couple who were visiting her parents' house. Her mother caught her, scolded her severely. The child innocently answered: "Why, what's wrong? I just wanted to see how they played. Don't you watch me when I play with my blocks?"

I have analyzed many theater people and have discovered that this kind of guilt-laden peeping scene recurs regularly in their childhood histories. In every case guilt had been so pervading that they attacked it, saying it was "unreal," merely a "play." The alibi of unreality became their guiding pattern. Added to the standard alibi of exhibitionism, it led them to the world of make-believe, the stage. Acting is a normal, productive occupation approved by the environment, and therefore a defensive weapon in the inner battle of the conscience.

Stage fright superficially pertains to exhibitionism: the actor fears he will forget his lines and make a fool of himself in front of his audience. On a deeper level, his fear is masochistic; what reaches the surface in consciousness represents the guilt accepted for a lesser crime. Accused of psychic masochism, the actor suffering from stage fright pleads guilty to pseudo-aggression and proves his contention by suffusing with guilt his "aggressive" flouting of the educational command not to exhibit.

At the bottom of every masochistic fear is one of the septet of baby fears present in every child. Often the exact fear can be pinpointed in analyzing a specific case of stage fright.

All this left one important question unclarified for Mrs. E. Why had her stage fright mounted during marital conflicts?

"Simply because exhibitionism, which had previously been used as a normal sublimatory defense, became suspect to your inner conscience. You intended to use it masochistically," I told her. "Remember the 'dirty marital linen washed in public' and how you paraded your marital misery?"

Working through the actress's stage fright required many weeks. In the meantime, her gambling debts had grown huge. She could no longer contend that her gambling addiction was "a triviality." It was time, I said, to look for the inner reasons that had led her to choose the dangerous diversion of gambling as a distraction from unhappiness in marriage.

Mrs. E.'s history of self-created defeats revealed not only psychic masochism but also a persisting infantile belief in her own omnipotence. She could hold on to this illusion only by paying the price of conscious suffering. In her two marriages she attempted the impossible task of recreating the image of her uncle. But the infantile illusion of absolute power, as an unconscious motivation for an adult, guarantees eventual external defeat, and therefore failure (made palatable by masochism) became her predominant pattern. This accounted for hopeless marriages and for her addiction to gambling. The impersonal roulette wheel (she had lost most of her money at this game) was Mrs. E.'s substitute for "the bad, refusing mother." Every time she lost she confirmed her inner conviction that mother was "unjust."

"According to you, roulette is my third husband," said Mrs. E.

"You are finally catching on."

"Where does my megalomania come in? In predicting defeat?"

"Partly, partly in the perpetuation of megalomania *per se,* possible only under self-damaging conditions."

As soon as Mrs. E. understood, emotionally, the foolishness of her self-damaging aims, she began to change. After months of working through, Mrs. E. agreed to divorce her husband. She found gambling "silly," and gave it up. Several stage and screen successes followed, and a third marriage, apparently successful.

Comment: Mrs. E.'s parents were happy in their marriage; both of them loved the child. Still she felt excluded—because they loved each other. Early in her childhood she found a suitable point of attack in the person of her crooked and homosexual uncle, then in jail. She reproached her mother for having betrayed "her own flesh and blood." Freely disregarding reality factors (what is a family to do with a criminal relative—hang his picture, in prison garb, prominently in the living room?) she idealized her homosexual uncle. This provoked her mother. She also put a suitable pseudo-moral connotation into operation: hadn't mother taught her to love her family and her relations? Psychic masochism became the leading pattern in Mrs. E.'s life, as her two marriages to unreliable homosexuals showed in later life.

There is another interesting detail in this case. In Mrs. E.'s second marriage, both she and her husband tried to escape their masochism but only succeeded in plunging more deeply into it. Before and during his marriage to Mrs. E., Mr. E. was in love with a "bitchy" woman—his real type. After the collapse of her first marriage, Mrs. E. rescued herself into "love," only to find herself again face to face with her real counterfeit-love—psychic masochism.

To remind the reader of what had already been stated in the beginning of this chaper, these case histories were chosen from many summaries (written to illustrate themes completely different from the subject of this book) included in four of my recent publications. They have all been considerably shortened.

They present clinical proof that *no direct congruity* exists between parental behavior and the child's reaction to it.

This group of cases presents portraits of all kinds of parents: loving and kind, neurotically cold and detached, easily provoked and hard to provoke. Despite the wide variety of parents and upbringers, one common denominator links all the portraits. It is masochistic misuse of reality by neurotic children. Thus the propelling factor is always the child's *specific* solution of his *specific* infantile conflict, which uses the *specific* behavior of the parents as a starting point and *not* as a photographic negative to be reproduced.

The best proof that neurotic children tendentiously misuse the home situation was the fact that these neurotics were cured through psychoanalytic-psychiatric treatment. This in itself is indicative. Analytic treatment brings the neurotic to the identical plateau of psychic health he would have reached of his own accord if his psychic masochism had not interfered.

The hunt for neurotic repetitions is not a sport which ends with finding the logic. The search itself has a "case history." One must find within the child the specific inner conflict that preceded and prompted the repetition.

Schematization is meaningless. Although it is true that every neurotic, in his transference repetitions, is like a man who owns one record and perpetually searches for a record player on which he can play it (and finds it in friends, acquaintances, even strangers), the record was still "made" by himself!

The main problem: *it seems to be the tendency of the neurotic child to attach himself to, instead of detaching himself from, early "disappointments."* These alleged disappointments are frequently self-created; any child who consistently asks the average parents for "too much" will manage to achieve "disappointment," "rejection," and "lack of love." What the child in his total self-centeredness does not want to understand is that even good parents can only devote a part of their energy to their children. They have lives of their own.

Moreover, the neurotic child's constant provocations make even cooperative parents impatient and angry. Later on, those provocations are conveniently repressed and memory retains only the picture of "mean parents."

In short, *the masochistic elaboration is the child's own contribution to the educational process. By shifting the blame, parents are the "culprits."*

CHAPTER 6

PARENTAL EXPECTATIONS
AND THE "REAL" CHILD

ASK a couple about to be married and looking forward to becoming parents, about their expectations; probably their reply would be a lyric on the theme of "baby—cute, lovable." The fantasy makes no provision for a postscript; people forget that cute, lovable babies can grow up into troublesome children.

There is little doubt that a procreative instinct does exist, although psychological inner reasons inhibit and impede it. Dr. Johnson, who prudently married a woman much older than himself, exhibited such fears when he said to Boswell in 1776: "I should not have had much fondness for a child of my own. At least, I never wished to have a child."

On the other hand, there is also a complex psychological overlay superimposed on the normal wish to have children.

First, there is a tendency to shift all hopes that have not materialized in one's own career upon children. This reduplication via identification partly explains the truly fantastic sacrifices parents do make.

Second, and this fact is less conscious, parenthood eradicates an infantile conflict of envy, dating from a time when having children was seen as a prerogative which adults reserved for themselves. They can now view themselves as adults.

The third element is totally unconscious. "Repetition in reverse" (see Chapter I) is at work; it is the active repetition of passively endured experiences, eradicating a lesion in narcissism, previously suffered.

221

Fourth, also unconscious, the adult amasses a certain amount of "normal" masochism in foreseeable problems connected with child rearing: inconveniences, worries, sacrifices, adjustments, expenses inevitable in parenthood.

These four points explain why logical arguments against having children have no effect upon prospective parents.

Here are a few other representative pronouncements:

> Some tormentor invented children, and I approved the opinion of Euripides, who said they who had no children are happy by being unfortunate in not having them. Boethius, *Philosophiae Consolationis,* 524 A.D.)

> Some would have children; those who have them moan or wish them gone. (Francis Bacon, *Life,* 1600.)

> When I consider how little a rarity children are—that every street and blind alley swarms with them—that the poorest people commonly have them in most abundance—how often they turn out ill, and defeat the fond hopes of their parents, taking to vicious courses, which end in poverty, disgrace, the gallows, etc.—I cannot for my life tell what cause for pride there can possibly be in having them. (Charles Lamb, "A Bachelor's Complaint of the Behavior of Married People," in *Essays of Elia,* 1823.)

> Children are a torment, and nothing else. (Tolstoy, *The Kreutzer Sonata,* 1890.)

Like all other relationships, that of the parent-child can be warped by neurosis. Some neurotic parents torture their children in a repetition of the torture they imagine their parents inflicted on them. Others exploit their children for neurotic reasons or involve them in family quarrels. Often a parent's attitude conceals a labyrinth of unconscious motivations.

A patient, father of a two-year-old girl, was trying to persuade his wife to have a second child. His reasoning embraced the familiar story of psychic difficulties an only child is bound to encounter—difficulties that could be eliminated by adding other children to the family. In addition, he had a nostalgic rationalization: he wanted a boy because he remembered the fun he had playing with his brother when he was a child. When his wife finally agreed to have a child, however, his potency failed him.

This patient had been the oldest child in his family, though only a year older than his brother. He believed that he had been weaned prematurely because of the brother, and seemed to remember hating the baby suckling at mother's breast. It was evident that his desire for a second child reached back to this situation: unconsciously he wanted to repeat actively what he had himself passively endured as a baby, in order to cancel his infantile humiliation. He wanted, in other words, to watch his own child subjected to the disappointment he had experienced. This was the dynamic unconsicous wish concealed behind his plausible arguments. But when his wife consented, the inner torturer entered the picture, vetoing his wish as forbidden. To establish a moral alibi, the defense of impotence went into effect.

Inevitably parents approach parenthood with narcissistic inner expectations. This does not make for an easy transition to acceptance of the fact that every child has a personality of his own. In favorable cases parents do accept it; in unfavorable ones this very fact becomes a fertile field for injustice collecting. Generally the parents' complaints center around their children's "ingratitude."

To the parent it all seems simple. A steady stream of benefits has flowed to the child; the benefactor does not ask that the direction of this stream be reversed but only that it be acknowledged, testifying to the generosity of the benefactor. It is not that simple, however, to the child.

Parents can teach the outward forms of gratitude, the correct "thank you," and even the less perfunctory expressions of appreciation. But spontaneous and genuine gratitude is not a matter of etiquette; it has an unconscious genetic base.

The baby's yardstick for measuring the world and all that is in it consists of his own megalomania, his illusion of magic power. This yardstick is joined by others as he grows older and more experienced, but it still retains a good part of its influence over his judgments. To some extent he will still tend to think in the terms defined by his illusion of absolute power and to view the "good" as a gift which he makes to himself and only the "bad" as an action entirely controlled by the external world. Since everything "bad" includes restrictions imposed for the sake of his own welfare, this makes a poor start for gratitude.

When the child reaches the stage in which he attempts to compromise between the need to save face and to give in to restrictions and taboos, he identifies with some parts of his parents' codes and makes some of their taboos his own, accepting certain standards of conduct "of his own volition." The identification can develop in the child the ability to accept with appreciation the gifts made to him by the outside world. How willing he is to recognize these actions as gifts, and how willing he is to be grateful for them, depends on whether he has been willing to adapt himself to reality and abandon the misconceptions of earliest childhood.

But the child who has been completely successful in this adaptation is relatively rare. Most children conform to some extent, but with their own individual and secret reservations. This makes a continuance of conflict with the parents inevitable. Since restriction is one of the essential weapons of education, the neurotic child will have ample opportunities to interpret his parents' actions as malice. The likelihood is that he will feel justified in retaliating against these "cruel tyrants." The frustration that arises upon first encountering a taboo is quickly followed by hatred. He then has only two ways of contending with this hatred. If the taboo fits into the private bargain of identification he has made and happens to match one of his newly internalized restrictions, hatred can be dissipated. If it does not, he must take the neurotic, masochistic way out of his dilemma, and pay the price of suffering in exchange for the privilege of continuing his old slave revolt in disguised form.

It is this neurotic streak in the child and later in the adult that stifles gratitude. The more neurotic the individual, the more thankless it is to do him a kindness; in extreme cases an act of kindness seems to trigger an ungracious or even aggressively malicious response. What happens here is that the favor "types" the benefactor as a surrogate parent. The neurotic repetition compulsion ("repetition in reverse") then goes to work and impels the neurotic to take his "revenge" for the injustices allegedly done him as a child. It does not matter that the benefactor is not the real parent and had nothing to do with the fantasied disappointment. All that is needed to stir the unconscious mechanism is an initial identification of benefactor with parent.

Another typical infantile attitude governs the ability to show gratitude. The young child's desire for love and attention has no limits; the more he gets, the more he wants. And within the magic circle of neurotic repetition the standards of reality do not apply, no more than they do in infancy. The benefactor's act of kindness, once it has become part of the process of neurotic repetition, takes its place as part of the childhood picture of alleged neglect and denial of love. As such, it can be no better than a small payment attempting to balance an enormous debt.

Psychic masochism also plays its part in the ability to feel and express gratitude. Typically, the psychic masochist is submissive to people he classifies as stronger than himself and aggressive in his dealings with weaker people. The benefactor, having contributed a deed of kindness, falls into the category of "weak people" and as such is aggressively attacked. Without the data supposedly supplied by the act of kindness, the psychic masochist had no way of deciding whether the benefactor was "weak" or "strong" and therefore approached him cagily, saving his defensive inner aggresssion for a certain target. The degree to which this tendency shows itself varies, of course, with the extent of the individual's self-damaging tendencies.

If all these unconscious processes operate in a neurotic's relations with strangers and acquaintances, they must be even more obtrusive in a neurotic child's—or a neurotic adolescent's—relationships with his parents. The parent does not accidentally enter the magic circle of neurotic repetition; he is there in the beginning. The areas of love and kindness allegedly due the neurotic are the parents' sins of omission. The fact that the supposed crime, in either case, is buried in the dim past and was not a crime in the first place, is not considered.

Even a parent who has become resigned to his children's ingratitude feels some resentment when the child exhibits, as he often does, unexpected and spontaneous gratitude for a kindness extended by another adult. The mechanism here bears a close resemblance to the unconscious process underlying the magic gesture. A kindness from a stranger provides the neurotic child with a ready-made reproach to pass on to his parents: "You never did anything for me, and here is a stranger putting himself out to make me happy!" The gratitude shown the stranger points the moral: "See how grateful I would have been to you, if only you had given me a chance!"

A child's ingratitude is an old story of which the aphorists will never tire. Here are a few of their conclusions:

> How sharper than a serpent's tooth it is
> To have a thankless child! (*King Lear,* Shakespeare)

> Children suck the mother when they are young and the father when they are old. (English proverb)

> Infancy loves nothing. . . . A rascal of a child—that age is without pity. (La Fontaine)

> Children are always ungrateful. (Napoleon, on St. Helena)

> Children begin by loving their parents; after a time they judge them; rarely, if ever, do they forgive them. (Oscar Wilde)

In recent decades the increased divorce rate has created a new important problem for parents: How will their children react to divorce?

It has already been pointed out that divorces fall into two well-defined categories. There is the divorce which corrects an error made by inexperience. Here the probability is that the partners are not-too-neurotic, capable of learning from their own mistakes, and have a good chance of correcting these mistakes in a successful second marriage. There is also the neurotic divorce, in which the failure of the marriage reflects the failure of the partners to abandon their unconscious, infantile, neurotic aims.

This is not, of course, the opinion of the neurotic divorcee (to consider the female partner as typical). She firmly retains her illusion that all her problems will be cleared up, if only she could change husbands. Since she will choose her next husband to complement her own neurosis, the chances of such a solution are exactly zero.

The unconscious purpose of all neurotic marriages is masochistic pleasure. This calls for a facade of conscious misery to serve as an alibi for the unconscious gratification supplied by the marriage. When inner tension becomes too great or the alibi of "misery" no longer serves as a bribe to the inner tyrant, conscience, a strategic retreat is planned. "Misery" mounts until it becomes "intolerable," and divorce—always in the offing—ends the marriage. But this is not a surrender; it is only a postponement. The masochistic aim, spelled out in terms of marriage, remains constant, and therefore the divorce is only the preamble to another triumphantly unsuccessful alliance.

In the meantime, because even the most neurotic individual has some normal sectors, all divorced and divorcing parents are concerned about the effect of a broken home upon their children. There is no doubt that the child reacts strongly, but it does not mean that he will react by becoming neurotic. An unhappy marriage is an equally ominous factor in the child's development. No environment—no matter how favorable—offers any guarantees that a child will *not* develop neurotic traits.

The best the environment can do is to provide a situation which encourages healthy attitudes and minimizes the opportunities for unhealthy ones.

In a harmonious marriage, the child's Oedipal problem is simplified. In the boy's rivalry with his father, a limit is automatically set to his fantasy by the obvious fact that his parents love each other and that theirs is a partnership which leaves no room for him. Since it is pointless to go on asking for the impossible, the boy modifies his fantasy and adjusts to reality. In an unhappy marriage, however, the boy's aim does not seem to be unattainable. Nowhere does he see evidence that the parents are an indissoluble unity: all he sees is conflict. In a divorce, when one parent disappears from the stage, forbidden wishes actually seem to be encouraged.

The usual pattern of divorce, where children remain with the mother, may increase the child's conflict, strengthening the boy's attachment to his mother or the girl's antagonism to her. And this is true in puberty, when these unconscious wishes temporarily revive, as well as in early childhood. Sometimes the parents' separation may help to tip the balance, when the child is inwardly incapable of solving his problem.

A harmonious marriage eliminates the danger point and gives the child a sounder basis from which to work out the entire problem. Happy parents, to begin with, are more likely than neurotic parents to give their children tender love. It is the parents' love that provides children with the cushion they must have if they are to endure the painful deprivations of early childhood, such as the great loss of the cherished fantasy of omnipotence and also the necessity of giving up a long list of forbidden wishes. Humiliated, injured, stripped of his dearest aims, the fortunate child can still save face by considering: "If I give up some 'impossible' wishes, my parents will go on loving me. It's worth it, so I will."

A child explains the reasons for his parents' separation in terms of his own misconceptions. As he sees it, the parent who has left could have done so only if he ceased to love the child. Looking about for a reason to explain this loss of love, the child finds it in his own misdeeds and in his unconscious deposits of guilt stemming from many other sources. Guilt is therefore heightened, and the loss of one parent is taken as proof that this guilt is justified and that the child has separated his parents.

Divorce is not the only factor that the child sees through a mist of preconceptions and misunderstandings. The entire outer world, for him, is an instrument serving only his own fantasies. The farther from reality these are, the more difficult it is to maintain them and the easier it is for him to yield to the requirements of reality. A happy home is less conducive to these self-damaging fantasies than a home threatened by divorce. When there is conflict between the parents, the child is furnished with an abundance of raw material to knit into his fantasies. He takes sides with one or the other parent, partly because he is involuntarily drawn into their quarrels and partly because he projects his own emotional conflicts into their situation. If we take as an example the boy of four or five, at the high point of his Oedipal rivalry with his father, this becomes clear. This child watches a violent quarrel between his parents. Mother reproaches father. The boy is uneasy, because his unconscious wishes have suffused him with guilt. Yet the quarrel unexpectedly makes him feel better. He uses it to diminish his own feeling of guilt, assuring himself: "Father is mean to Mother, but I wouldn't be." In the long run, of course, these quarrels have the reverse effect since the total result of the boy's self-justifying arguments is to strengthen his attachment to his mother. This means that he clings to an irrational, guilt-laden wish instead of abandoning it.

There is no compromising with this fact: every child must overcome and psychically digest the pre-Oedipal and Oedipal attachments, both libidinous and aggressive. If his reality situation provides him with an excuse for refusing to accept the defeat that is at the same time the solution to his problem, he may very well avail himself of that excuse. This does not mean, of course, that he must or will.

A remarriage of the parents undoubtedly leaves a mark on the child, although the results may not become visible for decades.

The stereotype of the "unhappy child of divorce" calls for a mental image that closely resembles a charity appeal: the unhappy child is not only pitiably forlorn and under-privileged but usually very young. Nobody ever visualizes the unhappy victim walking up to the offending parent on size-eleven feet and asking for an accounting in a voice as deep as his father's. Nevertheless, a large proportion of the children of broken homes are adolescents, and the effect of divorce on them is by no means to be ignored.

I have encountered this situation frequently when analyzing middle-aged men who are passing through the period of "middle-age revolt." (*The Revolt of the Middle-Aged Man,* Hill & Wang, N.Y., 1954.) These patients are violently discontented with the pattern of their lives and certain that their middle-aged wives provide the clue to their discontent.

Divorce and "a new beginning" are virtually every rebel's aim in this situation. His primary concern is his own welfare. He acknowledges a certain financial duty towards his wife and children but he is too absorbed in his own crisis (and it is a deeply unhappy, infinitely perplexing period for him) to have many emotional resources left over for them. He rationalizes this coldness without too much difficulty, both by his willingness to make financial amends for his absence and by standing fast on a few defiant arguments. Typical statements are: "I cannot be penalized all my life because I once took on fifty per cent of the responsibility for a child," or "Self-defense first; my duty as a parent can wait."

What he is not prepared for and has no defense ready to meet is a situation in which his children actively take sides in their parents' quarrel.

One patient said: "Today I was faced with something I hadn't foreseen, even in my nightmares. My nineteen-year-old son is in town for his Christmas vacation from college, and he asked for a personal talk with me. We talked. He acted very superior and rather indignant. His mother informed him of 'my disgraceful behavior.' Those were his exact words."

After a parental rebuke in no uncertain terms, the boy "changed his tune" and politely asked for his father's side of the story.

"I told him," the patient continued, "a child has no business setting himself up as a judge of his parents. I've made enough sacrifices for the boy! If he doesn't like it, he's welcome to work his way through college, as I did. Or he can quit and get a job. . . . It obviously took him by surprise; he expected to deliver a lecture to a penitent sinner. First he was furious; he accused me of damaging his future, of being irresponsible, a bad father, and so on. I started to leave the room. Then came tears and apologies. Then, very humbly and timidly, a question: 'Why are you making Mother unhappy?' "

"Did you answer?"

"I said he wasn't old enough to understand. I also asked why he took it for granted I was making his mother unhappy, and not the other way around. Do you know why? 'Because Mother is such a darling!' ... I told him that his mother could be a darling and I could still find her impossible to live with. Even darlings can be incompatable."

"And do you expect him to understand that?"

"No, I don't. The whole situation is ridiculous. And his attitude is infuriating! 'You're old, anyway' is written all over his face. 'Why should you make a fuss about the few years you have left?' "

"Do you expect a boy of nineteen to understand the problems of a man of your age?"

"Of course not. But why does he think he has a right to interfere?"

"Isn't he directly and indirectly involved?"

"Listen. I've made enough sacrifices for the boy. It would be different if he were still a child. He isn't, and that settles it. He can't be psychologically damaged at his age. He has to face facts."

This last statement was the patient's official platform, but he was not as firmly balanced on it as he would have liked. Instead of handling his son's complaint as he would have handled a less barbed situation, in a "man-to-man" or "you're my pal" manner, he had become furious, supercilious, aloof. This indicated that inner guilt had been awakened by the boy's reproach, a guilt too strong to yield to a simple reiteration of the patient's official point of view on the subject.

Sometimes the adolescent child unexpectedly appears as the supporter of rebellion instead of the defender of the status quo. He has his reasons, of course, and these are closely and exclusively related to his particular problems.

"I am depressed and puzzled," said another patient. "More puzzled than depressed. Something happened yesterday—"

"You look as if someone had hit you with a brick."

"Wait till you hear what happened. My son, a typical soph-omore in every way, invited me to go out to lunch with him."

"At your expense?"

"Naturally. Of course I was on guard: did he want an ad-vance on his allowance, or a bigger allowance, or had he eloped with a girl, did he have a social disease, did he need money for an abortion, had he been playing the horses? . . . I canvassed the usual list. No. It was something quite different."

"Such as?"

"It was a ceremonial lunch. I might almost say an official visit of condolence."

"Meaning?"

"My younger friend, as he called himself, informed me that he was quite aware of the domestic conflict. He sympathized with me. Why? On sociological and religious grounds."

"Strange formulation."

"I thought so too. He had authorities for his point of view; peculiarly enough, they are usually quoted by the opposing party. St. Augustine and First Corinthians VII."

"That's interesting."

"Isn't it! It seems that he and his friends had been discussing the value of marriage, and their conclusion is that marriage is nothing but an 'anti-sex institution.' Here's their proof from First Corinthians: 'To avoid fornication, let every man have his own wife, and let every woman have her own husband.' And from St. Augustine: 'Marriage is not a good, but it is a good compared with fornication.' Then, probably for variety, they dug up this from a woman, George Sand: 'The marriage vow is an absurdity imposed by society.' How do you like that?"

"I like the humor of the situation. You, the *pro tem* re-bel against marriage, put into the ironic position of defending marriage."

"I had to. It's my job as a father."

"Which made you, the rebel, revert to your own position of

the conservative. And your son became the rebel against established authority."

"Crazy situation."

"Not so crazy. The joke is that first adolescence, represented by your son, stood face to face with second adolescence, meaning you, and presto, you became a mature adult again—at least temporarily. . . . What hit you hardest when your son benignly gave his permission for your revolt was the fact that you seem to agree with his conclusion."

"Are you sure he is wrong?"

"I am sure. Marriage has deep emotional roots."

I explained how the concept of monogamy—one father and one mother—becomes firmly and unchangeably fixed in the child's mind during the upheavals of the Oedipal period.

"Very impressive," said the patient. "But I don't see how it disposes of the argument that marriage is an anti-sex institution."

"It does if you read between the lines of your son's quotations. The infantile idea of sex is full of misconceptions and mystery. Sex is always, for the child, *the* forbidden-mysterious. This connotation—that sex equals the forbidden—is normally relinquished. But in neurotics it remains in control. The consequences are tragic: neurotics find that legal marriage makes sex worthless for them, since it eliminates the element of the forbidden."

"I'll grant you this point. But it doesn't dispose of the argument that marriage cuts down sex interest in *everybody*."

"The purposes of ecclesiastical authorities (and rebels like George Sand) are not identical with the purposes of those who interpret psychological and medical facts. Marriage—the duality —is a normal solution for the relatively healthy individual. Normal marriage—and I can quote the Bible, too—is 'built on a rock,' on a solid, though unsuspected, psychological substructure. Now promiscuity is one of the possible *neurotic* solutions for sex. Marriage has been made a shibboleth in order to limit promiscuity and to avoid the worst of the problems that go with it. Moralists undoubtedly have their own reasons for their anti-sex propaganda, which has nothing to do with the fact that a healthy person knows from experience that sex with a person he loves is better than sex without love."

"But isn't it suspicious that the anti-sex group and the so-called healthy group should come to the same conclusions?"

"Only if you judge an argument by the person who is promoting it instead of by its contents. Two dissimilar groups may arrive at the same result even though their reasons are different. For example, take a puritanical sect that forbids its members to eat a certain sinful food. In the meantime a group of nutrition chemists discovers that this particular food is detrimental to the digestive systems of normal people. It does not follow that the chemists have been bribed by the puritanical sect."

"The deduction smacks of a lawyer's trick."

"Better ask yourself if you haven't specific reasons for your disbelief in what you call a trick. Isn't it true that you want to prove your point—the shibboleth of promiscuity—and therefore reject clinical evidence as an argument? Are you yourself an unbiased observer?"

"Biased or not, I still feel that the idea is to close one particular avenue to pleasure."

"That's an understandable reaction—for a second-edition adolescent. Every adolescent feels that the surest way to discover the truth is to assume that things are exactly the opposite of what his teachers and elders have told him. Isn't this storming at authority the predominant philosophy of the crisis of maturing? And doesn't it strike you as odd that the results of your son's reasoning should be identical with your own?"

"Now I can use your own argument against you. Didn't you just say that two groups, reasoning quite differently, can still reach the same conclusion?"

"That's another adolescent technique: reduction to absurdity. In your example the two groups are different—your son and you; the reasoning is exactly the same. Your middle-age-adolescent reasoning is only a duplication of your son's sophomore-adolescent reasoning. The idea that a few women in your life mean a few pleasures and many women mean many pleasures, is just neurotic. The wolf is not a man who has discovered a short cut to Paradise. He just runs from one woman to another as a preventive measure; he wants to make sure he doesn't reveal his limited potency. He is a neurotic driven to his behavior by inner forces over which he has no control."

One cannot help feeling a certain sympathy for the perplexed father in this situation. His son was old enough to be half-free of parental protection and influence. At the same time, the father was fully aware that he still owed the boy both influence and protection, and this automatic reaction came into play when he found himself defending marriage against the attacks of his son. Undoubtedly the boy could and would have taken some position of rebellion against established custom without the help of his father's example, and the father was fully aware of this. One nagging question, however, persisted: "Did I have the right to give him so authoritative a precedent?" There is no answer to this question, of course—except guilt.

The fact is that there is a long-term as well as a short-term requirement in parental responsibility. Short-term responsibility applies during the child's growing years; it involves regulating the parents' lives for the children's sake, providing them with material care, love, and a stable home life. Long-term responsibility —moral support, encouragement, kindness, love, material help when needed—never ends.

This does not mean that the parent has no right to self-protection. It is senseless, for example, to sacrifice oneself for a neurotic child past the uncertainties of youth. But self-protection does not justify cold detachment.

The majority of normal parents love, protect, and care for their children and like it. But the pronounced neurotic, or the parent caught in a neurotic crisis, will project his own neurotic conflict into all of his relationships, not excepting his relationships with his children. This behavior will not automatically create neurosis in the children; it will merely offer them convenient hitching posts for their own inner conflicts arising from other sources. The parent's neurotic attitudes need not necessarily be misused by the child, but they *may* be misused.

The pattern of marrying early and having several children

in quick succession while the marriage is still young has been widely adopted in this country since the war. The advantages to both parents and children are undeniable—as long as the marriage is a happy one. But the wife enmeshed in an unhappy union sees her children, in one sense, as jailers who are keeping her tied to her husband. The refrain is always the same: "How can I divorce him? There aren't any men who will marry a woman with children!"

But there are. A surprisingly large percentage of divorcees with children find suitable husbands.

Both experience and common sense appear to be confounded by this fact. A child-loving man wants children of his own; a man who does not care for children is not likely to be attracted by a ready-made family. And even when the material needs of the children from a former marriage are fully supplied by the terms of the separation agreement, the new husband automatically assumes a responsibility to the children by marrying their mother. To the many divorcees this responsibility, although it may be emotional only and not financial at all, looms as a burden that "any normal man would run away from."

Perhaps the "normal man" would run away if his actions depended on common-sense considerations alone. But in emotional situations the influence of the unconscious outweighs that of common sense. I have analyzed many prospective husbands of divorcees with children and have been convinced that in many cases the existence of the children was the unconscious factor which made these men decide in favor of the marriage. The reasons for this paradoxical reaction are not uniform. Three main types are distinguishable: the man in search of a loving woman, the man afraid to have children of his own; and the man who does not "run away" because he does not have normal attitudes towards either marriage or children. The latter belong to the category I have called "playboy neurotics." (*Money and Emotional Conflicts,* second edition, Pageant Books, Inc., 1959.)

To start with the third type: All wealthy divorcees know that the impostor draped in respectability is not a myth, and that they are the preferred prey of the playboy neurotic who exists by selling his looks and his "charming coldness" for cash. Analytically these emotional cripples are psychopaths whose disease has a complicated inner basis.

The divorcee's children are neither an obstacle nor a consideration to the playboy neurotic. His concern is exclusively for his own welfare. He wants to know whether the divorcee will support him in comfort and preferably in idleness, and how long she will tolerate his coldness and infidelity. Invariably he sponges on his wife and is aggressive in his dealings with her; usually he attaches himself to a girl friend who exploits him aggressively. In marriage the playboy neurotic takes money and gives mistreatment; in his relationship with his girl friend he gives money and submissively accepts cruelty.

The psychology of these people can be measured by this case:

A man who made it clear that he thought the world owed him a living, not in payment for work done but in acknowledgment of his sex appeal, consulted me because of depression and "drinking too much." He had begun to worry about his slight alcoholic addiction, because it was bad for his reputation. This euphemism meant that he was disturbed because his drinking habits threatened the success of his program of commercialized marriages. He had repeatedly tried to "taper off," but was unable to do so.

At twenty-seven he had been divorced twice. He did not consider his marital record unusual and was not consulting me because he needed to clear up any emotional difficulties arising from these fiascos. He had come simply to be cured of his alcoholism, he insisted.

"What is your profession?" I asked.

"I've worked in different fields," he answered evasively.

"For instance?"

"Well, first I went to college. After college I looked around...."

"What were you looking for?"

"A job. Then I became engaged to a girl whose father owned a big iron manufacturing outfit. After we were married I finally went to work in her father's office."

"What does the word 'finally' allude to?"

"Well, there was no real reason for me to go to work. My

wife had an income of her own, from her grandmother's estate. In the beginning we just traveled and had a good time, but then her father began working on her and she on me. I wasn't too happy over the prospect of being tied to a desk—who cares about iron, anyway?—but finally I did give in. Unfortunately our drinking interfered with my job. How can anybody work with a hangover?"

"What kind of husband did your first wife want? Did she want you to be a drinking companion or a hard worker?"

"You get the point exactly. I told her, either let me work—in which case you dispense with me as your night-club companion, or let me get out of that stupid office so we can have a good time."

"Did she understand what you meant?"

"Well, you know how these girls with money are. She blew her top and called me a playboy and a parasite. She was a parasite herself, but when I pointed that out to her she jumped on her high horse and said, 'Nobody could expect *me* to work— with a man it's different.'"

"And the end?"

"That *was* the end. I stayed away from the office for a couple of days, and then she started divorce proceedings. An unreasonable bitch, to put it mildly. I just went along with her, doing the kind of thing she wanted, and then she called me a playboy and walked out. I think her old fool of a father gave her the idea. She got rid of me just to cover up her own drinking."

"What happened sexually in the marriage?"

"She was a cold fish—although she accused me of coldness. She began an affair with another man, and later on married him. I got a lot of satisfaction out of hearing that her second marriage went on the rocks too."

"And you?"

"I was left out in the cold. After a while I hooked up with another girl in the same set. But it was the old story all over again. This time the family business was a shipyard. I had to learn something new, and I'll admit I wasn't too good at it. My second wife didn't drink so much, but she was insanely jealous."

"Did you give her reasons?"

"Well, I'm not claiming I married her for love. But she just thought she owned me. She became more violent and eventually went to Reno. I wouldn't repeat the names she called me. All I can say is, when you marry a wealthy girl you marry nothing but stinginess and complaints."

"Why *did* you marry for money?"

"I didn't exactly. I just never had too much confidence in my ability to work hard. I like a good time, and I imagined that these wealthy women would be glad to get a good-looking husband. But what did I get out of the deal? Nothing—except that I was typed as a playboy. Those two bitches made an alcoholic out of me—I had to drink to forget what they had done to me."

"And now?"

"Well, I managed to save a little money—"

"How?"

"Well, somewhat indirectly through my second wife. I saw Reno coming well in advance, so I managed to save some of *her* money—you know, little gifts, and so on."

"I see."

"Nothing spectacular, you understand. She was furious when she found out. She threatened to sue, and I threatened right back. I knew she couldn't afford a scandal."

"All in all, not too successful a business venture."

"Reasonably successful—no business is doing too well these days."

"And now?"

"Now I'm through with that crowd of wealthy parasites. All they want is a good time, but if a fellow gives it to them they get full of moral indignation and call him a playboy. And if he doesn't, they call him a washout. It's a hard world."

"Have you ever considered the possibility of supporting yourself?"

"What are my chances? A fifty-dollar-a-week job? Can I help it if I haven't got a talent for business?"

"Is your prospective third wife already in the picture?"

"No—I told you I'm wise to the whole crowd now. I want to

enjoy my freedom as long as I can—meaning as long as my money holds out."

"Why do you want to get rid of your drinking habit?"

"Well, you figure that one out for me."

"I have figured it out. It's a prerequisite for the next marriage deal."

"You can only sell what you have, you know. In my case that happens to be looks and personality."

"No illusions about yourself?"

"Not any more. A few years ago I had some, and they were nice and consoling. But by now they've evaporated."

"And what remained?"

"A correct evaluation of my chances. You can call it cynicism or cold-blooded calculation; I'm immune to that kind of criticism. The point is to get the best out of a poor deal."

"Has it occurred to you that you are emotionally sick? That your attitude bars you from all the feelings that give color to life?"

"Don't give me that. I don't believe in any romantic nonsense about love."

"Apparently it hasn't dawned on you that your over-drinking can't be isolated from the rest of your personality. Psychoanalysis of one trait must, out of inner necessity, bring in all others. And changing your personality may change your view that sex and marriage are business propositions in which commodities are bought and sold."

"Look, Doc, let's face facts. I don't need a face-lifting or morale-building job. I want you to remove my drinking compulsion, that's all. Everything else will take care of itself—and believe me, there's nothing a good-sized bank account can't cure."

"You said a little while ago that you're immune to criticism, meaning reproach. You will find out that you are very sensitive to inner reproaches: your drinking and depression are intimately connected with that."

"You don't say."

"And you'll discover that your cynicism can be psychologically explained, and so can your emotional coldness."

"Just do your job and we'll get along fine."

"I'm telling you just for the record. And one day I'll remind you of my warning."

"Don't worry. You 'warned' me and I know it. And I'll give you that in writing."

The not-too-neurotic divorcee will give this type of man a wide berth, provided her own unconscious wish to suffer is not in control. If this unconscious wish is sufficiently strong, she will prefer the playboy neurotic to other men because she will be sure the playboy can provide her desired masochistic diet of mistreatment and unhappiness.

A playboy's marriage is a business venture; the man sincerely in search of a loving woman wants a relationship with emotional value.

In a series of analyses of men, I have treated patients of the following type: A self-made man, a hard-working and successful business executive or member of a profession in his middle thirties, who has freed himself from an unhappy marriage to a shrew whom he had strangely misjudged, and believed to be "a sweet girl." Throughout that marriage he has been more or less indifferent to his children, temporarily coming closer to them only when his wife's coldness became pronounced.

Some time after the divorce, the man meets a divorcee with children. He observes that she is kind and loving in her treatment of them. "Somehow" (invariably vague about how or why) her attitude is so reassuring that he dismisses his qualms about raising the children of another father. He focuses on his satisfactory relation to the divorcee and marries her. More frequently than not, these marriages work out very well.

It is precisely the point that is always left unexplained that furnishes the clue to the real—unconscious—state of affairs. Three interwoven factors in the man combine to make him welcome the divorcee with children as a prospective wife.

First, the man's inner conscience held him responsible for the failure of his first marriage: he had discovered his wife's "shrewish nature" when it was too late to do anything about it. In reality, of course, he had discovered what was always in plain sight as soon as his inner needs drove him to acknowledge the facts. Unconsciously he always wanted to be mistreated; unconsciously he had married his first wife for the sake of her "cruelty" and not in spite of it. Consciously, of course, he was entirely unaware of his hidden wish. Consciously he now rejects this wish and looks for a new partner with whom he can achieve a relationship of loving warmth and trust.

Such a man's readjustment after a divorce is largely a matter of attempting to reduce his burden of inner guilt. In some way he must provide proof that he was not guilty, that he did not ask to be kicked around. It was *her* fault, he pleads unconsciously; if *she* had been kind and loving, the marriage would have been a success. If *she* had been like—; the name of the divorcee with children then becomes part of the unconscious argument. The divorcee's kind and loving way with her children is a revealing point; undoubtedly she is the woman he has always claimed to be looking for. This inner defense appears in consciousness as love.

The second factor is also unconscious. The man identifies with the divorcee's children. Aside from the naïveté which he claims was responsible for his unhappy marriage, the man of this mildly neurotic type is influenced, in his original choice of a wife, by a distorted and repressed infantile image which can be traced back to earliest childhood. It was in the nursery that he became an unconscious glutton for punishment. Since every unconscious wish that is disapproved of by the tyrannical inner conscience must be consciously disclaimed in the process of constructing a defense, the man is consciously aware only of his wish to be loved—the exact opposite of (and therefore an alibi for) the wish to suffer. This conscious wish to be loved is his defense against the accusation that he unconsciously prefers to be miserable. To fit this defense, he revamps his own infantile setting and fantasies himself as the divorcee's cherished child.

Third, a good deal of inner guilt connected with his own children is included in his approval of the divorcee's family. Whether he admits it or not, his own children are lost to him. Seeing them once a week, or for a few weeks during their summer vacation, cannot alter the bitter fact that they will at all times be influenced mainly by the person with whom they make their permanent home. That person, of course, is his ex-wife. To assuage this guilt the man performs a shift: he accepts the divorcee's children, often with genuine feeling.

Sometimes the divorcee's suitors include a man who loves children but has avoided becoming a father for reasons that have nothing to do with financial responsibility or other practical considerations. Such men, too, belong to a recognizable type; this becomes clear when their rationalizations have been punctured. Often the real reason has its roots in an unsolved infantile conflict. Instead of the normal solution to the Oedipal rivalry, the man of this type emerges from the conflict with a peculiar aftereffect: the fear of begetting a child. Denying himself this privilege is the man's unconscious method of proving to his inner tyrant that he has really relinquished the ambitions of the Oedipal period and become "a good boy." In later life he attaches himself to widows or divorcees who already have children. He thus becomes a part of a family situation when it is an accomplished fact, and in this way bypasses his inner fears.

This unconscious fear, too, works out to the advantage of the divorcee with children.

It would of course be wrong to assume that all men who emotionally approve of children from their wives' previous marriages are impelled by the mildly neurotic reasons of men in search of a loving woman and men afraid to have children of their own. There are other reasons, reflecting deeply neurotic conflicts, which also promote this attitude of approval. I applaud the caution of an ever increasing number of divorcees who approach psychiatrists asking for "premarital repair jobs" on their prospective husbands.

CHAPTER 7

WHEN THE CHILD GOES WRONG

NEWS that a child—or an adolescent or post-adolescent —is in trouble evokes a single, cut-and-dried response from the environment: "The parents are to blame." And the parents accept the blame, feel guilt, reproach themselves, and each other.

These self-accusations are senseless. The parents could just as reasonably blame themselves for the Second World War.

A child who has "gone wrong" may be involved in any one of a long list of difficulties. He or she might be:

a. Failing in school work, a truant, suffering from pseudo-mental deficiency
b. A liar or petty thief
c. A juvenile delinquent
d. Involved in an illicit pregnancy
e. A homosexual
f. A dope addict
g. Exhibiting impostor-like traits
h. Involved in crime

All these diversified masochistic ways of solving conflicts (each specific subdivision showing its individual characteristics) are beyond the reach of parental influence.

A survey of the psychological backgrounds of these techniques shows where parental influence ends and why it cannot be expected to prevail.

In the following pages, five of these traits will be singled out for detailed discussion.

I. PSEUDO-MENTAL DEFICIENCY

Psychoanalytic literature includes a long series of investigations of partial inhibition of the intellect. Most of these studies pertain to the difficulties children have in reading, learning and remembering. In them, authorities since Freud have pointed out the connection between inner conflicts and external attitudes. Here is a simple example of such a connection: An unconscious association is suggested by the approved study of geographical location of cities and the unauthorized study of the sexual "geography" of the body. An unconscious taboo becomes operative on the harmless knowledge, and the consequent result is that the child's school work suffers. This banal common cause and effect has been generally recognized.

When the unconscious taboo is not limited, however, and the end effect is to present a picture of wholesale stupidity so marked that it appears as mental deficiency, both parent and analyst face a situation which still remains comparatively unexplored.

More than thirty years ago I successfully treated a patient suffering from pseudo-mental deficiency, and from this and succeeding similar clinical experiences derived the knowledge which enabled me to outline the theoretical explanation and therapeutic accessibility of this previously unacknowledged disease.

A "pseudo-imbecile" is a person who to all intents and purposes is a moron. The use of the word "pseudo" does not refer to a conscious mask of stupidity but to the fact that there is no organic reason for the appearance of imbecility, and to the curability of the disease when psychoanalytically treated.

The pseudo-imbecile, untreated, is capable at best of primitive and mechanical work, which he performs in a robot-like manner. He can never support himself or become independent in any way. In addition, he is often subject to outbursts of aggression. On these occasions he is really dangerous.

The young man of twenty-three who supplied me with my first insight into the disease of pseudo-imbecility came to me in Vienna in 1930.* I was not his first analyst; he had spent several

* Described in "The Problem of Pseudo-Mental Deficiency," *Internationale Zeitschrift fuer Psychoanalyse,* 18:528-538, 1932.

months in treatment with a female colleague. He had requested treatment for a peculiar reason: he wanted prostitutes to urinate at him, but lacked the courage to make his wishes known. Analysis, he believed, could instil that courage in him. The first analyst he consulted made no attempt to handle the problem but passed him on promptly to another. His second analyst treated him as a typical Oedipal case. When she had to interrupt treatment for a few weeks (she was in the last stages of pregnancy) the patient quickly became unmanageable. Jealousy now made its appearance; the patient called the analyst's child "Mr. Baby" and became unbecomingly familiar in his attitude towards the analyst. More important, his mother reported that he had become "a raving maniac" at home. This was when I was called in to take over the situation.

In our initial interview the patient at first appeared to be quite rational. He readily admitted that his transference to the female analyst had become too much for him. After this hopeful beginning he trembled, sweated, and began to shout: "Don't understand! Don't understand!" There was nothing to understand, since I had not even opened my mouth. This state of affairs continued for three appointments.

At this inauspicious point I had an "intuitive" idea, the meaning of which I could not explain. I felt that the thing to do was to disregard the patient's shouts of "Don't understand," and talk to him—for weeks and weeks, if necessary. This was the program that I followed. I recited hundreds of simplified examples of fear from analyses of other patients. The man would listen quietly, but if I stopped for a moment he would fill the silence with his familiar shout: "Don't understand!"

One day I used an example from an analysis in which a patient had misunderstood the word "resistance." That patient happened to be an individual with a very low I.Q. When I told him, "You are under the influence of your resistance," he replied: "You are quite right, one should have a good resistance." He knew of resistance only when it fought against infection.

This story broke the ice. Instead of his usual battle cry, the patient said: "What a dope! He must have known what resistance in analysis means."

This was the end of the "don't understand" period. What had happened, unconsciously, was that my generous "giving" of words had made it impossible for him to maintain his identification of the analyst with the "bad" mother who refuses. That identification, with its masochistic overtones, called for a show of aggression that would testify to his alleged wish to get and not to be refused. My giving attitude enabled him to substitute a new defense: "That's what I want—kindness and generosity." This new defense made analysis possible.

The patient had deeply disappointed his parents; he was not consciously aware that he had provoked their rejection. His aggressive mother had dreamed of an "intellectual career" for him, but she knew when he was still very young that this ambition was futile. In the first grade he was expelled from school for masturbating in class. He was then sent to a small boarding school, where he remained until he was eleven. There he continued the pattern of provocation and stupidity that had become evident in his first year at school. He could not grasp anything new or remember anything old. He felt "rejected" by his parents and his environment.

His entire life appeared to be concentrated on defensive "getting," and doing so on the level of an infant. He was a voracious eater, drinker, and smoker. He was always sucking on something. His conscious motto was "the important thing is the juice." This motto prevailed in his sexual habits as well. The desire which brought him into analysis—the wish to be urinated on by a woman—stemmed from the same source.

His relationship with his mother proved that these wishes were not to be accepted at face value. He constantly provoked her refusal and masochistically exploited every rejection. At the same time he overflowed with pseudo-aggression against her. Although he acted as manager of the family business after his father's death, the job was beyond him. He would give orders that impeded reasonable management, wasted money, and decreased productivity. This pseudo-aggressive defense took some curious forms. On one occasion, when he had to prepare an income tax report for the family bakery, he exaggerated production figures so that his mother "would have to pay."

There were many interlocked unconscious reasons for his pseudo-imbecility. The decisive cause, however, had to do with his identification of intake of food with intake of knowledge. When he refused to take in knowledge, he was pseudo-aggressively dramatizing one of his denials of masochism: "I don't want to be refused; I refuse." This was a way of achieving masochistic pleasure while denying any wish for it; it was not exactly pleasant to be universally known as a moron. His stupidity had still another purpose. It allegedly proved that his mother had "starved" him. This alibi even penetrated into consciousness in the form of a fear: he suspected his mother intended to eject him from the family business, throwing him to the dogs and leaving him to starve!

It was amazing to see the patient change in analysis. The "moron" became director of a foreign bakery, after having been called in as a specialist in the delicacies featured by the family business.

In a series of similar cases I found the basis of the disease to be, again, masochistic attachment to the image of the mother of earliest infancy. The disease is curable.

Less radical inhibitions of intellect have usually been explained in terms of a single theme: the effect on the child of losing his parents' love or of being unable to achieve their love. This means that the child is left without any person "for whom" he wants to become a good pupil or acquire knowledge.

The entire deduction seems spurious to me.

First, the parents' reaction usually grows out of the child's own masochistically designed provocations. When the parents look forward to a bright future for the child, a future which will make up for their own insufficiencies, they cannot help being profoundly disappointed when the child sacrifices his intellectual powers to the demands of an unsolved infantile conflict. The parents are his ostensible enemy in his rejection of intellectual ability; behind this show of pseudo-aggression is the eternal aim of self-damage.

Second, there is the insistent question: why will one child take an unfavorable situation in his stride and overcome it, while another will not? One can take as an example the not infrequent case of the neurotic parent who can never be satisfied ("B-plus is not good enough for a Zimmerman," as the *New Yorker* cartoon had it) because he is unconsciously using his child to repeat his own unsolved infantile conflict and to work towards his own unfulfilled ambitions. Here again, one must remember that neurosis never uses a photostatic copy of the environment; the child's own inner elaborations of his external circumstances are decisive.

Third, it is a clinically observable fact that children often react to a crisis or a tragedy such as the loss of a parent, a household disrupted by divorce, the birth of a preferred brother or sister, by retreating to the refuge of books. Disappointment can stimulate as often as it impedes the acquisition of knowledge. It all depends on what the child chooses as a defense against his unconscious use of the crisis for masochistic pleasure. One of the standard defenses denies the wish for refusal and rejection by proving that the real wish is "to get." In the language of the unconscious, the "taking in" of knowledge is equated with the absorption of milk and the reception of love and attention. The child thus can prove that he "wants to get" by eagerly absorbing knowledge from books. The specialized knowledge of many scholars has rested on exactly this basis.

My fourth reason derives from another clinical observation. The child will often "forget" and blot out whole sectors of usable knowledge because he believes his parents do not wish him to know these facts. This is a typical occurrence in *happy* homes. I have analyzed a series of professional people with similar (middle-class) backgrounds. These were families determined to keep up appearances despite modest incomes, and the climate of these households disparaged the "dirty money-grubbing" of competitors. The child would accept this surface attitude literally and build it into his scale of values, naturally overlooking the element of envy hidden behind the parental statements. Later in life he might be considered financially "stupid."

Fifth, though the influence of external factors in activating an inner conflict cannot be denied, this actually casts a doubt on the theory of a direct and inevitable connection between the home situation and the child's unconscious rejection of intellectual pursuits. When masochism is a large part of the child's problem, the effect of external factors is particularly marked.

A successful business man in his early thirties proudly told me during analysis, "Nobody can call *me* an intellectual." This man read no books, saw no plays. He read a tabloid every day, which meant that he read the comics, sports page, and the headlines. "Is that the exact order?" I asked him. His answer was a grin.

In the first three grades of elementary school he had been first in his class and the "teacher's pet." The other children teased him about this and he decided to put an end to his prominence. He stopped learning, deliberately answered questions incorrectly, and put up a convincing show of general ignorance. Later on he found it impossible to stay awake in school and slept through nearly all classes.

Clearly, he had sacrificed scholarship in the interest of a double inner conflict. The theoretically enviable position of teacher's pet endangered the masochistic inner fantasy that "everybody was mean to him"; to safeguard the fantasy he had to be rejected by the teacher, and therefore provoked her deliberately until she did reject him. Having solved this part of his conflict, he had to set up a defense. The defense consisted of a display of aggression: he refused to learn, refused to admit that he knew his lessons.

The entire technique was of course self-damaging; his intellectuality, one could say, died of deliberate starvation. But this was merely incidental; intellectuality was the innocent bystander killed in a feud between two inner giants. Aside from the man's mental void, he gave the impression of being quick, cunning, and sly. His evident success in business confirmed this impression.

II. JUVENILE DELINQUENCY

Juvenile delinquency is a catch-all term applied to any action in conflict with the legal code, when the offender is below a certain age.

In *Our Troubled Youth* by Frederick Mayer,* the author gives the following list of the characteristics of the delinquent:

(1) he admires physical strength
(2) he yearns for material satisfaction
(3) he hates to be alone
(4) he despises the squealer
(5) he loves freedom, yet he escapes from it
(6) he despises authority
(7) he looks upon sex in sensate terms
(8) he regards work as an activity fit for squares
(9) most of the time he daydreams about impossible schemes
(10) he needs new thrills and adventures all the time
(11) he feels that the world is conspiring against him; "no one understands him"
(12) he enjoys annoying adults
(13) he looks upon life as a jungle
(14) he is governed by impulse

This book is typical of current studies on this subject; in all of them the decisive role is assigned to the cult of aggression and the execution of aggressive aims. Nothing is further from the inner truth. These sick adolescents are overdimensional psychic masochists who use pseudo-aggression as their typical defense. (Despite the violence that is often an accompaniment to their actions, the use of the prefix "pseudo" is justified: these actions must always be self-damaging because self-damage is their inner aim.)

It is ironical that in this age of psychological sophistication no one has translated the juvenile delinquent's tragic confession, "*I* killed the guy," into the language of his unconscious, which

* *Public Affairs Press,* Washington, D.C., 1959.

explains the purpose of his action. In inner reality his confession means: "I just bargained for the electric chair or a life sentence."

Authorities on juvenile delinquency often point out that all felonies and misdemeanors committed by adolescents have one characteristic in common—"the sadistic hatred of authority," a hatred, presumably, that knits them together in gangs. But they do not reach the crux of the matter, which is the question: Is this "hatred" real, or does it cover a more deeply repressed emotion?

The phenomenon of the gang is one item of evidence pointing to the defensive nature of the delinquent's actions. In submitting to the dictatorial gang leader, the delinquent is passive and not aggressive. Since this is the case, we cannot take his rationalizations at face value. The "defenders of the gang" are only defenders of their own inner defenses.

In analyzing delinquents one finds that these boys and girls are indeed filled with a feeling of savage indignation. They are convinced life has cheated them. Life is unjust—some people have everything, some nothing. Some people have fun; others only misery. These boys and girls want the injustice corrected and they believe that they are doing so in their gang activities.

What they mean when they complain about the injustice of life is, of course, the injustice inflicted by their parents. The complaints deal with externals, and actually amount to routine injustice collecting, with the parental figures supreme but in the background. Their unconscious masochistic submission to the first of all authorities is what they are trying to ward off with every act of violence—in other words, with every show of pseudo-aggression. Underneath the defiant surface of delinquent adolescents lurks the masochistic complainer, the self-pitying "victim" of someone's "cruelty."

It is not by chance that juvenile delinquency becomes a weighty problem during the advent of puberty. There are two reasons for this: one arises from the newly activated inner secretory glands. In boys, this results in a push of activity, both sexual and asexual. In girls, puberty normally produces the opposite effect. This is the time when the "tomboy" generally becomes the ex-tomboy, falling under the feminizing influence of the physiological "passivity and receptivity push."

The second reason is not biological. It is at puberty that the individual's specific solution of his infantile conflict is finally tested. When the psychic ledger shows a superabundance of psychic masochism, the physiologically induced "push" of puberty is pressed into service as a defense against masochism. In the boy, activity becomes highly aggressive. He attacks "adult values" both within and outside the bounds of parental and legal toleration. In the masochistic girl, the process is somewhat different. The normal passivity of puberty is mistaken for masochistic passivity, and the usual pseudo-aggressive defense is constructed to withstand it. Violence and "revolt" are also the delinquent girl's response.

Strictly descriptive discoveries in juvenile delinquency tend to bypass psychological and unconscious factors, except for a purely conventional consent to the importance of a stable home life that offers the child love and security. Emphasis falls mainly on three points in addition to the influence of the parents: on slum surroundings, on the general insecurity of world conditions leading to a widespread breakdown of morality, and finally on the phenomenon of "the gang."

The fact is that a good deal of blame-shifting must always be involved in singling out any individual factor. At the same time, no one can deny that in some way each of these conditions has an influence on juvenile delinquency. The missing ingredient here is specifically the psychological viewpoint.

Regarding slums, there is no doubt that sordid conditions can contribute to the child's feeling that he has been neglected. Objectively viewed, of course, a child who lives in the slums has not been deliberately placed there by his malicious parents. Here again, the masochistic propensity for misusing reality is decisive. Some children unconsciously blame their parents; others are aroused to ambition by the identical conditions and work with determination for future improvement.

That the slums alone do not create delinquency has been definitely established by the findings of the Senate Subcommittee on Juvenile Delinquency. This report made it clear that delinquency is not only a condition of underprivilege; a detailed description of widespread delinquency among adolescents in Oklahoma City, for example, dealt almost exclusively with the children of prosperous and prominent families.

As to the general breakdown of morality as an explanation of juvenile delinquency, this seems to be a "last resort" form of reasoning, brought forward only when other specific causes cannot be found easily.

The gang system may be responsible for many delinquent actions, although here, too, the end result is studied almost to the exclusion of the original impulse. Some authorities claim that in the criminal gang the unruly adolescent who sneers at all rules finds a code with which he can identify and which he can adhere to enthusiastically. This deduction does not explain why these youngsters sneer at established rules.

The truth is that such adolescents all have a masochistic aim to pursue. Their actions are designed to deny masochistic passivity and to dramatize their artificial defense of aggression. Knowing (unconsciously) that their criminal activities will be discovered and punished, they are only too ready to submit to the strict criminal code of the gang. This phenomenon of willing submission has its parallel in the criminal-ideological gangs that arise in extremist political parties. In these politically oriented gangs, people who pseudo-aggressively rebelled against the existing governmental order passively and masochistically submit themselves to the rule of the revolutionary "party leader."

This leaves us, again, with one alleged culprit: the parent. It would be absurd to minimize the parent's role in bringing up and influencing either a juvenile delinquent or a normally promising, well-adjusted child. Although the parent is the key—it does not mean that he can unlock all doors. A large part of the error that sends these investigations of juvenile problems off on a tangent comes from the tendency to judge a group in terms of its resemblances rather than its differences and to ignore the possibility that external similarities may stem from widely different unconscious elaborations. Psychoanalytic investigations, probing individual conflicts in terms of specific, unconscious details, have proved that in dealing with the human being no formula—no matter how intelligently contrived—can guarantee results, nor even foresee them with dependable accuracy. It is this element of individuality in the child that limits the parents' effectiveness and therefore must limit their guilt as well.

III. HOMOSEXUALITY

This subject has already been touched on in Chapter 5, where a short outline of the unconscious reasons for homosexuality introduced several case histories.

What about the adolescent or young adult homosexual?

A distinction must be made between the experimental homosexuality of the early teens, before unconscious patterns and unconscious solutions have become fixed, and homosexual fantasies and activities taking place well after puberty.

When the boy is emerging into the first stages of puberty he must contend with the unconscious revival of the inner conflicts of early childhood. This revival is marked by an excess of passivity and guilt. The awakening sex drive, because it is active, serves as a defense against these guilt feelings. At the same time there are sexual taboos to be considered. In this particular stage the strongest of these taboos bars contacts with girls. Touching another boy, curiously, is the weakest taboo and is less guilt-laden than masturbation. In a boy with pronounced inner conflicts, who needs to call upon his biological drive as a defense against inner passivity and masochism, the result will be "homosexual" experimentation. Later on, with comparative maturity, the unconscious sexual code changes. The most stringent taboo then becomes the ban on contacts with other boys, the least stringent the ban on contacts with girls. Contacts with other boys cannot be classed as truly homosexual acts unless they take place after the revision of the boy's unconscious list of sexual taboos.

The popular—not the scientific—interpretations of homosexuality are evenly split between the theory that homosexuality arises from an inborn proclivity (the "third sex" idea), and the assumption that it results from a childhood deprived of a strong father figure to identify with. These theories persist in the face of scientific studies that have repeatedly disproved them.

If homosexuality were a biological endowment, it could not be cured by psychoanalytic treatment. The high percentage of cures achieved in my own analyses of homosexuals, and in cases referred to colleagues, proves without a doubt that homosexuality is a neurotic disease, and as such often accessible to psychiatric help.

As for the other widespread notion, which shifts all responsibility upon the parents, the true facts show that the parents' role cannot be decisive in homosexuality any more than it can be in any other disease rooted in unconscious attitudes.

To recapitulate: The homosexual is a psychic masochist—plus. He is an individual who has found a neurotic solution—the pleasure-in-displeasure pattern—for the inner conflicts that beset every child and has added a specific elaboration—homosexuality—to this neurotic pattern.

The potential homosexual's essential problems are no different from those of any other child, but two exaggerations of the universal troublemakers are typical. The homosexual's inner fears (the "septet of baby fears," in which the mother is the dreaded enemy) are more overpowering than those of other neurotics and his masochistic elaboration of them is more extensive.

Ordinarily the boy counteracts his passive dependence on his mother by discovering that he too possesses a magical and powerful apparatus which, like the mother's breast, "produces" fluid. Identifying breast and penis, he sees himself as independent of his mother. In the homosexual, however, fear and passivity are too great for the identification to serve as more than a partial reassurance. What he needs is a reinforcement of his defense, and he looks for it in the penis of his homosexual partner. This is the unconscious basis for sexual pursuit of other men.

The homosexual is a man *unconsciously* eager for mistreatment at a woman's hands, consciously unaware of this deeply buried desire. Still unconsciously, he fears this wish but clings to it and instead of relinquishing it gives up its object, woman. His external defense against this wish consists of the claim that he has turned to men instead of women to find peace, quiet, love, understanding, and safety. The external defense does not alter the compelling inner need to be mistreated. In his relationships with men, therefore, he will inevitably discover that he is being mistreated, misunderstood, unjustly and cruelly treated, and rejected. These wrongs he will enjoy masochistically—though unconsciously. And, since his sex glands have remained unaffected throughout the emotional turmoil, secondarily he elevates his antidote against the feared sex to the status of a sexual attraction. Men will become his sexual objects and his providers of masochistic satisfaction.

Instead of blaming themselves for not having "corrected" or influenced attitudes that are too deeply buried for external influence or correction, the parents of the young homosexual should realize that something constructive can be done for him. The younger he is the more accessible he will be to psychiatric help. Neurosis, whatever its form, increases and becomes more formidable with age. Psychiatric help should be sought for the young homosexual, provided he *inwardly* wishes to change.

IV. IMPOSTORS

This is a term little used in ordinary speech, but the traits which it implies are by no means rare. The impostor is a person who pretends to a social or professional standing higher than his own and uses his assumed identity to provide himself with illegal, or at best irregular, profits. Usually his weapons are charm, a gift for ironic humor, and superb acting talent. He plays his chosen role with great skill and charm.

The impostor also has an ironic scorn of the people who believe his lies. At the same time he does not inwardly enjoy his successful hoax. His apparent optimism covers a prevailing depression, and he has a tendency to bow out of a successful situation while he is still riding high. Boredom, it appears, overtakes him. He concludes his success by disappearing from the scene, allegedly to prevent exposure. He is cynical about his victims. "So what?" is his substitute for remorse. He does not believe in work except to set the stage for the impression he wants to create. He feels superior to people who work for a living. His yardstick is the moment only; he has so little sense of timing that he continues to play his part often after he has been exposed and could gain nothing by maintaining the pretense. He is a chronic lawbreaker, but his crimes are invariably minor: he does not murder, rape, steal state secrets, or even embezzle on an ambitious scale.

Finally, the impostor is incorrigible. Exposed, punished, and eventually released to a new environment, he embarks on precisely the same campaign of fraud that has served him before.

Part of the explanation for this pattern of behavior is to be found in the mechanism of criminosis, which explains the psychological background of all chronic criminals, whatever their specialty. (Criminosis will be discussed at some length in the next section of this chapter.) The impostor adds to this mechanism the specific features of his own group.

One of these features deals with the innate and overabundant narcissism of these people. As young children they believed firmly in their gift of magical omnipotence so that the inevitable disappointments of childhood left irreparable wounds. As adults they respond to the unconscious necessity to prove their "superiority" and do so by courting and achieving love and admiration. But masochism enters the picture almost at once, counteracting the face-saving device which led them to seek approval. Consequently, the impostor provokes rejection from exactly the people who admire him.

These admirers are unconsciously identified with the original enemy, the mother of the earliest period of childhood. The impostor's provocations are a form of pseudo-aggressive revenge. In effect, he is saying: "I wanted to prove that I could get your love if I wanted it—but I don't want it."

Throughout this unconscious drama runs an element of guilt, discernible in the depression which always underlies the impostor's easy, optimistic surface. This guilt pertains to the masochistic need to reduce the mother substitute to absurdity as a giving person and to enjoy her refusal unconsciously.

The impostor defends himself against his psychic masochism by assuming a variety of devil-may-care poses: he cynically attacks the standards of his environment and appears to be impervious to reproaches either from the environment or from his own conscience. These are futile defenses; the wounded self-esteem that he attempts to negate with his humorously cynical remarks makes itself evident in his depression, and the masochistic aim he attempts to deny by assuming his other poses comes to the fore each time he invites the environment to expose the emptiness and falsity of his pretensions.

Why does the impostor choose to cheat people of money instead of using his dubious talent to gain power, influence, or other advantages? Part of the reason comes from his continued use of an old, childish irony as an unconscious reproach addressed to his mother: "You don't love me; you only love money." In retaliation for this alleged rejection he takes the money "that is loved" away from the mother substitute.

In addition, the impostor has chosen money as his medium because he can in this way be certain his offenses will neither be forgiven nor overlooked. Of all offenses on this level, those involving money arouse the greatest moral odium and the most intense resentment. Cheating a person financially is certain to make him your irreconcilable enemy. Even a psychic masochist, bent on humiliation and defeat, puts up a show of righteous indignation and justifiable aggression on these occasions. He clamors for the sheriff before going home to nurse his wounds in secret inner satisfaction. The impostor guarantees himself both moral odium and realistic punishment when he chooses money as the ostensible objective of his trickery.

It is not easy to effect psychiatric cure of these psychopathic people. They never enter analysis of their own volition. If they consult an analyst at all, they do so under pressure from their desperate families. Often their relatives have paid to keep the impostor "out of real trouble," cashing the checks he has forged and the money he has in other illicit ways managed to extort.

Theoretically, it is possible to mobilize the impostor's unconscious guilt feelings and utilize them for therapeutic purposes. Practically speaking, however, the chances are not good. The impostor tends to fend off therapy with a solid barrier of stoicism, cynicism or hypocrisy. However, if he has entered analysis because of some other neurotic symptom, an entering wedge is provided and his impostor-like trends respond to analysis of the entire personality. The patient does his best to keep it out of the picture, of course, protesting against "dragging in things that are nobody's business but my own."

The impostor almost invariably combines this psychopathic tendency with other neurotic traits, such as gambling, alcoholism, kleptomania, drug addiction, homosexuality. He is generally unstable, like all psychopaths. As a result, he tends to treat analysis as a joke and may even run away as soon as he catches a glimpse of the seriousness of the situation. A kleptomaniac patient once said to me: "Yesterday I understood for the first time what you are really after. You want to turn me into a good citizen. There is no fun in that. Goodbye!"

After repeated experiences with impostors, I now begin their treatment by tracing the various unconscious steps of their pattern of proving that they achieve love only so that they can disprove their psychic masochism. I then point out the absurdity of using this means of re-establishing self-esteem. This technique makes it possible to keep the patient in analysis, at least for a time. Furious and ironic objections appear, of course, but the procedure touches the patient at his single vulnerable point: the fear of appearing ridiculous. The idealized self-portrait of the impostor does not allow him to appear as a clown. In a series of cases in which I have used this approach patients have been helped, a few even to a degree which virtually justifies the use of the word "cure."

The impostor is an example of what a patient ironically and consolingly called "the pre-determined neurotic." His problem began with his biological endowment of megalomania, the illusion of omnipotence that was his only reality in earliest childhood. This was so overabundant that he could never surmount the natural and necessary disappointments that accompany the maturing process, so insatiable that no amount of love and approval could be considered "enough."

The impostor exists in loving families and in neglectful ones, in "privileged" and "underprivileged" environments.

V. CRIMINOSIS

The adolescent in collision with the law is perhaps the least understood, as he is logically the most publicized of all juvenile delinquents. Who is to blame, how is the criminal to be punished, how is the crime rate to be kept down—these are questions hotly debated and too often contradictorily resolved.

Much of the debate concerns the matter of punishment as a deterrent; it applies to adult criminals as well, but is more often broached in discussing the problem of the young criminal. The conviction of many psychiatrists that punishment is not a successful deterrent is often assumed to mean that psychiatry denies the right of society to protect itself and its law-abiding citizens against those who refuse to accept its laws. No one suggests that the criminal be left to his own devices or that his infractions be condoned. But many psychiatrists see no need to cling to unsuccessful formulae because they are time-honored. Scientific progress can make its contribution to this field, too.

Punishment has always been an unsatisfactory solution to the problem of the criminal because the criminal unconsciously *wants* to be punished: the prospect of arrest and punishment constitutes an alluring rather than a sobering factor. One should add that this is true only in inner reality; consciously, the criminal wants to escape the legal consequences of his act.

To the unconscious factors responsible for criminosis one must of course add sociological factors; these cannot be dismissed. But the important question is this: Which set of factors has priority? Some criminals turn the social factor into a convenient cover, unwittingly using it to disguise hidden unconscious motives or to provide opportunities for repetition of undigested injustices, real or fantasied, dating from childhood. To keep

these injustices alive after childhood, neurotics shift them to society or the social order in general. Unconsciously, the fantasy of
the parents as culprits remains unchanged. This type of rationalization is highly successful; perhaps its very banality makes it
convincing. But it cannot be the real unconscious reason for
the criminal's attitude; if it were, he could not be consciously
aware of it. Only defenses against genuine unconscious wishes
can emerge upon the psychic surface.

The science of criminology has gone through many phases.
Social, economic, biological explanations have been offered as
solutions to the riddle of criminal addiction, but it was not until
the advent of modern psychiatry, based on Freud's discovery of
the dynamic unconscious, that any explanation produced a practical solution. With knowledge of the unconscious finally available, it became possible to study the deeply hidden origins and
the true characteristics of criminosis.

In my opinion, we can accept the assumption that the key to
the criminotic is to be found in his failure to overcome the first
and most important disappointment of his life, the discovery that
his belief in his own omnipotence is only an illusion and that he
is in reality a helpless dependent. Throughout life he is haunted
by the bitter conviction that he is too weak to prevail against the
"ruler" of the nursery. During the Oedipal period, like every
child, he attempts to overcome the masochistic passivity built up
during the pre-Oedipal stage by borrowing strength from the
father and assigning to his mother his own passive role. But the
attempt does not succeed, and in inner reality he remains a passive baby throughout his life. In his unconscious scale of values
nothing that he can do (and this includes the most violent of
revengeful actions) impresses the formidable "cruel" mother.
When he performs his criminal actions he is trying to force her
to admit that he too has power. Like a dwarf trying to impress
a giant, he makes up for his alleged ineffectuality as a person by
resorting to the most powerful of weapons. Dwarf plus dynamite,
he reasons, makes a combination even the giant cannot ignore.

The desperate measure is of course self-damaging. To abandon the comparison, the criminal's "dynamite charge" consists

of his crime, and the legal penalty for it may be the extreme one. This is of little *unconscious* importance to him. What is important is the need to force an acknowledgment of his anger and his power and the more deeply buried need to satisfy the masochistic appetite that is a part of his entire pattern of unconscious dependence and passivity.

The criminotic must always balance external violence against his concealed masochistic helplessness. The real target of this compensatory violence is his mother. Society, which is his victim, is only her substitute.

Here is the core of the criminotic's unconscious conflict, but it explains only the constant factor in the criminal action, the "motor act." In addition to the constant factor, which accounts for the criminal attitude on the whole, there is a variable factor covering the unconscious contents of the specific criminal act.

The motives that thrust the criminal forward into his specific crime are as diversified as any other unconscious motivations. They can be partially explained, like any other aspect of human behavior, by searching for the unconscious wishes, defense mechanisms, projections, identifications, attempts to atone for unconscious guilt feelings that color and direct all human aims. What these mechanisms fail to explain is the added twist that enables the individual to go beyond the motive and undertake the criminal action. What, in the unconscious, makes possible the motor act?

The answer is pseudo-aggression, the defensive elaboration of the most primitive of all human trends. But the criminal's pseudo-aggression, which differs in every way from normal aggression, is not a rubber-stamp copy of the typical neurotic's show of violence. It does have the same secret purpose, masochistic self-damage; it successfully achieves this purpose, since all illegal acts are punishable acts. The greater seriousness of the self-damage that is the aftermath of crime, however, makes for a difference in quality as well as degree. There is a wide gulf between the personal, consciously experienced unhappiness that follows neurotic provocations and the jail sentence or legal execution that the criminal unconsciously bargains for. Moreover, criminotic aggression involves social ostracism, while neurotic aggression does not.

Exhibitionism is another element that appears in criminotic aggression and is absent from the neurotic's behavior. Most criminals unconsciously cooperate with the police, leaving a little trail of "inadvertent" evidence that eventually traps them. Here is a case where a familiar truism—"There are no perfect crimes"—makes sound psychological sense. The criminal, without knowing it, deliberately betrays himself by making "one little mistake." He does so partly because of inner guilt but also because he is using his crime to prove to his mother (and to her substitute, society) that he is strong enough to take his revenge for the wrongs done him. His crime must therefore become known to society.

Criminotic aggression shows persistent traces of the infantile illusion of omnipotence; this accounts for the criminal's conviction that he will "get away with" his job of larceny, forgery, arson, fraud, or even murder. His faith in his own magical power combines with his unconscious desire for punishment to prevent him from perfecting his plan of escape or concealment. This is why, when he arranges for a camouflage, he leaves one corner exposed to provide the authorities with the clue they need.

Inwardly the criminal accepts the fact that he will inevitably pay for his crime. Inner acceptance explains his apparent failure to feel remorse or guilt. He is neither remorseless nor guiltless; his inner tyrant mercilessly reproaches him for every infraction. But the inner tyrant in this case, as in all neurotics, is corrupt and will accept bribes. The criminotic's bribe is the punishment meted out to him for his crime.

What can be done, in childhood, to prevent the formation of the criminotic's unconscious pattern?

Many people believe that criminals are formed because in childhood they were exposed to "bad influences." If good advice had been substituted for evil example, they reason, the results would have been different. This theory stresses consciously performed imitation.

Unhappily, results cannot be guaranteed even when parents

provide a set of exemplary rules for the child and surround him with excellent examples. Some children accept the implied invitation and identify with their environment. Some do not. Some children, exposed to "bad influences," remain unimpressed and uninfluenced; others, exposed to the identical situations, succumb.

One must ask why the "bad example" has such devastating effects in one case and not in another; why some people should accept and profit by good advice while others remain impervious to it; why some people, without the benefit of ethical teaching, seem to do the right thing "instinctively." All these contradictions demonstrate, again, that the formula is not what counts. How the child reacts to external influence depends on his specific inner problems.

It is clinically observable that the example, in itself, does not have the slightest influence on the psychic apparatus. But if the child's unconscious situation calls for an unconscious identification, the environment is scanned for a hitching-post and the good example (or the bad) is "followed." Only under these conditions does the example have any effect. People who have not been psychologically trained see this unconscious identification as an "imitation." It is not an accurate description.

When an unconscious identification occurs, the identifier takes over someone else's opinions or repeats his actions without consciously realizing that he is doing so. The pupil who copies his teacher's gestures, uses his tones of voice, or parrots his opinions acquires these traits by means of unconscious identification. If his attention is called to what he is doing, he will indignantly deny that there is any resemblance between the teacher's mannerisms and his own. This denial will be sincere; consciously, he has not been imitating. The identification took place behind the scenes of his personality, in the deep recesses of the unconscious mind.

A person setting a good or bad example unknowingly offers himself as a model for identification. Here is an example that will clarify the process:

A patient had been orphaned at the age of two. His parents left him destitute, and he was raised by a wealthy uncle and aunt, who had a son of the same age. Both children were extremely fond of the patient's aunt but feared the uncle, a rigid and cold individual addicted to preaching. The patient was five years old when he came under the bad influence (as the family saw it) of a male servant, imitating this man's thefts and swindles. Clearly, there was a strong identification with him.

In analysis the steps that led to the identification were clarified. The boy had been strongly attached to his aunt; he had been frightened out of this Oedipal attachment in the usual way by the potential threat of his much feared uncle. While still hating his uncle and resenting him as a competitor, he unconsciously identified with his aunt (a kind and submissive person) in the hope that his uncle would love him as his aunt was loved (negative Oedipus). As an adult he could remember how people had teased him, at that time, for his shyness and "girlishness."

A few months later his behavior changed once more. He began to provoke both uncle and aunt, broke the household rules and became generally delinquent on the small scale suited to his age. The family explained this change by attributing it to the servant's influence; they attempted to correct it by dismissing the servant. But the boy continued to cheat and steal until late in life.

In his case the patient was exposed to good example (his highly moral uncle) and bad example (the thieving servant). Why should he have chosen to identify himself with the bad example? In theory, both possibilities for identification were present at the same time. The child's choice can only be explained in terms of his inner needs. If he had taken the path toward normality, he would have relinquished his futile campaign to displace his uncle and would have identified himself with him instead, thus accepting the taboo on his incestuous wishes. But the boy identified with his aunt, which meant that he accepted the threatened punishment (castration) while relinquishing the wish that prompted the threat. A strong inner feeling of guilt counteracted this identification, however. He had to find some means of denying the passivity accepted during this period (a continuation of masochistic passivity stemming from the pre-Oedipal stage), and did so by finding a new object for identification: the pseudo-aggressive servant. However, he managed to smuggle his passivity into the defense against it, for his thieving and swindling involved him in more serious conflicts.

One of the tempting factors involved in "bad advice" and "bad examples" consists of the use to which these external authorities can be put in the inner battle of the conscience. If the inner tyrant can be confronted with proof that "the authorities" are no more innocent than the individual under attack, a decided point has been won. The inner tyrant is bound by the precepts of the upbringers, whether these precepts are good or bad. If a "bad example" is conveniently at hand during the situation of inner conflict, unconscious identification can take place as part of the process of building a defensive alibi.

The mere presence of good or bad examples will not, therefore, prompt either good or bad behavior. Examples are used or misused according to the individual's specific unconscious needs, at the specific moment.

The role of good advice is not very different. Nobody is wholeheartedly grateful for good advice; the neurotic person distrusts it more than the normal individual does. This distrust goes back to the nursery. The neurotic has never overcome his childhood conviction that his parents are hypocrites and believers in a double standard of ethics. They forbade sex to their children, for example, but permitted it to themselves! The eternal rivalry between the generations puts up another barrier here. Sound-advice-givers, by force of logic as well as tradition, come from the older generations and base their counsel on their own experiences. Advice-seekers, on the other hand, are usually young, and as a general rule automatically distrust their elders' conclusions and depreciate the value of their experiences.

In his attitude towards advice, the young adult is very much like the child who refuses to believe the stove is hot until he touches it to make sure. Someone else's experience tends to remain unreal; it has to become one's own in order to register. What is more, people do not learn from their own experiences, in spite of the Latin proverbs which declare that they do. This is why generation after generation repeats the same mistakes,

and individual human beings repeat their individual mistakes
year after year.

These habitual errors are not failures of logic. They are direct
outgrowths of an unconscious pattern. The need to reap masochistic returns, which is embedded in the individual's neurosis
or neurotic traits, makes them inevitable.

One of my patients constantly loaned money to unreliable
friends. Repeatedly his loans turned out to have been unwilling
gifts. He was repeating an infantile situation and using this
means to prove that he was always unjustly treated. "How often
do I have to go through this nonsensical routine?" he asked me
in despair. "As long as you cling to your neurosis" was the
answer.

By and large, good advice fails to be effective because it conflicts with the advice-taker's still persisting infantile belief in his
own omniscience. It is surprising to discover how many people
think of themselves as "exceptions" to whom general rules do
not and cannot apply. For these people, "experience" resolves
itself into a hopeless attempt to reconcile the irreconcilable—
to make fact fit fancy.

Advice, whether good or bad, takes root only when it fits into
the requirements of the unconscious personality. The criminotic
cannot accept good advice or absorb good example because the
defensive tactics that obtain in his unconscious are entirely foreign to these influences. Preaching cannot impel him into normality, nor can punishment—which he unconsciously seeks.

The entire problem of criminosis is complicated by the fact
that there is a paucity of actual clinical analytical experiences
with criminals in prison. Only a few attempts have been made to
conduct organized analysis in jails. This is still largely unexplored
territory. The situation is surprising, since there is no scarcity
of prison inmates, nor any lack of experienced psychoanalytically
trained psychiatrists who would be interested in helping to conduct such exploratory analyses. What seems to be missing is the
means of implementing such a project: money, and an organization.

We just don't know enough about the future possibilities of

the therapy of criminals, of incipient criminals, who are too young to be branded with the hopeless adjective "hardened." In this, as in so many other neurotic and psychopathic problems, the stumbling block may well prove to be the large amount of psychic masochism deposited within the unconscious of the criminotic.

CHAPTER 8

PARENTS TAKEN OFF THE PILLORY

IT is rather ironic that the *century of the child,* having bestowed every advantage on the newest generation by taxing to the limit parents' endurance and capacity for sacrifice, should not have given the child credit for his own unconscious choice of selected items from the mass of raw material presented to him. In the name of the unconscious (a concept generally both watered down and misunderstood), parents' attitudes have been radically revamped, always under the naive assumption that changing the educational climate will automatically change the unconscious of the child.

Externally a change has been accomplished. In the past children were afraid of their parents; today, parents are afraid of their children. This shift has not succeeded in improving the emotional health of the children. Its most marked result has been to provide some parents with a new point of deposition for their psychic masochism.

It is time to take parents off this pillory. They don't belong there in the first place. Nor is there any justification for subjecting them to medieval tortures while "freeing" the children.

This cannot be overemphasized: Parents cannot be responsible for the neuroses of their children simply because they do not have the power to create a disease of the unconscious. Those who make the opposite claim have naive ideas about the genesis of neurosis.

A neurosis is based on faulty unconscious elaborations of conflicts connected with the long maturation time of the human being. During the growing-up period, the child who has come into the world with drives he is incapable of handling, must still accommodate himself to them and live with them. Impulses which should be expended outwardly and are inhibited because of the weakness of the child's muscular apparatus are consequently turned inward, against the child himself. The child becomes the victim of his own inborn aggression, of his own frustration, and of his untenable belief in his own magical omnipotence.

This boomerang effect, especially with respect to the aggressive drive, leads to the establishment of an internal "misery machine" which manufactures self-punishment on the conveyor belt. To counteract this, the child's inner trouble-shooter (his unconscious ego) creates the defense of psychic masochism, a scourge that infects the whole of humanity.

In short, there seems to be an inherent flaw in the psychic system, which is apparently centered on the infantile illusion of absolute power. Reality persistently encroaches on this illusion; the child stubbornly and sometimes cunningly resists. In the psychic-masochistic solution, remnants of the illusion are preserved and enthroned. The flaw, like the dangerous crevasses encountered in Arctic ice formations, can be narrow enough to cross without too much difficulty. Children with adaptability do cross it to develop into not-too-neurotic human beings. But the child who is unwilling to adapt is, in terms of the Arctic simile, coping with a wide crevass. He must travel miles out of his way to find a place where it is narrow enough for him to get to the other side. (Sometimes he cannot cross over at all.) This extra mileage represents the extent of his subsequent neurosis.

There are five immutable unconscious facts which have convinced me that parents cannot be responsible for their children's neuroses.

1. The child is born with a certain biological endowment of megalomania; the quantity seems to be a troublemaker later on.

2. Inborn aggression inevitably boomerangs against the child himself, and this leads directly to the establishment of the inner tormentor, the superego.

272 PARENTS NOT GUILTY!

3. The "masochistic solution" is the counteraction *always* set up by the unconscious trouble-shooter (the unconscious ego) to contend against the inner torturer.

4. Pseudo-aggression *must* in some way be expressed by the child. The masochistic solution, invariably reached, is taboo, and therefore it opens the way to a constant barrage of reproaches from the inner tyrant. Pseudo-aggression is the standard and necessary defense against unconscious accusations of psychic masochism. How essential it is can be seen from this "clinical picture" of the psychic masochist's actions:

Step I: Through his behavior or the misuse of an external situation, the neurotic unconsciously provokes disappointment, refusal or humiliation from the environment. The enemy thus made is unconsciously identified with the mother of earliest infancy, the neurotic's first alleged "refuser."

Step II: The neurotic does not consciously realize that he has provoked his own defeat. He tells himself that he has been attacked and he retaliates with pseudo-aggression, full of righteous indignation and appearing to act in self-defense.

Step III: He is defeated and humiliated by his "enemy," which was his real unconscious aim. He now bewails his fate, complaining that "these things happen only to poor little me." Unconsciously he experiences masochistic pleasure.

Pseudo-aggression (see table, Chapter 4) is inextricably entwined with psychic masochism, and therefore its appearance is no more accessible to parental influence than is its unconscious partner. The parent does, however, influence the means through which the child expresses his pseudo-aggressive defense. All children cleverly capitalize on some parental prohibitions. These precepts provide them with the raw material for their provocations. But parentally enounced precepts follow cultural requirements, so that the parents' opportunities for choice are decidedly limited, and even within these limitations, minor.

5. The child's exhibitionistic defense is doomed at an early age (see Chapter 2).

The absence of congruity between the moral dicta laid down in the educational process and the moral inhibitions which the child builds up from these precepts is especially visible in cases in which the child becomes, as a patient expressed it, "more papal than the pope." I have repeatedly observed patients from a permissive childhood background, also neglected children (where the enforcement of restrictions pertaining to "bodily decency" were concerned) who were severely inhibited in this sphere. Current theories suggest that these patients, who viewed their parents in various stages of undress, would have developed a lenient attitude towards peeping. If the theorists' claim were correct and example invariably led to acceptance, these approved opportunities for peeping would indeed have resulted in laxity and tolerance in the visual sphere on the part of these children. But exactly the opposite is frequently observable.

Here are two examples:

In the analysis of a blocked writer, aged forty-eight, there emerged a recollection dating from the patient's seventh year. His mother called to him from her bedroom. He found her standing in front of a mirror, dressing. Her breasts were exposed. The boy immediately responded "But you aren't dressed," and left the room. His mother called impatiently "Come in! I have to talk to you."

Another writer, in analysis because of his homosexuality, remembered specifically that "no special emphasis was placed on being fully clothed at home." However, it was difficult for him to talk about peeping during his analysis. He neither touched nor opened the books on the shelves in my waiting room, although he was tempted to do so. Otherwise he had, as he proudly stated, "no sexual inhibitions."

Two reasons account for the sternness illustrated by these patients. First, when the fiction of "mean" parents has to be maintained, the child magnifies the most casual educational dicta. In this situation, the parents are falsified into "sight-deprivers," too. Second, the *battle for privacy* enters the picture. *The child is under constant parental supervision, but the parents arrogate to themselves the right to privacy whenever they retire to their bedroom. In exaggerated form, and in some kind of reversed reciprocity, the child shows his parents how he would have liked to be treated: with his privacy respected.* (This is a form of "magic gesture.")

The culture enforces its rules on the parents; they in turn must pass cultural moral dicta on to their children. But the immaturity of the child imposes certain amendments on all these dicta. Can a three-year-old, for example, claim his right to "privacy" as justification for his wish to be left undisturbed when he is trying to burn the house down with the matches he has just found? The one-sided situation arises repeatedly. The parents should not be blamed for this fact, but the child does blame them.

"Injustice" of this type, involving the misuse of a realistic and unchangeable fact, comes graphically alive in a statement made to me by a woman patient. She had been discussing her grievances against her mother, and she said forcefully that the mere fact that the mother is not naked when bathing the child—and the child is—proves to the child that peeping is a prerogative of adults. As such, it must be forbidden to children, and the child sees it as forbidden whether the mother tells him so or not.

These five points of infantile conflict, all of which arise independently of the parents' power to interfere, have convinced me that it is entirely senseless to accuse the parents of creating neuroses in their children. The appearance of parental guilt, even when it seems highly plausible, cannot stand up against scrutiny of the child's individual problems.

Freud's acknowledgment that no direct relationship exists between severity of education and severity of the superego has already been quoted at the end of the Preface. Freud followed up this statement by making a reservation which led to a compromise between his earlier and later views:

> Nevertheless, it would be erroneous to exaggerate this independence; it is not difficult to convince oneself that the severity of education has a strong influence on the development of the infantile superego. What it amounts to is that inherited constitutional factors and influences of the real environment work together in the making of the superego and the development of

conscience. This is by no means surprising but the general etiological condition of all such phenomena.

Freud's stress on the unknown X of "inherited constitutional factors" seems to me to lose much of its mystique if we consider the quantitative factors of inherited "infantile megalomania." Some children, as already pointed out, "cannot take" the *unavoidable* infantile frustrations that contradict their grandiose illusion of supreme power. Their demands are insatiable; to satisfy them, the parents would have to be selfless beings without lives of their own and with a touch of that same legendary magical power.

Infantile megalomania is the chief troublemaker because it is a major ingredient in the masochistic solution. When the child, and later the adult, is in the midst of one of his "humiliations," the innocent bystander sees only the mistreated "victim." But the unconscious picture in the mind of the so-called underdog is quite different. Its caption reads: "That fool believes that he is humiliating and punishing me. That's what *he* thinks. *I,* through my initial provocation, *made* him punish me!" Once more, megalomania triumphant.

The idea that neurosis is something *artificially created* in the child by severe, indifferent or selfish parents is erroneous. It is an approach that fails entirely to take into account the *pleasure gain* embedded in neurosis. Neurotics are not victims only. Unconsciously they pursue a specific pleasure—and get it.

It has been recognized in analysis that neurotics enjoy "substitute gratifications" in their symptoms and personality distortions. In stressing the masochistic pleasure gain (and demoting the previously overrated libidinous pleasures in neurosis as secondary rescue stations), as I suggest, one still reaches the identical substratum: pleasure gain. The "trade balance" may seem to the uninitiated to be unfavorable: *every ounce of unconscious pleasure must be paid for with tons of conscious unhappiness.* One cannot help concluding from the evidence that an "ounce of unconscious pleasure" must be worth the expenditure of conscious suffering.

Since the masochistic solution of infantile conflicts is universal and people who are not full-fledged neurotics do exist, there must be present in some people a special affinity to that sweetest and most dangerous of all mental poisons, psychic masochism. One is tempted to see a comparison between the neurotic and a certain type of drug addict. Repeatedly we hear tragic reports of people who became drug addicts as a result of receiving morphine to alleviate pain. What about other sufferers who received repeated doses of the drug but did not become addicted? Perhaps the affinity to the narcotic may be organically conditioned. Perhaps the affinity to psychic masochism also consists of a biological over-endowment of infantile megalomania.

It is naive to assume that in this prodigious battle within the unconscious during infancy, parental influence plays the decisive part. It doesn't, simply because a series of inner conflicts arises independently of parents' influence.

In my book, *Principles of Self-Damage*, the human tragedy was summed up in the following passage:

A megalomaniacal philosopher of the last century (who, to counteract his own overdimensional inner passive-masochistic deposits, created the "superman" concept which was subsequently exploited for political purposes) numbered among his minor defensive efforts the statement that man's suffering is so excruciating that he was driven to invent laughter.

The suffering to which Nietzsche referred pertains to shortness of life, disease, misfortune, inequities, disappointments, but his observation also—and decisively—pertains to incalculable, unconscious, self-inflicted mental misery. It is a terrifying thought that each of us, in earliest childhood, installs an internal "misery machine" in his superego, and thereafter must—in self-defense —learn to enjoy suffering, once more unknowingly and unwittingly. On the other hand, life may possibly be unendurable without a certain amount of masochism, though one should distinguish between productive and unproductive depositions.

The purpose of science is not to deplore but to investigate. And in investigating psychic phenomena, one finds that the real responsibility for human misery must be ascribed to that impersonal factor, biology. Biology decrees both the long maturation time of the human child and the fact that the newborn, helpless human child is endowed with drives that are potentially as strong as those he will have at his disposal as an adult. The three inborn drives rebel helplessly from the first moment of life: megalomania is offended, aggression rebounds against the ego, and libido sheds its saving grace on the unfortunate solution known as psychic masochism. In psychic masochism self-aggression is libidinized and megalomania artificially satisfied by provoking, and thus allegedly decreeing, punishment.

The majority of analysts avoid as unpalatable the fact that psychic masochism is universal; they show even more distaste for the fact behind this fact—the unremitting cruelty of the superego. But science cannot be converted to the program of happy endings adhered to by the slick magazines. Even distasteful facts must be swallowed when their accuracy has been demonstrated.

Biologically conditioned unfavorable depositions of rebounding aggression in earliest infancy result in the installation of the superego. Again in earliest infancy, unplaceable megalomania, coupled with the libido's rule of thumb, the pleasure principle, which tries to make the best of an impossible situation, results in the installation of the only possible defense against the constant torture emanating from the superego—psychic masochism.

Unlike contemporary politics, where "too little and too late" is the main trouble, human biology presents the problem of "too much and too early."

"All humanity is pathetic," was Mark Twain's summing up, and not the least pathetic aspect of humanity deals with the fact that people forge their unconscious happiness out of conscious misery, and are aware of the misery alone.

The statement has been made here that parents should be taken off the pillory. But do they always want to be?

It might be assumed that this is an absurd and unnecessary query. What innocent person wants to suffer? Not the innocent person who is at the same time relatively healthy. The not-too-neurotic parent wants very much to be "taken off the hook." A neurotic parent would rather suffer.

This should not be overlooked: psychic masochism is a universal human trait. It does not bypass parents.

Generally, the parents of patients in analysis are off-stage figures, represented in the analysis only by their child's judgments of them (often fantasies). When young homosexuals are analyzed, however, the preamble to analysis is frequently an interview with the parents. Here is an area in which parents invariably begin by acknowledging their own guilt and their own failure. How do they react to information which should rid them of this burden?

A New England industrialist and his wife consulted me on behalf of their son, who was twenty-three. His mother had been led to suspect him of homosexuality because of the unreasonably late hours he kept. She had then found and read his diary; it contained detailed descriptions of homosexual experiences. She "nearly had a nervous breakdown," and the father then confronted the son with the evidence. He did not relish having his parents know about his homosexuality, but he firmly maintained that "there was nothing wrong" about it.

This discovery gave the industrialist two domestic problems to handle, a homosexual son and an hysterical wife. To protect his family and himself from scandal, he considered asking his son to leave home and change his name. His wife objected violently to this idea and made hysterical scenes. At this point they thought hopefully of persuading their son to go into analysis.

I interviewed the son; he was not cooperative. I pointed out the legal dangers of homosexuality. He replied, with naive assurance, "I'm too smart for them." His outlook on life was cynical; his father would not let him down, he was sure, because his mother "could not live without" him. I described the inner dangers of self-damage. He shrugged his shoulders and loftily informed me that these dangers would not touch him.

I asked him: "Are you so sure you are invulnerable to self-damage? What about the infection you described in your diary?"

"Accidents will happen."

"I wouldn't be so sure this was just an accident. Is your promiscuity an accident too?"

"No. That's my fun."

"You are an immature boy who is bound to get into trouble. I wouldn't put much reliance on your mother's attachment to you; your father will convince her that self-protection comes first."

"I don't think so."

"We shall see. If you deny you have any self-damaging tendencies, how do you account for the fact that you indirectly informed your parents about your homosexuality? Why did you leave your diary where it could be found?"

"I took it for granted that they wouldn't dare touch any of my personal possessions!"

"That pseudo-naïveté of yours is exactly what will get you into trouble again and again."

The mother viewed her son's homosexuality as a major tragedy. After making her discovery, she spent virtually all her time in an agonizing appraisal of the past: what was the "mistake" she had made that led to her son's "disgrace?" Every attempt to explain to her failed.

A widow who lived in Baltimore consulted me about her son, aged twenty-five. The "boy" had always been reasonable and pleasant until he entered the armed forces. There he seemed to become homosexual. "When he returned home again, I found out," she said. "He received suspicious telephone calls. I read some of his letters."

"Did you discuss the problem with him?"

"Yes. He said that I'm still living in the last century and don't know what's going on. I insisted that he see a minister or a psychiatrist. He became indignant and gave me an ultimatum: if I didn't leave him alone, he would move out."

"He is obviously not ready for a change. But I believe he should know about the self-damage always present in homosexuality. You could tell him that you consulted me about your own nervous state and I asked that he give me information about you. This might be a way of persuading him to listen to information about self-damage."

"I will try that. Please, please tell me: Am I responsible?"

"Homosexuality is an illness, and you are not responsible."

She did not seem to be relieved or at all convinced. Her next questions made it clear that her masochism would have welcomed a different reply. I never saw her again, nor her son.

A business man and his wife traveled from the Middle West to tell me the problem of their twenty-three year old son. The father accepted the situation with some resignation; his wife did not. She was in a fighting mood, though streaked with self-reproach.

"First I heard rumors," she said. "Then I overheard some telephone conversations, and then I caught a peculiar glance my son gave another boy. That was disgusting and heartbreaking—the kind of look a boy gives a beautiful girl. It turned my stomach and broke my heart. What can be done for him?"

"Nothing, without his inner cooperation. How does he feel about it?"

"He's one hundred per cent for that dirty business. I have only one explanation for the whole mess. I was forty-one when he was born, and I had toxemia. Is God punishing me?"

"Neither toxemia nor the age of the mother can account for homosexuality. You are torturing yourself needlessly."

"If I could only believe that!"

I suggested to them, as I had to my Baltimore patient with the same problem, that their son be told his mother had consulted me about her own condition and that I had asked to talk to him about her.

The father exerted a good deal of pressure and eventually the son came down from college to see me. He scoffed at my accusation of self-damage; his attitude combined anger with irony.

A few weeks later I heard through the mother that her son's boy friend (and roommate) had been arrested. Although the college year had just ended, her son stayed on in the college town. The parents now tried to force him to leave, but the boy insisted on remaining despite his own danger so that he could help his friend.

Over the telephone the desperate mother asked me: "Now

that he's face to face with real danger, will that be frightening enough to push him into treatment?"

"I believe he needs a few more shocks," I replied.

So far I have not heard from this young man, who had told me with much assurance that he "did not believe there was danger."

The modern approach to education poses an insoluble problem, and one that has so far not become clear to parents and educators. This problem concerns the need which has been omitted from a list of the child's inalienable rights: his need for a point of deposition for the unconscious psychic masochism which he, like every other human being, possesses to one or another quantitative degree.

The now outmoded punitive approach to education encouraged psychic masochism, which was certainly not the ideal state of affairs. Today's permissive technique however leaves the masochistic tendency homeless and unabsorbed—not an ideal state of affairs, either. The child's provocations (his "naughtiness") tend to grow to a periodic peak, eventually exasperating even his lenient parents. They, having reached a limit of endurance, temporarily revert to the old technique and become punitive instead of permissive. One of the results of this drastic action is a persistent feeling of guilt. The philosophy of permissiveness contains another defect. The unconscious "philosophy" of every psychic masochist (and this is a theory constructed by the very young child) interprets both kindness and cruelty in a very primitive way: kindness represents weakness, cruelty means strength. The psychic masochist takes merciless advantage of the "weak" person, yields with appalling submissiveness to the "strong." This tendency is most evident in children. Witness their almost savage treatment of the "sissies" or "misfits" in their midst.

Advocates of modern permissive education must face the fact that the end results of their methods have been as unsatisfactory as those of the punishment advocates. Neurosis has certainly not decreased.

In more than thirty years of psychiatric practice on two continents, I have had the opportunity to observe achievements of both the punitive and the permissive techniques. By the only standard that has any validity in this discussion—how healthy, emotionally, is the product of the system?—neither method can be approved. Neuroses bloom under both regimes.

The real enemy of human contentment is the individual's inner torture machine, and the universal unconscious defense against it, psychic masochism. These two foes of conscious happiness are not even touched by modern educational procedures.

The forces molding the child's inner conflicts are bigger and stronger than parental influences. Trying to combat them is comparable to a struggle described by that formidable eighteenth-century wit, the Reverend Sidney Smith, in a speech at Taunton in October of 1831:

> [This] reminds me very forcibly of the great storm at Sidmouth, and of the conduct of the excellent Mrs. Partington on that occasion. In the winter of 1824, there set in a great flood upon that town—the tide rose to an incredible height: the waves rushed in upon the houses, and everything was threatened with destruction. In the midst of this sublime and terrible storm, Dame Partington, who lived upon the beach, was seen at the door of her house with a mop and pattens, trundling her mop, squeezing out the sea water, and vigorously pushing away the Atlantic Ocean. The Atlantic was roused. Mrs. Partington's spirit was up; but I need not tell you that the contest was unequal. The Atlantic Ocean beat Mrs. Partington. She was excellent at a slop or a puddle, but she should not have meddled with a tempest.

From the vantage point of the psychiatrist there are three possible steps towards educational progress:

1. Parents and educators should be informed of the existence of the two inner dangers facing every child (the inner tyrant, the psychic-masochist solution) and should know that these unconscious enemies are inaccessible to educational measures.

2. Educators and other related specialists should stop making

naive external rules for governing the nursery. These accomplish only one purpose: they burden the parents with undue guilt, since the naive code can never be faithfully and completely adhered to. The ineffective as well as impossible principle of forgiving all for forgiveness' sake results only in unendurable suppressions on the part of the parents.

3. This basic psychological truth should be clarified: Neurosis is the outcome of the clash of inner forces, above and beyond the educational process, and it is not a creation of the parent.

An acute observer can discern important truths about human behavior even if he lives in an era that has not benefited by scientific discovery. To quote Sydney Smith again, this time from a letter written to Francis Jeffrey in 1803: "Children are horribly insecure; the life of a parent is the life of a gambler."

The rest of the letter makes his meaning very clear. As he saw it, the outcome of the educational process was as uncertain as the eventual destination of roulette's little ball. Allowing for the exaggeration inherent in a witticism, this remark still represents a point of view that should be included in every parent's philosophy.

Even though there can be no guarantees, there still must be standards of optimum parental performance. Stated very simply, these call for essential and ungrudging kindness, plus firm discipline and staunch insistence on the child's obedience to cultural precepts.

This modest listing *is* the optimum; it defines the restricted field over which the parents can hope to govern. Every other area is beyond their power.

It is a simple program. What makes it complex is that parents do not realize this—yet.